Zen and the Art of Storytelling

Andrew Parry

Published by Andrew Parry, 2024.

ZEN AND THE ART OF STORYTELLING

First edition. October 14, 2024.

ISBN: 979-8227210791

Written by Andrew Parry.

Table of Contents

Storytelling is often viewed as a creative storm—a swirling combination of ideas, emotions, and inspiration. For many writers and creators, the challenge lies not in finding ideas but in organizing them into a cohesive story. In the midst of this creative chaos, the Zen approach offers an antidote: calmness. By embracing a Zen-like mindset, you can unlock a more focused and intentional way of storytelling, one that allows you to tap into your natural creativity without being overwhelmed by it.

At the heart of Zen is the concept of mindfulness, the act of being fully present in each moment. When applied to storytelling, mindfulness invites you to quiet the noise of your thoughts and focus solely on the task at hand—whether that's conceptualizing characters, plotting the arc of your story, or visualizing a specific scene. This practice of mindfulness can be the key to unlocking your potential as a storyteller.

In this chapter, we begin with a simple yet powerful idea: storytelling starts within. Before you create worlds, characters, or conflicts, you must first find a calm center in your own mind. Only then can you clearly visualize the complete story, see the relationships between plot points, and understand the nuances of your characters.

Tapping into Inner Stillness

Imagine sitting down to write. Your mind may initially race with ideas, insecurities, and distractions. The first step in Zen storytelling is to acknowledge these distractions without judgment. Allow your thoughts to settle, much like sediment falling to the bottom of a still lake. The goal is not to banish thoughts but to observe them from a distance, letting them come and go naturally. Once the mind quiets, you will find space for true inspiration to arise.

In this stillness, stories begin to form more naturally. Rather than forcing ideas, you're now allowing them to emerge organically, as if they were always there, waiting for you to uncover them. When your mind is calm, you can see the whole story laid out before you—a complete arc, characters moving with purpose, and settings alive with detail. This visualization becomes much clearer when your mind is free from clutter.

Breathing Life into the Creative Process

A key element of Zen practice is breathing, and in storytelling, mindful breathing can become an essential tool for grounding yourself before you begin writing. Take a few moments to focus on your breath—inhale slowly, and exhale fully. With each breath, imagine yourself letting go of distractions and opening up to the flow of creativity. This simple practice helps to ground you in the present moment, bringing your full attention to your writing.

When you're grounded in this way, storytelling becomes less about constructing an idea from scratch and more about discovering the story that already exists within you. Much like a sculptor chipping away at a block of marble to reveal the figure inside, your job as a storyteller is to uncover the narrative hidden within your imagination.

The Power of Visualization

One of the most profound benefits of the Zen approach to storytelling is the ability to visualize your story from beginning to end. Visualization is not just about seeing the surface of the scene or the outline of a character; it's about diving deep into the layers of your narrative. By visualizing, you can see the emotional journey of your protagonist, the tension in key moments, and the overarching themes that thread your story together.

Begin by meditating on the ending of your story. Visualize the resolution—the moment where the protagonist reaches their goal or fails in their mission. See this climactic scene in your mind's eye, paying attention to the emotions, the setting, and the stakes. When you have a clear sense of the ending, you can work backwards, allowing each preceding scene to fall into place. This practice aligns with Zen principles, encouraging you to start with the end in mind and let the journey reveal itself naturally.

Letting Go of Control

In Zen, there's an emphasis on letting go of attachment, whether it's attachment to a particular outcome or to preconceived notions. When you apply this to storytelling, it means being willing to let your story evolve as you write. Many writers cling to rigid outlines or try to control every element of their story, but this often stifles creativity. Instead, embrace the idea that the story may shift as you write. Characters may reveal themselves in unexpected ways, or plot points may develop that you hadn't anticipated. This flexibility is a hallmark of Zen storytelling.

Letting go of control also means quieting the internal critic that tells you your ideas aren't good enough or that you're not skilled enough to execute them. The Zen storyteller acknowledges these fears but does not let them take hold. You must allow your story to flow through you, trusting in the process and the journey.

Storytelling as Meditation

Writing can become a form of meditation. When you're fully immersed in your story, you enter a state of flow where time seems to disappear, and you're entirely present in the creative process. This is the essence of Zen: being fully engaged in the present moment. In this state, you're no longer struggling to find the right words or force ideas into place; you're simply allowing the story to unfold as it should. By treating storytelling as a meditation, you turn it into a practice that nourishes you, rather than one that drains you. Instead of feeling overwhelmed by the enormity of the task, you approach it one moment, one scene, one sentence at a time. There is no rush, no need to finish quickly. The process is just as important as the product. The Zen of storytelling invites you to step away from the noise and distraction of the outside world and find a stillness within. It's in this stillness that your most authentic stories will emerge—stories that are rich, purposeful, and deeply connected to who you are as a creator. As you move forward, remember that the journey of storytelling is much like the practice of Zen itself. It's not about perfection or rushing to the finish line. It's about staying present in the process, finding joy in the act of creation, and trusting that your story will reveal itself in time.

Meditation as a Creative Tool: Tapping into the Mind's Eye

Meditation, often associated with relaxation or spiritual exploration, is also a powerful tool for tapping into the creative mind. For storytellers, whether novelists, screenwriters, or directors, meditation can serve as a gateway to visualizing entire worlds, characters, and plotlines. It quiets the mind and creates the space needed for ideas to emerge organically. In this chapter, we explore how meditation can become an essential part of your creative process, enabling you to access the depth of your imagination and bring clarity to your storytelling.

The human mind is constantly bombarded with distractions—work, social media, personal worries. Amid this noise, it can be difficult to summon the focus needed for deep creative work. Meditation helps by teaching you how to calm your thoughts and narrow your attention, allowing your creative ideas to rise to the surface. When you meditate before writing or brainstorming, you're preparing the mind to enter a creative flow state, where visualization becomes effortless, and the connections between story elements are easier to see.

The Connection between Meditation and Creativity

At first glance, meditation and storytelling might seem like unrelated practices. One is about stillness, while the other often involves dynamic characters, conflict, and action. But both practices share a common thread: focus. In meditation, the goal is to focus the mind on a single point, whether it's the breath, a mantra, or an image. Similarly, in storytelling, you must focus on the story's core elements—characters, plot, themes—while shutting out distractions that might dilute your vision.

Meditation teaches you how to be fully present. This presence is invaluable when you sit down to create, as it allows you to become fully immersed in your story. By eliminating external and internal distractions, you create the mental space needed to visualize your characters in detail, see the settings clearly, and understand the emotional beats of your narrative. This kind of deep focus is essential for storytelling that is rich, layered, and coherent.

Meditation also fosters creativity by training the mind to let go of rigid thought patterns. Often, the greatest barrier to creativity is overthinking—trying to force an idea into existence or being overly attached to one outcome. Through meditation, you learn to release control, allowing ideas to flow more freely. You begin to see the story not as something you must wrestle into shape, but as a living thing that you are uncovering moment by moment.

Preparing for Creative Meditation

Before you can use meditation as a creative tool, it helps to establish a simple practice that centers and grounds you. Set aside a quiet space where you won't be interrupted. This space should be free from distractions, a place where you feel calm and comfortable. Sit or lie down in a relaxed position, and focus on your breathing. Inhale deeply through your nose, hold for a moment, then exhale slowly through your mouth. Allow yourself to settle into this rhythm, feeling your body relax and your mind quiet.

As thoughts arise, acknowledge them without judgment and let them pass, like clouds drifting across the sky. The goal here is not to empty your mind entirely, but to distance yourself from your thoughts, observing them without becoming entangled. This practice of observing and letting go creates the space for creative ideas to surface.

Once you've established this sense of calm, shift your focus inward. Begin to visualize an open, blank space in your mind—this is your canvas. It is from this place of stillness and openness that your story will begin to take shape.

Tapping into the Mind's Eye

The mind's eye is your internal visual center, the space where ideas are seen, felt, and experienced before they are expressed on the page or screen. Tapping into the mind's eye requires both focus and openness. You need to direct your attention to the story you want to tell, but also remain open to whatever the story reveals to you.

To begin, choose a single element of your story to focus on. It could be your protagonist, the climax of the plot, or even a specific scene. Close your eyes and bring this element into the center of your mind. Visualize it as clearly as possible. What does your protagonist look like? What is their emotional state? What is happening in the scene? Don't rush this process—allow the details to emerge gradually. The more time you spend in this meditative state, the more vivid and specific the images will become.

In this way, meditation becomes a creative tool, not only for generating ideas but for refining them. The mind's eye allows you to see the scene unfold with a level of detail that you may not achieve through conscious thinking alone. You can imagine the setting, hear the dialogue, and even feel the emotional tension in the room. When you finally sit down to write, these visualized moments will come to life on the page with greater clarity and purpose.

Meditation as Story Incubation

Meditation can also serve as a tool for story incubation. Sometimes, you have a rough idea of a story or a scene but haven't yet figured out all the details. Rather than forcing the idea, meditation allows you to let the story "breathe." During meditation, bring your incomplete idea into your mind's eye and simply let it sit there. Don't try to fix or solve it. Instead, observe it, turn it over in your mind, and notice how it feels.

As you sit with the idea, new elements may begin to emerge naturally. You might see how a character reacts differently in a scene or realize a plot point that wasn't clear before. This process of letting go and allowing the story to develop at its own pace is a hallmark of using meditation as a creative tool. It taps into your subconscious, the wellspring of creativity, and allows it to guide you toward the solution without overthinking.

. . . .

INTEGRATING MEDITATION into Your Writing Practice

To make meditation an effective part of your creative process, integrate it into your daily routine. Before you sit down to write, take a few moments to meditate. Use this time to center yourself, clear your mind, and focus on the story you want to tell. You can use guided meditations specifically designed for creativity or simply sit in silence, focusing on your breath and allowing ideas to rise naturally.

You may also find it helpful to meditate during moments of writer's block. When you feel stuck, step away from the page and spend a few minutes in quiet reflection. This practice helps to reset your mind, allowing you to return to your writing with fresh energy and insight.

Over time, you will notice that meditation sharpens your ability to visualize your stories with more depth and detail. You'll begin to trust your mind's eye to guide you through complex scenes, characters, and plot twists. By making meditation a regular part of your creative process, you unlock a deeper level of storytelling, one that is both intuitive and intentional.

Meditation is not a quick fix for creativity, but rather a practice that deepens over time. As you commit to it, you will find that it becomes easier to access your inner creative wellspring. Storytelling will become less about "trying" to come up with ideas and more about letting ideas emerge naturally from a calm, focused state. You will begin to see your stories with greater clarity, visualizing scenes, characters, and plots with more ease. In the end, meditation is a pathway to creative clarity. By tapping into your mind's eye, you unlock the power to visualize and create stories that resonate deeply with both you and your audience.

Visualizing the Whole Story: A Zen Approach

When it comes to storytelling, one of the most important elements is seeing the entire picture—the characters, the plot, the setting, the emotional beats, and the resolution—before you even write the first word. This might seem like a daunting task, but with a Zen approach to visualization, you can tap into your innate ability to perceive your story as a cohesive whole. By stepping into a meditative state, you'll learn to view your narrative from a higher perspective, allowing the details to fall into place naturally. In this chapter, we'll explore how to use visualization as a tool to see the full arc of your story and then translate that vision into words.

The Power of Story Visualization

Story visualization is much more than simply thinking about your plot or outlining a series of events. It's a deep, immersive process where you engage your mind's eye to see the world, characters, and events unfold in real time. This process requires focus and presence, two key tenets of Zen philosophy. When you bring a mindful, meditative focus to storytelling, you can visualize with greater clarity and precision.

Think of your mind as a projector. When it's cluttered with distractions, the images are fuzzy, and the story seems fragmented. But when you find stillness, the projector sharpens, and suddenly, the entire story is in view. You can see the interactions between characters, the flow of events, and the emotional progression. Visualization in this way allows you to engage with your story as if it's happening in front of you, making it easier to capture the nuance and complexity that may be missed in traditional brainstorming.

Starting with the End: A Zen Perspective on Storytelling

A Zen approach to storytelling often begins with the end in mind. Rather than trying to work from the beginning and hoping the story will come together, we begin by visualizing the resolution—the moment where all the threads come together and the story's purpose is revealed. This gives you a clear destination and allows you to work backwards, mapping out how your characters and plot points must develop to reach this point.

In meditation, focus your mind on the final scene of your story. What happens? What is the emotional tone? How do the characters feel in that moment? The end of the story is where the resolution lies, where the protagonist has faced their challenges and either overcome them or succumbed to them. By holding this image in your mind, you create a clear goal for your narrative to work towards. Visualizing the end provides you with a framework and allows the rest of the story to unfold naturally from this point.

Once you have a solid grasp of your ending, you can begin to trace the steps back, one by one. How did the characters arrive here? What events led to this resolution? By working backwards, you avoid the risk of losing direction or getting tangled in subplots that don't serve the ultimate story.

Visualizing the Hero's Journey

The hero's journey is central to many stories, and visualization can help you explore this journey in its entirety. Picture your protagonist at the start of their quest: Who are they at the beginning? What do they believe? Now, fast forward through their journey. What challenges do they face? How do they evolve? And ultimately, what transformation do they undergo?

In a Zen approach, focus on the transitions. The hero's journey isn't just about external events but internal growth. In your mind's eye, watch the protagonist's arc unfold. Visualize them in key moments of crisis or doubt, and notice how they change. By mentally walking through these steps, you gain a clearer understanding of your character's motivations and emotional trajectory, making it easier to write their development with authenticity and depth.

Seeing the Settings and Worlds Come to Life

Settings are not just backdrops for your story; they are living, breathing parts of the narrative. Through visualization, you can immerse yourself in these environments, exploring them as though you were walking through them. Start by choosing a specific location in your story—perhaps it's the bustling streets of a futuristic city, a quiet room in an old house, or a vast alien landscape. Close your eyes and place yourself in this world.

What do you see? What does the air feel like? What sounds are in the background? Allow the details to materialize in your mind, focusing on the sensory elements. The more vividly you can visualize the setting, the more easily you'll be able to translate it into words that create an immersive experience for your audience.

Visualization can also help you see how your settings interact with the characters. As you imagine your protagonist moving through these spaces, notice how the setting influences their actions, emotions, and decisions. Perhaps the claustrophobic feel of a small room increases their anxiety, or the expanse of a desert forces them to confront their isolation. These details enrich your storytelling by creating a dynamic relationship between character and environment.

Visualizing the Flow of Conflict

Every great story is driven by conflict, and visualization allows you to trace the flow of tension and resolution throughout your narrative. In your meditative state, watch the story unfold in your mind, paying close attention to the rise and fall of conflict. When does tension escalate? When do your characters face their greatest challenges? And how do they eventually overcome—or fail to overcome—the obstacles before them?

As you visualize, focus on the emotional undercurrents that drive the conflict. Who is at odds with whom? What are the stakes? See these conflicts play out in real time, as if you were watching a film. This practice helps you understand the emotional beats of your story, ensuring that the pacing feels natural and the tension builds in a satisfying way.

Letting the Story Flow

One of the core principles of Zen is the concept of flow—the natural, unforced movement of events. When visualizing your story, allow it to flow. Don't try to control every detail or force the plot in a specific direction. Instead, trust your mind to guide you. Let the story unfold as it wants to, and observe the natural connections between scenes, characters, and events.

This process is particularly helpful when you encounter moments of writer's block. When you feel stuck, return to meditation and visualization. Allow yourself to step back from the pressure of creating and simply observe the story in your mind. Often, you'll find that the solution presents itself once you've created the space for it to emerge.

Integrating Zen Visualization into Writing

To make visualization a regular part of your storytelling practice, dedicate time to it before you write. Spend a few minutes in meditation, visualizing different aspects of your story. You might start with a broad view—seeing the entire arc of your narrative—then zoom in on specific scenes or characters. The more you practice this, the easier it will become to see your story as a whole, and to move fluidly between the big picture and the smaller details.

When you sit down to write, draw on these visualizations. Because you've already seen the story play out in your mind, the act of writing becomes a process of transcription. You're not inventing something from scratch; you're simply describing what you've already witnessed in your imagination.

Visualizing the whole story from start to finish is a powerful tool for any storyteller. By taking a Zen approach, you can access a calm, focused state that allows you to see your narrative with clarity and depth. Whether you're working on a novel, screenplay, or film, visualization helps you create a cohesive, purposeful story where every element is connected. Through this practice, you not only unlock your creative potential but also bring your stories to life with greater intention, clarity, and flow.

In a world filled with constant noise—both external and internal—finding moments of true silence can seem like a rare luxury. Yet, for storytellers, silence is a crucial ally in the creative process. It is in the stillness of the mind, away from the chatter of daily life, that ideas take shape. Silence allows you to access deeper layers of creativity and intuition, where stories are born not from noise but from clarity. In this chapter, we'll explore how cultivating stillness can unlock new levels of creativity, revealing the powerful connection between silence and the birth of ideas.

The Art of Stillness

Stillness is a fundamental concept in Zen philosophy. It refers not only to physical silence but to the quieting of the mind. For many of us, the mind is rarely still. It's filled with thoughts, worries, plans, and distractions that crowd out the subtle voice of intuition. Yet, when we can create moments of mental stillness, even if only for a few minutes, something extraordinary happens. Ideas that were once elusive begin to surface. Scenes, characters, and plot twists reveal themselves with surprising clarity.

In Zen, stillness is often cultivated through meditation, but it can also be found in other practices that quiet the mind, such as walking in nature, sitting in solitude, or simply being present in the moment. For storytellers, this stillness becomes a fertile ground for creativity. When the mind is not busy processing external information or dwelling on tasks, it becomes more receptive to inspiration.

Think of stillness as a blank canvas. When the canvas is cluttered with distractions, there's no room for new ideas to take shape. But when you clear the space—both mentally and physically—you create room for creativity to flow freely. In this way, stillness is not just the absence of sound or thought; it is an active state of openness and receptivity.

The Relationship between Silence and Ideas

Some of the greatest creative breakthroughs happen in silence. In the absence of external stimuli, the mind can wander into unexplored territories, connecting ideas that may have previously seemed unrelated. This is why many creative professionals—writers, artists, musicians—often speak of their best ideas coming to them in moments of solitude or quiet.

The reason silence breeds ideas is that it allows your brain to enter a state of "diffuse thinking." Unlike focused thinking, which is highly analytical and deliberate, diffuse thinking is more relaxed and open. It's the state of mind you experience when daydreaming, drifting, or allowing thoughts to flow without trying to control them. In this state, your brain makes connections that it wouldn't otherwise make, leading to fresh perspectives and new ideas.

When you invite silence into your creative process, you are inviting this diffuse thinking. Rather than forcing yourself to come up with the next plot point or the perfect line of dialogue, you allow ideas to emerge organically. Silence gives your mind the space it needs to explore without pressure, and it is often in these moments of stillness that the most original and unexpected ideas come to life.

Creating a Space for Stillness

To harness the power of stillness in your storytelling, it's important to create both a physical and mental space for it. Find a place where you can be alone, free from distractions. This could be a quiet room, a park, or even your own backyard. The key is to be in an environment where external noise won't interfere with your internal stillness.

Once you've found your space, engage in a practice that helps quiet your mind. This could be as simple as sitting in silence, focusing on your breath, or taking a walk in nature. The goal is to remove the clutter from your mind—the constant stream of thoughts, plans, and worries that usually dominate your mental space. As you sit or walk in silence, observe your thoughts without judgment and let them pass. Gradually, you'll notice your mind becoming quieter, creating room for creativity to emerge.

It's important to note that this practice doesn't require long stretches of time. Even five or ten minutes of stillness can have a profound effect on your creativity. The key is consistency. The more you cultivate these moments of stillness, the more natural they will become, and the more readily ideas will flow.

The Creative Void: Embracing Emptiness

In many creative disciplines, there's a fear of the blank page or the empty canvas—a feeling that emptiness represents a lack of ideas or direction. But in Zen, emptiness is not something to be feared. It is, in fact, where all creation begins. The void is not a symbol of nothingness; it is a space of infinite potential.

When you sit in silence and embrace the creative void, you are not waiting for ideas to appear out of thin air. Rather, you are creating the conditions for them to emerge. The void is a space of possibility, and it is only in stillness that you can fully access it. As you sit in this emptiness, you are allowing your mind to wander freely, exploring new connections and concepts that would otherwise remain hidden beneath the surface noise.

Stillness in creation is about trusting that the ideas will come. When you stop trying to force inspiration and instead create a quiet, open space, your mind will naturally gravitate toward new ideas. The act of storytelling becomes less about "finding" ideas and more about receiving them, about being in the right state of mind to recognize them when they arise.

Silence as a Writing Practice

For storytellers, stillness and silence can become part of your daily writing practice. Before you sit down to write, spend a few minutes in silence. Let go of any expectations or pressure to create something specific. Instead, focus on your breath or simply observe the quiet around you. This small ritual can help center your mind, preparing it for the creative process.

As you write, practice returning to moments of stillness. If you find yourself stuck, rather than pushing through or forcing the next sentence, take a pause. Close your eyes, breathe deeply, and sit in silence for a minute or two. Often, the idea you're searching for will appear once you've quieted your mind and released the need for control.

Incorporating silence into your writing routine can also help you stay connected to the essence of your story. In the noise of everyday life, it's easy to lose sight of the emotional core of your narrative. Silence brings you back to that core, helping you focus on what truly matters in the story you're telling.

Listening to the Silence

Silence is not an absence of sound; it's an opportunity to listen more deeply. In the stillness, you can hear your intuition more clearly. You can feel the subtle shifts in your story, understand your characters on a deeper level, and see the connections between plot points that weren't obvious before. This deep listening is what allows you to write with authenticity and purpose.

When you listen to the silence, you also become more attuned to the rhythms of your own creativity. Every writer has their own creative cycle, periods of intense productivity followed by lulls. By embracing silence during these lulls, rather than resisting them, you can gain insight into your creative process and learn to work with it, rather than against it.

Stillness is not simply a technique for generating ideas; it is a gift you give to yourself as a creator. It is in these quiet moments that your mind has the freedom to roam, to explore new possibilities, and to uncover ideas that may have been buried beneath the noise. By embracing silence and making it a regular part of your creative practice, you allow your stories to unfold naturally, with clarity and purpose.

The next time you sit down to write, don't rush to fill the page with words. Instead, take a moment to pause, breathe, and listen to the silence within. You may find that the most powerful ideas are already there, waiting to be heard. Through the art of stillness, you can tap into a wellspring of creativity that is always available, as long as you are willing to create the space for it.

The Power of Focus: Unlocking Creative Energy

In today's fast-paced world, the art of focus is increasingly elusive. Our attention is constantly being pulled in multiple directions—by technology, responsibilities, and the demands of daily life. For storytellers, this fragmented attention can be particularly draining, as creative energy dissipates in the noise of distractions. But what if focus was the key to unlocking a vast reservoir of creative energy? What if honing your ability to concentrate could not only improve your storytelling but also transform how you approach the entire creative process? In this chapter, we explore the power of focus and how cultivating it can enhance your storytelling by tapping into deeper levels of creativity and insight.

Focus as a Gateway to Creative Flow

At its core, focus is about being fully present in the moment. When you focus, you give your full attention to one task, one thought, or one scene, allowing yourself to become immersed in it. This immersion is where creative flow begins. Flow is that magical state where time seems to disappear, where ideas come effortlessly, and where you feel completely connected to your work. It's in these moments of deep concentration that your best ideas are born.

Think about the times you've been in flow—when the writing seemed to flow through you rather than from you. These moments are not accidents. They are the direct result of intense focus. When you focus, you free yourself from distractions, allowing your creative energy to channel directly into the task at hand. Rather than spreading your attention thin across multiple ideas or tasks, you invest deeply in one, and this investment pays off in the form of clarity, insight, and inspiration.

The challenge, of course, is that focus does not always come easily. In a world filled with distractions, focus is something you must cultivate. But once you begin to develop this skill, it can unlock creative energy that was previously out of reach.

Clearing Mental Clutter to Make Room for Creativity

Before you can focus on your story, you must first clear away the mental clutter that often occupies your mind. This clutter might include worries, to-do lists, or unrelated thoughts that have nothing to do with your creative work. In Zen philosophy, this mental clutter is sometimes referred to as "the monkey mind"—a mind that jumps from thought to thought, never staying still long enough to fully engage with one idea.

To combat the monkey mind, begin by setting aside time for quiet reflection or meditation before you start writing. This practice helps clear away distractions and allows you to center your mind. Focus on your breath, and let go of any thoughts that aren't related to your story. As these thoughts arise, acknowledge them, and then gently bring your attention back to your breathing. Over time, this practice of mindfulness will help you develop the ability to clear your mind more quickly and focus more deeply on your creative work.

When your mind is uncluttered, your creative energy can flow more freely. You'll notice that ideas come more easily, your writing feels more fluid, and you're able to connect with your characters, plot, and themes in a deeper way. This is the power of focus: it allows you to access a purer form of creativity, one that is not diluted by the noise of everyday life.

Single-Tasking: The Key to Creative Focus

One of the biggest enemies of focus is multitasking. We live in a culture that often celebrates the ability to juggle multiple tasks at once, but research has shown that multitasking can actually reduce productivity and creativity. When you divide your attention between tasks, you lose the ability to dive deeply into any one of them. Your creative energy becomes fragmented, and as a result, the quality of your work suffers.

To unlock your full creative potential, embrace the art of single-tasking. This means focusing on one task—whether it's outlining your plot, writing a scene, or developing a character—and giving it your undivided attention. When you single-task, you allow yourself to go deeper into the creative process. You become more attuned to the nuances of your story, more aware of the emotions driving your characters, and more connected to the larger themes of your narrative.

Single-tasking requires discipline, especially in a world that constantly encourages distraction. But with practice, you'll find that single-tasking not only improves the quality of your work but also makes the creative process more enjoyable. When you're fully immersed in one task, you experience the joy of creative flow—the feeling that you're fully present and engaged in the act of creation.

Harnessing Focus in the Writing Process

So how do you harness the power of focus in your daily writing routine? It begins with intention. Before you start writing, set a clear intention for what you want to accomplish. Whether it's drafting a particular scene, outlining a chapter, or brainstorming ideas for your protagonist, having a specific goal helps direct your focus.

Once you've set your intention, create an environment that supports your focus. Eliminate distractions by turning off notifications, closing unnecessary tabs on your computer, and silencing your phone. If possible, create a dedicated space for writing—one that is free from the distractions of daily life. This space doesn't need to be elaborate; it simply needs to be a place where you can focus fully on your creative work.

During your writing session, practice mindful awareness. If you find your mind wandering, gently bring it back to the task at hand. This practice is similar to meditation, where you continually refocus on your breath whenever your thoughts drift. Over time, this ability to refocus will strengthen, allowing you to stay engaged in your creative process for longer periods.

. . . .

THE ROLE OF BREAKS in Sustaining Focus

While focus is essential for unlocking creative energy, it's also important to recognize that focus is not something you can maintain indefinitely. The human brain needs regular breaks to sustain high levels of concentration. Just as a Zen practitioner might take short breaks during meditation to refresh the mind, you should build breaks into your writing routine to maintain your focus and energy.

The Pomodoro Technique is a popular method for managing focus and breaks. It involves working in focused bursts of 25 minutes, followed by a short break. After four "pomodoros," you take a longer break. This approach works well for many writers because it encourages deep focus without overwhelming the brain. By taking regular breaks, you give your mind the opportunity to rest and recharge, allowing you to return to your writing with renewed focus and creativity.

Embracing the Present Moment in Your Story

At the heart of focus is the ability to be fully present. When you're writing, being present means engaging deeply with your characters, your plot, and your setting in the current moment. You're not thinking about what happens later in the story or worrying about how readers will respond; you're simply immersed in the scene in front of you.

This sense of presence is what allows you to write with clarity and intention. When you're fully focused on the present moment in your story, you can see the details more vividly, hear the dialogue more clearly, and feel the emotions more intensely. Your writing becomes more authentic because you're not trying to control or manipulate the story—you're allowing it to unfold naturally in real-time.

To cultivate this sense of presence, approach each writing session as an opportunity to connect with your story in the here and now. Let go of any expectations about where the story "should" go and simply be with your characters in their current moment. Trust that by focusing on the present, the larger arc of your story will reveal itself in time.

The power of focus lies in its ability to unlock your creative energy, allowing you to write with greater depth, clarity, and purpose. By cultivating focus, you tap into a state of flow where ideas come effortlessly and your storytelling becomes more intuitive. Whether you're writing a novel, screenplay, or short story, focus is the key to accessing the full potential of your creativity.

Remember, focus is not about rigid control or forcing your ideas into place. It's about creating the space for creativity to emerge naturally, and being fully present in the process. Through the art of single-tasking, clearing mental clutter, and embracing the present moment, you can harness the power of focus to unlock new levels of storytelling and bring your most inspired ideas to life.

In Zen philosophy, much emphasis is placed on understanding the whole picture before getting lost in the details. When applied to storytelling, this concept translates into an approach that encourages seeing the conclusion of your story first. While many writers begin at the beginning, hoping the story will unfold naturally, starting from the end can provide a clear direction and purpose, ensuring that each scene, each character arc, and each plot twist serves a greater narrative goal. In this chapter, we'll explore how starting from the end can enhance your storytelling, giving it a sense of purpose and coherence that makes the writing process smoother and more intuitive.

Why Start from the End?

Starting from the end is counterintuitive for many storytellers, who are more accustomed to letting the story evolve from a starting point and finding their way through the plot as they go. However, beginning with the ending provides a valuable roadmap. Knowing where your story ultimately leads helps you determine how every preceding event, character decision, and subplot connects to that conclusion.

The benefit of working backward is that it forces you to think about the resolution of all the story's conflicts and the growth of your characters from the very beginning. With a clear picture of how your protagonist ends their journey, you can create a more structured path that logically and emotionally leads them to that destination. This process prevents aimless writing, ensures that your story has a strong emotional payoff, and keeps your themes consistent throughout.

Imagine you're trying to solve a maze. If you start at the beginning, it's easy to get lost in dead ends. But if you begin at the exit and trace your way back, every decision you make has direction and purpose. In storytelling, starting from the end allows you to trace the character's journey backward, ensuring that every choice and event naturally leads to a satisfying resolution.

Visualizing the Conclusion

Before you begin plotting or drafting your story, take some time to meditate on the ending. Close your eyes and visualize the final scene. Where are your characters? What is their emotional state? What have they gained or lost? By immersing yourself in the conclusion, you gain insight into the core message or transformation that your story is driving toward.

Ask yourself some key questions to guide this visualization:

- What is the emotional impact you want the ending to have on your audience?
- How has your protagonist changed from the beginning to the end?
- What conflicts have been resolved, and how were they resolved?
- What themes come to a head in this final moment?

By focusing on these questions, you'll create a vivid mental picture of the conclusion that will guide your storytelling journey. This visualization doesn't need to be perfect or detailed at first. The goal is to create an emotional and thematic blueprint that you can refine as you work through the rest of the story.

Working Backwards Through Character Arcs

Once you've established the ending, the next step is to work backward through your character arcs. Knowing how your protagonist ends their journey gives you the chance to map out the specific steps of their transformation. Character development is one of the most crucial elements in storytelling, and starting from the end ensures that every decision your character makes along the way is purposeful.

For instance, if your protagonist ends the story having overcome a major fear or achieved a long-sought-after goal, consider how you can introduce this fear or desire at the beginning. What events need to happen for this transformation to feel earned? How can you challenge your character along the way to help them grow into the person they become at the end?

By working backward through your character's emotional and psychological journey, you ensure that their arc feels authentic. You're no longer leaving character growth to chance; instead, you're carefully constructing a path that takes them from who they are at the start to who they are at the conclusion. Each trial, setback, and victory they face is in service of this ultimate transformation.

Reverse Engineering Plot Structure

Plot structure is another area where starting from the end can provide a clear advantage. Once you know how your story ends, you can reverse-engineer the events that lead up to that moment. This method allows you to ensure that every plot point is meaningful and builds toward the resolution, rather than existing simply to fill space.

Begin by identifying the climactic moment in your story—the point at which everything comes to a head. This moment is likely close to the ending, where the main conflict reaches its peak and the protagonist faces their greatest challenge. Then, work backward to figure out the chain of events that leads to this climax. What key decisions does your protagonist make that push them toward this point? What obstacles do they encounter along the way?

By reverse-engineering the plot, you can avoid the common pitfall of getting stuck in the middle of your story, unsure of how to move forward. Instead, you have a clear roadmap that leads you from one major event to the next, with each step logically progressing toward the climax and resolution.

Setting Up Themes and Symbols

Starting from the end also allows you to think about how to weave themes and symbols throughout your story. Often, themes become more apparent as you near the conclusion of your story, but by starting with the ending, you can plan these elements from the very beginning.

• • • •

FOR EXAMPLE, IF YOUR story's conclusion is about the protagonist finding inner peace after a long period of struggle, you can introduce visual and thematic motifs early on that support this theme. Perhaps there's a recurring symbol of water that represents serenity, or a specific piece of dialogue that foreshadows the protagonist's eventual acceptance of their fate. When you begin with the ending in mind, these thematic threads become easier to introduce early on and develop throughout the narrative.

Symbols and themes can be powerful tools for adding layers of meaning to your story, and starting from the end allows you to incorporate them in a way that feels organic and purposeful. Rather than tacking on themes or symbols after the fact, you build them into the very fabric of your story from the start.

Crafting a Satisfying Emotional Payoff

One of the greatest benefits of starting from the end is that it allows you to craft an emotionally satisfying payoff for your audience. A well-executed ending ties together the emotional and narrative threads of your story in a way that resonates deeply with readers or viewers. By starting with this moment in mind, you can ensure that every element of your story—characters, plot, themes—contributes to that final emotional impact.

Think about some of the most memorable endings in storytelling. Whether it's the bittersweet conclusion of a love story or the triumphant resolution of a hero's journey, the emotional payoff is what sticks with audiences long after the story has ended. Starting from the end helps you ensure that this payoff is not only impactful but also earned. Every scene, every piece of dialogue, and every character decision has led to this moment.

When you plan your story backward, you also have the opportunity to build in moments of foreshadowing and emotional tension that will make the final payoff even more powerful. The resolution doesn't come out of nowhere—it feels inevitable, like the culmination of everything that has come before it.

Trusting the Process

Starting from the end may feel strange at first, especially if you're used to letting your story evolve organically. But with practice, this approach can bring a new level of clarity and purpose to your writing. Trust that by knowing where your story ends, you're not limiting your creativity—you're giving it direction. As you work backward through your character arcs, plot points, and themes, you'll find that the story begins to reveal itself in ways you hadn't anticipated. Each scene, each decision, and each conflict feels more intentional, more grounded in the larger narrative. And when you finally sit down to write, you'll have the confidence of knowing that every word is leading toward a resolution that is both emotionally and narratively satisfying. Starting from the end is a powerful storytelling tool that helps you see the whole picture before you begin writing. By visualizing the conclusion first, you create a roadmap that ensures every element of your story works together to deliver a cohesive and impactful narrative.

Writing for Visual Moments: Capturing the Essence of a Scene

In storytelling, there are moments that leap off the page or screen—scenes that linger in the minds of readers or viewers long after the story has ended. These visual moments are more than just sequences of events; they are snapshots of emotion, action, and meaning that crystallize the essence of your narrative. Whether you are writing a novel or a screenplay, crafting these powerful moments requires a deep understanding of how to translate the visual into words. In this chapter, we'll explore how to write for visual moments, capturing the essence of a scene so that it resonates with your audience on a visceral level.

The Power of Visual Storytelling

At its core, storytelling is a visual medium. Even when we write words on a page, we are painting pictures in the minds of our audience. These pictures evoke emotions, create tension, and drive the plot forward. Great storytellers understand how to craft scenes that engage the reader or viewer not just intellectually, but visually. When done effectively, visual storytelling transcends language—it creates an immersive experience that pulls the audience into the world of the story.

Consider some of the most iconic moments in film or literature: the sweeping sunset at the end of *Gone with the Wind*, the first appearance of the T-Rex in *Jurassic Park*, or the charged silence between two characters in a love story. These moments stand out not only because of what happens, but because of how they are visually rendered. They make you feel something deeply because they show, rather than tell.

When writing for visual moments, your goal is to create scenes that evoke emotion and meaning through vivid description, pacing, and atmosphere. You want to capture the mood, the movement, and the visual elements in such a way that the audience can "see" the scene as clearly as if they were watching it unfold in real life.

Visualizing before Writing

To capture the essence of a scene, begin by visualizing it fully before you write. Close your eyes and imagine yourself in the setting of the scene. Where are your characters standing or moving? What are they wearing? What's happening in the background? What is the lighting like? How does the space feel? Use all of your senses to bring the scene to life in your mind's eye.

This process of visualization is like directing a film in your mind. You are not just writing about a scene—you are placing yourself inside it, seeing it unfold moment by moment. By immersing yourself in the details, you can bring greater clarity to your writing and help the reader feel as though they are present in the moment as well.

• • • •

AS YOU VISUALIZE, PAY attention to the most striking or emotionally charged images. Is it the expression on a character's face during a pivotal conversation? The way light filters through a window during a tense moment? The sound of footsteps echoing in an empty hallway? These are the visual cues that will guide your writing and give the scene its emotional weight.

Show, Don't Tell

The classic advice to "show, don't tell" is especially important when writing for visual moments. Telling describes events in a way that is abstract and detached. Showing, on the other hand, brings the reader into the experience by allowing them to witness it firsthand. Instead of telling the reader that a character is angry, show their clenched fists, the tension in their jaw, or the way they pace back and forth. Instead of telling the reader that a setting is beautiful, describe the shimmering sunlight on the water, the rustle of leaves in the wind, or the way the horizon stretches endlessly before them.

This focus on showing allows you to convey emotion, action, and atmosphere without spoon-feeding the reader. It invites them to engage with the scene more deeply, making them an active participant in the storytelling process. When writing for visual moments, always ask yourself: How can I show this, rather than tell it?

Pacing and Rhythm in Visual Scenes

Pacing plays a crucial role in how visual moments unfold. Just as a filmmaker controls the pacing of a scene through cuts, camera angles, and movement, a writer controls pacing through sentence structure, dialogue, and description. The rhythm of your writing sets the tone for the visual experience.

For action-heavy scenes, shorter, punchier sentences can create a sense of urgency and movement. For example:

The car sped around the corner. Tires screeched. He slammed on the brakes, but it was too late. Metal crunched. Glass shattered.

The quick pace mirrors the fast, chaotic energy of the scene, pulling the reader into the tension and immediacy of the moment.

In contrast, slower scenes benefit from longer, more descriptive sentences that allow the reader to soak in the atmosphere. For a quiet, reflective moment, you might write:

The sun dipped slowly beneath the horizon, casting a warm, golden light across the field. She stood there, watching the sky fade from orange to deep purple, her breath steady, her mind quiet for the first time in days.

The slower rhythm here creates a peaceful, contemplative mood, allowing the reader to experience the beauty of the scene at the same pace as the character.

By controlling the pacing of your visual moments, you can guide the emotional response of your audience, whether it's creating tension, excitement, or calm.

Creating Cinematic Imagery

Cinematic imagery refers to writing that feels as though it could be lifted straight from the screen. It's vivid, dynamic, and highly visual, making the reader feel as though they are watching a film unfold in their mind. To create cinematic imagery, think like a director or cinematographer. Consider how the scene would be shot on film, and then translate that into your writing.

For example, imagine a character walking down a dimly lit street at night. A cinematic version of this scene might focus on the interplay of light and shadow, the sounds of the character's footsteps, the tension in their posture, and the anticipation of what lies ahead:

The streetlights flickered, casting long, thin shadows across the cracked pavement. His footsteps echoed in the still night air, each one louder than the last. He pulled his coat tighter around him, his eyes scanning the empty street for any sign of movement. Somewhere in the distance, a dog barked. He quickened his pace.

This type of writing pulls the reader in by focusing on the sensory details that create a specific mood. It's not just about what happens in the scene, but how it feels to be in that moment.

Using Atmosphere to Enhance Visual Moments

Atmosphere is the emotional tone of a scene, and it plays a vital role in shaping how visual moments are perceived. Whether it's the eerie calm of a foggy night or the bustling energy of a crowded marketplace, atmosphere sets the stage for the visual experience. To capture the essence of a scene, think about how the atmosphere influences the characters and the action.

For example, in a suspenseful scene, you might describe how the oppressive silence heightens the tension:

The room was unnervingly quiet. Not even the creak of a floorboard or the hum of electricity broke the silence. Her heartbeat thudded loudly in her ears, each breath coming slower, heavier. She knew something was wrong before she saw it.

Here, the lack of sound becomes a tool to build anticipation and fear. The atmosphere amplifies the character's anxiety, creating a visual moment that is deeply tied to the emotional undercurrent of the scene.

The Emotional Core of Visual Moments

At the heart of every powerful visual moment is emotion. Visual storytelling is not just about painting a pretty picture; it's about using imagery to convey deep emotional truths. Whether it's joy, grief, love, or fear, the emotion behind the scene is what makes it resonate with the audience.

When writing for visual moments, always ask yourself: What is the emotional core of this scene? What do I want the audience to feel? Once you have a clear sense of the emotion, you can shape the visuals to support it. A scene that evokes sadness might use muted colors, slow movement, and quiet sounds. A scene that evokes excitement might be fast-paced, bright, and full of movement.

The key is to align the visual elements with the emotional experience, creating a seamless connection between what the audience sees and what they feel.

Writing for visual moments is about more than just describing what happens in a scene. It's about capturing the essence of that moment—the mood, the movement, the emotion—in a way that allows the audience to see and feel it as if they were there. By focusing on visualization, showing rather than telling, controlling pacing, and using atmosphere and cinematic imagery, you can craft scenes that linger in the minds of your readers or viewers long after they've turned the final page or watched the last frame.

Creating a compelling protagonist is one of the most vital aspects of storytelling. It is through the protagonist's journey that the audience connects emotionally with the story. But creating a truly memorable character, one that feels real and authentic, requires more than simply assigning traits or goals. In Zen practice, there's an emphasis on mindfulness, stillness, and intention. These principles can be applied to character creation, allowing you to breathe life into your protagonists with clarity and purpose. In this chapter, we'll explore how to take a Zen approach to crafting your characters, focusing on how to make them resonate deeply with both you and your audience.

Mindful Character Creation

In Zen, mindfulness is the act of being fully present, aware of your thoughts, and observing without judgment. Applying this mindfulness to character creation allows you to engage deeply with your protagonist, understanding who they are at their core before you begin shaping their actions, dialogue, and relationships.

When crafting a protagonist, the first step is to meditate on who they are—not just their role in the plot, but their inner essence. Close your eyes, breathe deeply, and visualize your character. What do they look like? How do they carry themselves? What emotions do they hold inside? Take the time to sit with them in your mind's eye, observing their traits, quirks, and behaviors without rushing to define them with labels or categories.

This process is about discovery rather than invention. Instead of forcing a character to fit into a preconceived mold, you're allowing their personality to emerge naturally. This mindful approach creates characters who feel more authentic, whose motivations are deeply rooted in their inner world rather than imposed externally by the needs of the plot.

Character as Reflection of Self

In Zen philosophy, there's a belief that all things are interconnected, and this applies to character creation as well. Often, the most compelling characters are those who reflect some aspect of the writer or creator. This doesn't mean that every protagonist is a direct mirror of the writer, but rather that they embody emotions, struggles, or desires that resonate with the creator on a personal level.

To breathe life into your protagonist, ask yourself: What part of me is reflected in this character? Are they struggling with something that mirrors a challenge you've faced in your own life? Do they embody a quality you admire or fear? By connecting your protagonist to your own experience, you give them a depth and authenticity that resonates with the audience. Readers and viewers can sense when a character is real—when they are crafted from a place of emotional truth.

This connection to self doesn't need to be literal. It could be as abstract as sharing a common emotional journey or fear. The key is to create a protagonist whose internal world feels authentic because it is tied to something you understand deeply.

The Importance of Character Stillness

Stillness is a central tenet of Zen. It's not just about physical stillness, but mental and emotional stillness—the ability to find peace and clarity within oneself. When applied to character creation, stillness means allowing your protagonist room to breathe. Rather than overloading them with traits, backstory, and action from the outset, give them space to develop organically.

This stillness can be found in moments of reflection for the character. Not every scene needs to be filled with action or dialogue. Some of the most powerful moments in storytelling are those of quiet introspection, where the protagonist is alone with their thoughts, facing an inner conflict. These moments of stillness allow the audience to connect more deeply with the character's emotions, giving them insight into their struggles, desires, and fears.

For example, a scene where a protagonist is sitting by a window, watching the rain fall, can reveal as much about their emotional state as a scene filled with action or dialogue. In these quiet moments, the character's inner life becomes more vivid. Allowing stillness within your protagonist's journey gives them the space to evolve naturally, making their arc feel more grounded and real.

The Protagonist's Core Conflict

At the heart of every great protagonist is a core conflict. This conflict doesn't have to be external (though it often is), but it should always have an internal dimension. In Zen, there's a belief that growth comes from within, through facing one's own mind and emotions. Your protagonist's journey should reflect this internal battle, even as they navigate external challenges.

To discover your protagonist's core conflict, ask yourself: What is their greatest fear? What do they desire most deeply, and what stands in the way of achieving it? This conflict should be something that shapes every decision they make, whether consciously or unconsciously.

For example, a character might be driven by a fear of failure. This fear could manifest in various ways—perhaps they're overly cautious, unwilling to take risks, or maybe they compensate by being overly ambitious. Whatever the external plot may be, this internal conflict will color how they react to challenges, relationships, and setbacks. By grounding your protagonist in a core conflict, you give them a strong foundation for growth and change over the course of the story.

Working Backwards from the End

As discussed in earlier chapters, starting from the end is a powerful tool in storytelling. This approach applies to character creation as well. By visualizing where your protagonist ends up—how they've changed or what they've learned—you can work backwards to understand how they got there.

What transformation does your protagonist undergo throughout the story? Do they overcome their core conflict? Do they come to terms with something about themselves or their world? By seeing the end of their journey first, you can craft a more intentional character arc, ensuring that every decision, mistake, and victory leads them toward this final state.

When you know the destination, you can create a path for your protagonist that feels purposeful and cohesive. Their growth isn't random or reactive; it's part of a larger design that makes their journey more satisfying to the audience.

The Balance of Strengths and Flaws

No protagonist is complete without a balance of strengths and flaws. In Zen, balance is key to understanding the nature of things—there is no light without darkness, no strength without vulnerability. Your protagonist should embody this balance, making them complex and relatable.

Start by identifying their key strengths. What are they good at? What makes them stand out as a character? Whether it's their courage, intelligence, compassion, or determination, their strengths should be an integral part of how they navigate the challenges in the story.

But just as important as their strengths are their flaws. No protagonist should be perfect, as it is their imperfections that make them human. Perhaps your character is overly proud, emotionally distant, or impulsive. These flaws create tension within the character's journey and provide opportunities for growth. More importantly, they make your protagonist relatable to the audience. Everyone has flaws, and seeing a character struggle with their own shortcomings creates a deeper emotional connection.

Allowing the Character to Surprise You

Zen teaches the value of openness—being receptive to what comes rather than trying to control every outcome. This principle can be applied to character creation as well. While it's important to have a clear idea of your protagonist's core conflict and journey, you should also leave room for them to surprise you.

As you write, you may find that your character takes unexpected actions or reveals aspects of their personality that you hadn't planned. This is a good thing. It means your character is alive, evolving beyond the initial blueprint you created. Embrace these moments of spontaneity, as they often lead to some of the most authentic and interesting developments in your story.

Allowing your protagonist to surprise you is part of the Zen approach to storytelling—letting go of control and trusting in the process. Your characters, much like real people, may not always behave predictably. By giving them the freedom to grow organically, you breathe life into them, making them feel real and dynamic.

The Zen of character creation is about more than just giving your protagonist a name, background, and goals. It's about breathing life into them, allowing them to evolve naturally from a place of mindfulness and intention. By connecting deeply with their inner world, creating space for stillness and reflection, and embracing both their strengths and flaws, you craft a protagonist who feels authentic and compelling. Remember, your protagonist's journey is not just about external events—it's about internal growth, transformation, and conflict. By applying a Zen approach, you can create characters who resonate deeply with your audience, whose stories are driven by emotional truth, and whose journeys feel purposeful and real.

In every great story, the protagonist's journey is defined by the challenges they face, and these challenges are often personified through the antagonist. The antagonist represents conflict, opposition, and, ultimately, a reflection of the protagonist's deepest struggles. But to craft a truly compelling antagonist, it's important to go beyond the surface-level villainy and explore the duality that exists within them. Just as the protagonist embodies growth, hope, or change, the antagonist reflects opposition, fear, or control. In this chapter, we'll explore how to create an antagonist whose path is not only believable but intricately tied to the protagonist's journey, embracing the duality that drives the story's core conflict.

Understanding Duality in Storytelling

In Zen philosophy, duality is seen as a natural balance in life—yin and yang, light and dark, creation and destruction. In storytelling, this balance is often represented through the relationship between the protagonist and the antagonist. These two forces are not just opposites; they are interconnected, each shaping and defining the other.

The antagonist is not simply an obstacle for the protagonist to overcome. They are a crucial element that drives the story's emotional and narrative stakes. By creating an antagonist who embodies duality—who has their own goals, motivations, and fears—you add depth to your conflict. The antagonist becomes more than just a villain; they become a mirror, reflecting the protagonist's challenges and testing their beliefs and strength.

The duality between the protagonist and the antagonist is often what makes conflict compelling. The antagonist's path should be as carefully crafted and considered as the protagonist's, giving both characters equal weight in the narrative.

The Antagonist as a Reflection of the Protagonist

To fully embrace the duality of conflict, the antagonist must be seen as a reflection of the protagonist. They may represent the dark side of the protagonist's traits or embody the fears and weaknesses the protagonist is trying to overcome. This reflection creates a powerful dynamic, where the antagonist's actions directly challenge the protagonist's growth.

For example, if your protagonist is someone who values freedom and independence, the antagonist might represent control and domination. Their conflict becomes more than just a physical or external battle—it becomes a philosophical struggle, where the core values of both characters are put to the test. The protagonist's journey to achieve freedom is intensified by the antagonist's desire to maintain control, creating a layered and meaningful conflict.

· · · ·

WHEN CRAFTING YOUR antagonist, ask yourself: What does this character represent that opposes the protagonist's values or goals? How can their presence force the protagonist to confront their own fears, flaws, or desires? By making the antagonist a reflection of the protagonist's internal journey, you create a more nuanced and engaging conflict that resonates on a deeper level.

Giving the Antagonist Clear Motivations

A compelling antagonist is never evil for the sake of being evil. Just as your protagonist has motivations and desires, your antagonist should have clear goals that drive their actions. In many cases, the antagonist believes that they are in the right, and their motivations are rooted in their own perspective of the world. By giving the antagonist a reason for their behavior, you humanize them and make their actions more believable.

Consider what drives your antagonist. What do they want to achieve? Is it power, revenge, justice, or something more personal? Their motivation doesn't have to be grand or complex, but it should be rooted in something that feels real to them. Even if their actions are morally questionable, they should be driven by a sense of purpose or belief in their cause.

This focus on motivation adds depth to your antagonist, making them a more formidable and interesting force for the protagonist to face. The audience may not agree with the antagonist's goals, but they should understand why the antagonist is pursuing them, even if it creates tension or conflict.

The Antagonist's Path of Growth (or Decline)

While the protagonist's journey is often one of growth or self-discovery, the antagonist's path can take different forms. In some cases, the antagonist experiences their own form of growth, though it may lead them deeper into their flaws or darker tendencies. In other cases, the antagonist may experience a decline, as their obsession with achieving their goal leads them to self-destruction.

Regardless of the direction their path takes, the antagonist should undergo some form of transformation over the course of the story. Just as the protagonist faces challenges that force them to evolve, the antagonist should also encounter obstacles that test their resolve and push them to change—whether for better or worse.

For example, an antagonist who begins the story with a strong sense of justice may become more ruthless as they pursue their goal, crossing moral lines they once held sacred. Alternatively, an antagonist who starts as a seemingly cold-hearted villain might reveal deeper vulnerabilities as the story progresses, showing that their motivations are driven by past trauma or loss.

By giving the antagonist their own arc, you make them a more dynamic and unpredictable character. Their path becomes just as engaging as the protagonist's, and the audience is drawn into the tension between these two evolving forces.

Balancing Symmetry and Contrast

When creating the relationship between the protagonist and antagonist, consider how symmetry and contrast play a role in their dynamic. Symmetry refers to the ways in which the protagonist and antagonist mirror each other—how their desires, fears, and motivations are similar, even if they're expressed in opposite ways. Contrast, on the other hand, refers to the stark differences between them, the qualities that make them fundamentally opposed.

A well-crafted antagonist often shares some core traits with the protagonist, creating a sense of symmetry. For instance, both might be ambitious, courageous, or driven by a desire for justice. However, where the protagonist seeks to achieve their goals through moral or selfless means, the antagonist might be willing to resort to manipulation, violence, or coercion. This balance of symmetry and contrast creates a tension that drives the story forward.

One powerful example of symmetry and contrast is found in the relationship between Batman and the Joker. Both characters are shaped by trauma and seek to impose order or chaos on Gotham City. However, while Batman represents controlled justice and order, the Joker embodies chaos and anarchy. Their conflict is heightened by the fact that they both seek to reshape the world in their own image, but in completely opposite ways.

By balancing symmetry and contrast, you create a relationship between the protagonist and antagonist that feels dynamic and inevitable. The conflict between them isn't just about good versus evil—it's about two opposing worldviews colliding, forcing both characters to confront their beliefs.

Humanizing the Antagonist

No matter how ruthless or villainous your antagonist may be, they should still possess some degree of humanity. Humanizing the antagonist makes them more relatable and complex, even if the audience disagrees with their actions. This doesn't mean making the antagonist sympathetic, but it does mean giving them emotions, relationships, or vulnerabilities that ground them in reality.

Perhaps your antagonist has a family they care about, a past trauma that shapes their worldview, or moments of doubt in their own mission. These humanizing details give the antagonist layers, making them feel like a fully realized person rather than a one-dimensional villain.

Humanizing the antagonist also deepens the conflict between them and the protagonist. The audience may be torn between rooting for the protagonist and understanding the antagonist's point of view. This emotional complexity adds richness to the story and prevents the conflict from feeling black-and-white.

The Antagonist's Ultimate Test

Every antagonist should face a moment of reckoning—an ultimate test that challenges their resolve and reveals their true nature. This test might come in the form of a confrontation with the protagonist, a betrayal by someone they trust, or a moral dilemma that forces them to make a difficult choice.

The outcome of this test often defines the antagonist's path. Will they double down on their goals, embracing their darker tendencies? Or will they experience a moment of vulnerability, showing a glimpse of humanity before their final confrontation with the protagonist?

This ultimate test not only shapes the antagonist's fate but also raises the stakes for the protagonist. The antagonist's decisions and actions directly impact the protagonist's journey, and their final showdown becomes the culmination of the story's central conflict.

The antagonist is not just an obstacle for the protagonist to overcome—they are a mirror, a reflection of the protagonist's own struggles, values, and fears. By embracing the duality within the antagonist, you create a character who is as complex and compelling as the protagonist, elevating the conflict to something more profound and meaningful.

Through thoughtful characterization, clear motivations, and a dynamic arc, the antagonist's path becomes an integral part of the story's emotional and narrative tension. Whether the antagonist represents a dark reflection of the protagonist or challenges their deepest beliefs, their presence in the story forces both characters to evolve, leading to a climax that resonates deeply with the audience.

In the end, the duality between the protagonist and antagonist is what makes the conflict real, intense, and unforgettable. By crafting an antagonist who embodies this duality, you create a story that goes beyond simple opposition, offering a rich exploration of character, motivation, and the nature of conflict itself.

Astory, like life itself, is in constant motion. It ebbs and flows, rises and falls, and follows a natural rhythm that carries the audience through a journey of emotions, challenges, and resolutions. The story arc is the framework that guides this flow, providing structure to the narrative and ensuring that every scene, character development, and conflict builds toward a meaningful resolution. Without a well-defined arc, stories can feel aimless or disjointed. In this chapter, we'll explore how to craft a strong story arc, how to let it shape your narrative, and how to guide your audience through a satisfying and impactful journey.

What Is a Story Arc?

At its most basic, a story arc is the path that a narrative follows from beginning to end. It encompasses the rise and fall of tension, the development of characters, and the eventual resolution of the central conflict. The story arc ensures that each part of the narrative serves a purpose, with every scene building on the one before it, leading to a climax, and finally resolving in a way that feels both inevitable and fulfilling.

The arc can be visualized as a curve, beginning with the exposition, rising through conflict, peaking at the climax, and then descending through resolution. It's the shape that gives the story a sense of direction and momentum. Without it, the narrative would feel flat, lacking the tension and payoff that makes storytelling engaging.

While there are many variations on the traditional arc, most stories adhere to some form of this basic structure. Even in non-linear storytelling or experimental narratives, the arc provides a hidden framework that guides the flow of the story. Whether you're writing a novel, screenplay, or short story, understanding the story arc is key to crafting a narrative that resonates with your audience.

The Components of a Story Arc

To understand how to guide the flow of your narrative, it's important to break down the key components of a story arc. These elements provide the foundation for how the story progresses and how the characters evolve.

Exposition: The beginning of the story, where the world, characters, and setting are introduced. This is where you establish the status quo—what life looks like before the central conflict arises. The exposition gives the audience the context they need to understand the stakes of the story.

Rising Action: The period during which tension builds. The protagonist encounters challenges, obstacles, or conflicts that propel the story forward. Each challenge raises the stakes, increasing the emotional and narrative tension.

Climax: The peak of the story, where the central conflict comes to a head. This is the moment of highest tension, where the protagonist must confront the antagonist or face their greatest challenge. The climax is often a turning point that leads directly into the resolution.

Falling Action: After the climax, the story begins to wind down. The consequences of the climax play out, and loose ends are tied up. The falling action allows the audience to process the climax and understand how it impacts the characters and their world.

Resolution: The end of the story, where the central conflict is fully resolved. The protagonist has either achieved their goal or failed, and the story reaches its conclusion. The resolution provides closure for the audience, bringing the arc to a satisfying end.

Understanding these components allows you to map out the flow of your story, ensuring that each part serves its purpose in guiding the audience through a journey of increasing tension, emotional stakes, and eventual resolution.

Starting with the End in Mind

As discussed in previous chapters, one of the most powerful techniques for crafting a story arc is starting with the end in mind. By visualizing the resolution before you begin writing, you create a clear destination for your narrative.

This approach helps you shape the arc with purpose, ensuring that every scene and event leads toward a meaningful conclusion.

When you know how the story ends—whether it's a victory, a tragedy, or a bittersweet compromise—you can work backward to design the rising action and climax. What challenges must your protagonist face to reach that ending? What decisions or sacrifices must they make along the way? By keeping the resolution in mind, you maintain a sense of direction and avoid unnecessary tangents that don't serve the larger narrative.

Starting with the end also helps you create a more satisfying resolution. Because the story arc has been carefully crafted to lead toward a specific goal, the resolution feels earned. The audience can see how every event and conflict contributed to the protagonist's journey, making the payoff more impactful.

The Protagonist's Role in the Arc

At the heart of every story arc is the protagonist's journey. The arc is not just about the external events that unfold but also about the internal transformation of the main character. As the protagonist moves through the rising action, climax, and resolution, they should undergo some form of change, whether it's growth, self-discovery, or even a tragic downfall.

To craft a compelling protagonist arc, ask yourself: How does the protagonist change over the course of the story? What internal conflicts mirror the external challenges they face? Whether your protagonist is learning to overcome fear, embrace vulnerability, or let go of control, their personal growth should be intertwined with the narrative arc.

The protagonist's arc also provides the emotional core of the story. While the external plot might revolve around battles, investigations, or romance, the real heart of the story is often found in the character's internal journey. By aligning the protagonist's development with the flow of the story arc, you create a narrative that is both emotionally and narratively cohesive.

Rising Tension and Escalating Stakes

One of the most critical elements of a story arc is the gradual increase in tension and stakes. As the story progresses through the rising action, each event should add new layers of conflict or challenge, making the protagonist's journey more difficult and the stakes higher.

If the tension doesn't rise, the story can feel stagnant. To keep the audience engaged, you need to build momentum, ensuring that each scene intensifies the central conflict. This can be achieved through external obstacles (e.g., a villain becoming more powerful, a relationship falling apart) or through internal struggles (e.g., the protagonist facing doubts, fears, or moral dilemmas).

The key is to continually raise the stakes, forcing the protagonist to make more difficult choices or face more dangerous situations. The climax should feel like the culmination of all this rising tension—a moment where everything the protagonist has faced comes to a head.

Climax: The Turning Point

The climax is the pivotal moment in the story arc—the point at which the central conflict reaches its peak. This is where the protagonist must confront their greatest challenge, whether it's defeating an antagonist, resolving a personal crisis, or making a life-altering decision.

The climax should feel inevitable yet surprising. The audience should sense that everything has been building toward this moment, but it should also contain an element of unpredictability that keeps them on the edge of their seat. Whether the protagonist succeeds or fails in their goal, the climax should be a turning point that sets the stage for the resolution.

In crafting the climax, think about the emotional stakes as much as the narrative stakes. This is the moment where the protagonist's internal and external conflicts collide, forcing them to make a choice or take action that will determine the outcome of the story. The climax should reveal something profound about the protagonist—whether it's their strength, vulnerability, or moral compass—and leave the audience with a sense of catharsis.

Falling Action and Resolution

After the intensity of the climax, the story needs to wind down, allowing the audience to process the events that have just unfolded. The falling action provides this space, offering a chance to resolve any remaining subplots and show the consequences of the protagonist's decisions.

The resolution ties up the story arc, bringing closure to the central conflict. This doesn't always mean a happy ending—resolutions can be tragic, bittersweet, or open-ended—but it should feel like a natural conclusion to the journey. The protagonist may have achieved their goal, learned an important lesson, or faced defeat, but the story's arc has come full circle.

In the resolution, it's important to leave the audience with a sense of emotional fulfillment. Even if the ending is not what they expected, it should resonate with the themes and conflicts that have been explored throughout the story.

Letting the Arc Guide You

As a storyteller, the story arc is your compass. It guides the flow of narrative, ensuring that every scene, character moment, and plot twist serves the larger purpose of the story. By understanding the arc and its components, you can craft a narrative that feels purposeful, cohesive, and emotionally satisfying.

Remember, the story arc is not a rigid formula—it's a flexible framework that can be adapted to suit different genres, tones, and narrative styles. Whether your story follows a traditional arc or takes a more unconventional route, the key is to maintain a sense of direction, with each part of the narrative building toward a meaningful resolution.

The story arc is more than just a structural tool—it's the heartbeat of your narrative. It's what gives your story shape, momentum, and emotional resonance. By guiding the flow of your narrative with a well-crafted arc, you take your audience on a journey that is both compelling and transformative.

Whether you're writing a sweeping epic, an intimate character study, or a fast-paced thriller, the arc is what ensures that your story has a beginning, middle, and end that work in harmony. By understanding how to create rising tension, build toward a powerful climax, and deliver a satisfying resolution, you can craft a story that stays with your audience long after the final page is turned or the credits roll.

The Hero's Journey: Discovering the Zen of Transformation

The Hero's Journey is one of the most enduring and universal storytelling structures. It is the story of a protagonist who embarks on an adventure, faces trials, learns valuable lessons, and returns transformed. While the journey itself is often fraught with external challenges, at its heart, the Hero's Journey is about inner transformation. In this chapter, we will explore the Hero's Journey through the lens of Zen philosophy, focusing on how the protagonist's journey is not just about achieving external goals, but about discovering inner truths and achieving personal growth.

By embracing a Zen approach to the Hero's Journey, we shift the focus from the hero's external battles to their internal transformation. This allows us to explore how the trials and conflicts in the story mirror the hero's inner struggles, and how the ultimate resolution is as much about self-discovery as it is about external victory.

The Call to Adventure: Awakening from the Ordinary

The Hero's Journey begins in the ordinary world, a place where the protagonist feels comfortable and safe. But inevitably, there comes a moment when the hero is called to leave this world behind. This "Call to Adventure" often appears as an invitation to step outside of one's comfort zone and embark on a journey of growth.

In Zen practice, this moment can be seen as a form of awakening—a realization that there is more to life than the ordinary routine. The hero becomes aware that something is missing, that there is a greater purpose waiting to be discovered. This sense of awakening can be sparked by a literal call (an external event, such as a crisis) or an internal restlessness, a desire for meaning and transformation.

For the protagonist, this moment of awakening is the first step toward transformation. It is the realization that the ordinary world is no longer enough, and that they must seek something greater. This echoes the Zen idea of stepping away from attachment to the familiar and embarking on a path toward deeper understanding.

Crossing the Threshold: Embracing Uncertainty

Once the hero answers the Call to Adventure, they must cross the threshold into the unknown. This is a pivotal moment in the journey, as it represents the hero's commitment to change. By leaving behind the familiar, the hero steps into a world of uncertainty, where they will face new challenges and encounters that test their resolve.

In Zen, crossing the threshold can be likened to letting go of preconceived notions and embracing the uncertainty of life. It requires a willingness to step into the unknown and trust that the journey itself will reveal the necessary lessons. The hero must learn to release control, allowing the experiences they encounter to shape their path.

This crossing is often accompanied by fear or doubt. The protagonist may hesitate, uncertain whether they are ready to face the trials ahead. But it is in embracing this uncertainty—this Zen acceptance of the unknown—that the hero begins their transformation. By stepping forward despite fear, the hero embarks on a journey of self-discovery and growth.

Trials and Tribulations: The Mirror of Inner Conflict

As the hero moves deeper into their journey, they encounter a series of trials and challenges. These external obstacles are often reflections of the hero's internal struggles, manifesting as monsters, villains, or difficult situations that force the hero to confront their own weaknesses, fears, and limitations.

From a Zen perspective, these trials can be seen as opportunities for inner reflection. Each challenge that the protagonist faces is not just a test of their strength or skill but also a mirror of their internal conflict. For example, a hero who is overly prideful may face a challenge that humbles them, while a hero who is afraid of vulnerability may be forced into a situation where they must rely on others.

The key here is understanding that these external trials are not meant to defeat the hero, but to transform them. They are the catalysts that push the hero to let go of old beliefs, fears, or habits that no longer serve them. In Zen, this process is akin to "non-attachment"—the idea that we must release our grip on the things that hold us back in order to grow.

The Dark Night of the Soul: The Moment of Surrender

In every Hero's Journey, there comes a moment of deep crisis—a "Dark Night of the Soul." This is the point at which the hero feels overwhelmed, lost, or defeated. They may question their ability to continue, feel isolated from their allies, or confront the possibility of failure.

This moment of surrender is central to the hero's transformation. In Zen, it is often through surrender—through letting go of the need to control outcomes—that one finds true peace and clarity. The Dark Night of the Soul is the hero's opportunity to relinquish their ego, their attachment to success or validation, and to fully embrace the uncertainty of the journey.

For the protagonist, this moment often leads to an epiphany—a realization about who they truly are and what they need to do to move forward. By surrendering to the process, the hero gains new insight into their path. This transformation marks the turning point in their journey, allowing them to rise from defeat with a deeper sense of purpose and inner strength.

The Reward: Inner Clarity and Outer Victory

Following the Dark Night of the Soul, the hero emerges with newfound clarity. They have confronted their deepest fears, let go of their old self, and embraced a new understanding of their purpose. This transformation is often symbolized by the hero receiving a reward—whether it's a physical treasure, knowledge, or a sense of inner peace.

In Zen terms, this reward can be seen as "enlightenment" or "awakening." The hero has achieved a state of inner clarity, having learned to accept the duality of life—both its challenges and its beauty. This moment of clarity gives the hero the strength to face the final challenge or defeat the antagonist, but it also represents a more profound transformation: the hero is no longer the same person who began the journey.

The reward is not simply about achieving external success; it's about understanding oneself on a deeper level. The hero's victory is not just over their external foes, but over their own inner conflict. They have grown, evolved, and are now equipped to face the world with a new perspective.

The Return: Bringing Transformation Back to the Ordinary World

Once the hero has achieved their goal and undergone transformation, they must return to the ordinary world. But this return is not a simple return to the status quo. The hero brings with them the lessons they've learned and the wisdom they've gained through their journey.

In Zen, this return symbolizes the integration of enlightenment into everyday life. The hero may have found peace or clarity in their journey, but the true test is how they apply that wisdom in their ordinary world. The return is a reminder that transformation is not just an internal process—it must also be reflected in one's actions, relationships, and choices.

The return is often bittersweet. The hero may have won, but they are forever changed, and the ordinary world may no longer feel like home. However, the hero's presence in the ordinary world now brings a sense of balance and understanding that was not there before.

The Hero as a Zen Practitioner

When viewed through the lens of Zen, the Hero's Journey is not just about adventure or achievement; it is about self-discovery, surrender, and transformation. The protagonist's journey mirrors the path of a Zen practitioner—starting with an awakening, facing trials that reflect inner conflict, and ultimately achieving a state of enlightenment or clarity.

This Zen approach to the Hero's Journey emphasizes the importance of the internal experience. The hero's trials and victories are not just physical or external—they are deeply rooted in their emotional and psychological growth.

The journey itself is a process of letting go, of accepting the impermanence and uncertainty of life, and of discovering the hero's true nature.

The Hero's Journey is more than a narrative structure—it is a reflection of the human experience. By approaching it through a Zen perspective, we see that the protagonist's journey is not just about battling monsters or winning wars. It is about facing oneself, embracing uncertainty, and discovering the true meaning of transformation. Through the Call to Adventure, the trials, the Dark Night of the Soul, and the ultimate reward, the protagonist embarks on a path of inner growth. Their victory is not just in the external world, but in their ability to let go of fear, ego, and attachment, finding peace and clarity within.

The Power of Simplicity: Creating Characters with Clarity

In storytelling, there is a temptation to overcomplicate characters by loading them with elaborate backstories, conflicting traits, and intricate motivations. While complexity can add depth to a character, it can also obscure their core essence, making them harder for audiences to connect with. Simplicity, on the other hand, has the power to create characters with clarity, focus, and impact. Simplicity doesn't mean the absence of depth; it means stripping away the unnecessary layers to reveal the true core of who the character is. In this chapter, we'll explore how simplicity can be a powerful tool in character creation, helping you craft characters that are memorable, authentic, and resonate deeply with your audience.

The Zen of Simplicity: Less Is More

Zen philosophy embraces the idea of simplicity as a path to clarity. By removing excess and focusing on the essentials, we find peace and understanding. This same principle applies to character creation. Rather than overwhelming your audience with a long list of character traits, relationships, and backstories, focus on the core aspects that define who the character is.

Think of it like carving a sculpture from a block of marble. The beauty of the sculpture lies not in adding more material, but in carefully removing the excess to reveal the figure within. In the same way, simplicity in character creation is about peeling away the distractions to reveal the heart of the character.

Ask yourself: What are the most essential qualities that define this character? What drives them? What do they fear? What do they want? By focusing on a few key traits, desires, and conflicts, you can create a character who is not only easier to understand but also more compelling. The audience doesn't need to know every detail of the character's life to connect with them. They need to understand their essence, their core motivations, and their emotional journey.

Finding the Character's Core Essence

To create a character with clarity, start by identifying their core essence. This essence is the defining quality or driving force that shapes everything they do. It's the lens through which they see the world and the foundation of their personality. Once you understand this essence, you can build the character around it, ensuring that every trait, action, and decision aligns with who they are at their core.

For example, if your protagonist's core essence is courage, then their actions throughout the story should reflect their bravery, even when they face fear or uncertainty. Similarly, if your character's core essence is compassion, their relationships and choices will likely revolve around helping others, even when it comes at a personal cost.

By focusing on this central trait or motivation, you can give your character a clear and consistent identity that the audience can latch onto. This doesn't mean your character has to be one-dimensional; it simply means that everything they do is anchored by a clear internal compass.

Streamlining Backstory

One area where complexity often creeps in is the character's backstory. Writers are often tempted to give their characters elaborate histories, filled with past traumas, family conflicts, and dramatic life events. While backstory is important for understanding who a character is, it can easily become a burden if too much emphasis is placed on it. Overloading a character with a convoluted past can distract from the present narrative and make it harder for the audience to connect with the character's current journey.

Instead of drowning your character in backstory, focus on the few key experiences that truly shape who they are in the story. What moments from their past define them? What formative experiences are most relevant to their current conflict? By choosing one or two pivotal events that influence your character's motivations, you keep the backstory focused and meaningful without overwhelming the audience.

For instance, a character might be driven by a single defining event—such as a betrayal that left them distrustful or a moment of failure that fuels their desire for redemption. By focusing on these key moments, you can give the character depth without overcomplicating their history. Every bit of backstory you include should serve a purpose in the story and reveal something important about the character's present conflict.

Simplicity in Character Arcs

A character arc is the journey of transformation a character undergoes throughout the story. While it's tempting to make this arc complex, with multiple twists and emotional shifts, simplicity often leads to a more powerful and coherent arc. The more focused the arc, the easier it is for the audience to follow the character's transformation and understand the emotional stakes.

To create a clear character arc, start by identifying the core change your character will undergo. What is the single most important lesson they will learn? What fear will they overcome, or what truth will they discover about themselves? By narrowing the arc down to one central transformation, you give the audience a clear sense of the character's growth.

For example, a character who begins the story as selfish and self-centered might undergo a transformation where they learn to put others before themselves. Every step of their journey should be tied to this central change, whether it's through the challenges they face, the relationships they form, or the decisions they make. By keeping the arc simple and focused, you allow the audience to track the character's growth and become emotionally invested in their journey.

. . . .

SIMPLICITY IN DIALOGUE and Action

When writing dialogue and action, simplicity often leads to more impactful moments. Characters don't need to speak in long, complicated monologues to convey their emotions. In fact, some of the most memorable characters are those who say little but express much through their words and actions.

In dialogue, focus on clarity and brevity. What is the most direct way for the character to express what they feel or want? Avoid over-explaining or using dialogue as a means to dump information. Instead, let the character's words reflect their core essence and reveal their inner world through subtlety and nuance.

For example, a character who is deeply guarded might say very little, but the few words they do speak carry weight and meaning. Their silence can be just as telling as their speech. A single, well-placed line can reveal more about a character's emotions than an entire paragraph of dialogue.

The same principle applies to action. A character's actions should be simple but meaningful, reflecting their core traits and desires. Every action should serve a purpose, whether it's advancing the plot or revealing something important about the character. By focusing on the essential actions that define your character, you can create moments that resonate with the audience without cluttering the narrative.

The Power of Symbolism and Minimalism

Another way to embrace simplicity in character creation is through symbolism and minimalism. Rather than relying on elaborate descriptions or convoluted backstory, use symbols or minimalistic traits to convey deeper meaning about your character.

For example, a character might wear a specific piece of jewelry that symbolizes their connection to a loved one, or they might have a particular habit that reveals something about their personality. These small details can carry significant emotional weight without requiring long explanations. By focusing on a few key symbols or traits, you can communicate a lot about your character in a simple and efficient way. Minimalism in character design doesn't mean stripping away all complexity, but rather distilling the character down to their most essential elements. A minimalist character might have a strong, defining trait or quirk that sets them apart, but the rest of their personality is expressed subtly, allowing the audience to fill in the gaps with their own interpretation. This approach can create a sense of mystery or intrigue, drawing the audience deeper into the character's world.

Simplicity as a Tool for Emotional Resonance

Ultimately, simplicity in character creation allows for greater emotional resonance. When characters are focused, clear, and defined by a few key traits or motivations, the audience can more easily connect with them. The story becomes less about deciphering the character's many layers and more about feeling their emotional journey.

By focusing on the core emotions that drive your character—whether it's love, fear, anger, or hope—you can create moments of raw, powerful emotion that leave a lasting impact on the audience. Simplicity allows you to cut through the noise and get to the heart of the character's experience, making it easier for the audience to empathize with their struggles and root for their success. Simplicity is not the enemy of depth—it is a path to clarity. By focusing on the essential traits, motivations, and actions that define your character, you can create a protagonist who is both compelling and easy to connect with. Simplicity allows you to strip away the unnecessary and reveal the core of who your character truly is.

The Art of Visualization: Writing Scenes from the Mind's Canvas

Visualization is a powerful tool in storytelling. It allows writers to see their scenes in vivid detail before translating them into words. By tapping into your mind's eye, you can create moments that feel real, immersive, and emotionally charged, as if you are painting with words on the canvas of your imagination. This chapter will explore the art of visualization—how to harness the power of mental imagery to write scenes that resonate with clarity and impact.

Whether you're a novelist, screenwriter, or short story writer, the ability to vividly imagine your scenes can elevate your writing, helping you capture not only the physical details of a moment but also its emotional core. By approaching writing as a form of visual storytelling, you learn to build your narrative from strong, evocative imagery.

Why Visualization Matters

Visualization is more than just picturing a scene in your head—it's about immersing yourself fully in the world of your story. When you visualize, you are not only seeing the setting, characters, and actions, but you are also feeling the emotions, hearing the sounds, and sensing the atmosphere. This level of immersion allows you to create scenes that feel authentic and grounded, because you've experienced them in your mind before putting them on the page.

When readers or viewers connect with a story, it's often because the imagery is so strong that they can picture the world as clearly as if they were living in it. Effective visualization creates this level of engagement, allowing your audience to step into the scene and experience it alongside your characters.

Visualization also helps with pacing, structure, and emotional beats. By seeing a scene play out in your mind, you can identify the moments that need to slow down for impact or the beats that need to accelerate for tension. The act of visualizing gives you a bird's-eye view of your story, allowing you to adjust the rhythm and flow of your narrative as needed.

. . . .

STARTING WITH STILLNESS

Before you begin writing a scene, take a moment to sit in stillness. Close your eyes, clear your mind, and focus on the blank canvas of your imagination. In this quiet space, allow the scene to take shape. Picture the location, the characters, and the atmosphere. Where are your characters? What is happening around them? What do they see, hear, and feel?

This moment of stillness allows you to center yourself in the scene, shutting out distractions and bringing your full attention to the world you're about to create. Visualization is like meditation for writers—a practice that helps you focus your energy and creativity on the present moment in your story.

As you sit in this stillness, let the scene unfold naturally. Don't force the details or rush the process. Allow your mind to explore the space, taking in the sensory details, the lighting, the mood. The more vivid your mental image, the more vivid your writing will become when you translate that image into words.

Seeing Through the Character's Eyes

One of the most effective ways to visualize a scene is to see it through your character's eyes. Imagine that you are inhabiting your character's body—what do they notice first? How do they perceive their surroundings? What emotions are running through them in this moment?

By visualizing the scene from the character's perspective, you create a more personal and emotionally resonant moment. Your descriptions become more subjective, colored by the character's thoughts, feelings, and state of mind. This approach draws the audience deeper into the character's experience, allowing them to connect with both the external setting and the internal emotions.

For example, if your protagonist is walking through a dark forest at night, what details stand out to them? Are they focused on the sound of twigs snapping underfoot, the flicker of shadows between the trees, or the tightness in their chest as fear creeps in? By seeing the scene through the protagonist's eyes, you shift the focus from an objective description of the forest to an emotionally charged moment of tension and anticipation.

Focusing on Sensory Details

Visualization isn't just about what you see—it's about engaging all the senses. A scene becomes more immersive when you include sensory details that evoke sight, sound, smell, taste, and touch. As you visualize, imagine how the scene feels on a physical level. Is there a chill in the air? A distant hum of traffic? The smell of freshly cut grass or the acrid scent of smoke?

These sensory details bring the scene to life for the audience, making them feel as if they are physically present. They also deepen the emotional experience, as certain sensations can evoke memories, feelings, or associations. For example, the smell of rain might trigger a sense of nostalgia, while the sound of footsteps in an empty hallway might create suspense or anxiety.

When writing your scene, focus on these sensory details without overwhelming the reader with too many at once. Choose a few key sensations that capture the essence of the moment and use them to draw the reader into the scene.

Building Atmosphere and Mood

Visualization also plays a crucial role in establishing the atmosphere and mood of a scene. The way you describe the setting, the weather, the lighting, and even the colors can create a specific emotional tone that shapes how the audience feels.

As you visualize, think about the mood you want to evoke in the scene. Is it tense, tranquil, eerie, or joyful? How can the environment reflect that mood? For instance, a tense confrontation might take place in a dimly lit alley with sharp shadows and muffled sounds, while a peaceful morning might be bathed in warm sunlight with the gentle rustle of leaves in the background.

Use your visualization to create a vivid emotional landscape that enhances the narrative. Every detail should serve a purpose, contributing to the overall mood and helping the audience feel what the characters are feeling.

The Role of Movement and Action

In addition to the setting and mood, visualize the movement and action within the scene. How are the characters moving? Is there a flow or rhythm to their actions? Is the scene fast-paced and full of energy, or slow and contemplative?

By visualizing the movement, you can create more dynamic scenes that feel alive and engaging. Think about how the characters interact with their environment—do they pace restlessly, stand still in contemplation, or move with purpose? Action reveals a lot about a character's emotions and intentions, and by visualizing it, you can write scenes that are more physically and emotionally expressive.

For instance, if a character is nervous, you might visualize them fidgeting, tapping their foot, or avoiding eye contact. If a character is confident, their movements might be more deliberate, with strong, purposeful gestures. By paying attention to movement, you add another layer of depth to the scene that helps convey emotion and tension.

Pacing and Flow in Visualization

One of the advantages of visualization is that it allows you to see the pacing and flow of a scene before you write it. By mentally playing out the events, you can identify moments where the action needs to slow down or speed up. You can sense where the tension builds and where it releases, ensuring that the scene unfolds in a way that feels natural and engaging.

• • • •

VISUALIZATION ALSO helps you anticipate the rhythm of dialogue, action, and description. Is there a balance between these elements, or does one dominate the scene? Are there moments of stillness that allow the characters and audience to reflect, or is the scene packed with rapid-fire exchanges and quick movements? By visualizing the pacing, you can create a more balanced and well-structured scene.

For example, in a suspenseful scene, you might visualize the buildup of tension as slow and deliberate, with each movement and word carefully chosen to increase the suspense. In contrast, an action-packed chase scene might play out in quick bursts of motion, with fast cuts between characters and events. By seeing the pacing in your mind, you can better control the flow of the narrative.

Translating Visualization into Writing

Once you've visualized the scene in your mind, the next step is to translate that mental image into words. This is where the art of description comes in. Your goal is not to describe every detail exactly as you visualized it, but to capture the essence of the scene—the mood, the emotions, the key details that bring it to life for the reader.

Use strong, vivid language to paint the scene, focusing on the most important elements. Trust your visualization process, and let it guide your descriptions. You don't need to explain everything; sometimes, the simplest images can convey the most meaning.

For example, instead of saying, *The forest was dark and eerie, with thick trees and an ominous atmosphere,* you might write, *Tall pines loomed like silent sentinels, their branches whispering secrets in the wind. Every step felt like an intrusion, the air thick with the weight of unseen eyes.* This description uses vivid imagery and sensory details to create a mood without overloading the reader with too much information.

Visualization is a powerful tool that allows you to create scenes with clarity, depth, and emotional resonance. By approaching writing as a visual art form, you can craft moments that feel alive and immersive, drawing the audience into the world of your story.

Through stillness, sensory detail, movement, and pacing, you build your narrative from the mind's canvas, shaping it into something that feels both real and meaningful. The art of visualization isn't just about seeing the story—it's about feeling it, living it, and then sharing that experience with your audience through words.

Zen and the Plot Structure: Building a Story with Purpose

Plot structure is the framework that holds a story together, guiding the narrative through its twists, turns, and emotional beats. But in the Zen approach to storytelling, plot is more than just a sequence of events. It is about creating a story with intention, one that unfolds naturally and with purpose. Rather than forcing the plot into a rigid structure, the Zen storyteller allows the plot to grow organically, shaping the narrative around the deeper themes and emotions at play. In this chapter, we'll explore how to build a plot that is both structured and purposeful, using a Zen approach to craft a story that resonates with meaning and flow.

The Zen of Plot: Finding Balance Between Structure and Flexibility

In Zen philosophy, balance is key. This principle applies to plot structure, which requires a balance between structure and flexibility. Too much structure, and the story can feel predictable or mechanical. Too little structure, and the story may become aimless, losing its momentum and direction. The goal is to create a plot that guides the narrative while leaving room for spontaneity, growth, and discovery.

Think of the plot as a river flowing toward its destination. It follows a natural path, moving around obstacles, sometimes speeding up and other times slowing down, but always progressing toward a goal. Like a river, the plot should have direction and purpose, but it should also be flexible enough to adapt to the changes that arise during the writing process. By allowing the plot to flow naturally, you create a story that feels organic and alive.

Zen storytelling encourages you to start with a clear intention—what is the ultimate goal or message of your story? What do you want the audience to feel or understand by the end? Once you have this purpose in mind, you can let the plot grow around it, shaping the events and structure to serve the larger narrative. This approach keeps your plot focused and meaningful, while still allowing for the unexpected twists and developments that make storytelling exciting.

Starting with the End in Mind: Crafting a Purposeful Climax

As with many aspects of Zen storytelling, building a plot often begins by envisioning the end. Knowing how the story will conclude gives you a clear sense of direction, allowing you to work backward and ensure that every event and character decision leads toward that final resolution.

The climax is the point at which the central conflict reaches its peak, and it is one of the most important moments in your plot. By visualizing the climax early in the writing process, you create a goal for the story to work toward. This helps you avoid plot threads that lead nowhere or events that don't serve the overall narrative.

• • • •

IN THE ZEN APPROACH, the climax is not just an action-packed scene or dramatic confrontation—it's the moment of transformation. It is when the protagonist reaches a new level of understanding, resolves their internal conflict, or confronts the truth of the situation. The climax is where the story's purpose is revealed, making it a powerful and emotionally resonant moment for both the characters and the audience.

Once you have a clear sense of your climax, you can begin to map out the rising action, ensuring that each plot point leads naturally to this transformative moment. This doesn't mean every scene needs to be intense or high-stakes, but it does mean that each event should contribute in some way to the protagonist's journey toward the climax.

Rising Action: Building Tension and Meaning

The rising action is the part of the plot where tension builds, conflicts emerge, and the stakes are raised. It is the journey that takes the protagonist from the familiar world of the exposition to the climactic moment of transformation. In Zen storytelling, the rising action should unfold with intention, each event and conflict deepening the story's themes and pushing the protagonist closer to their moment of growth.

Instead of viewing the rising action as a series of random obstacles or events, think of it as a progression. Each challenge the protagonist faces should serve a purpose, either by revealing something about their character, advancing the plot, or heightening the emotional stakes. The rising action is where you create momentum, guiding the story forward without rushing to the climax.

A Zen approach to rising action also involves patience. You don't need to throw every challenge at the protagonist right away. Allow the tension to build gradually, like the slow tightening of a bowstring. This creates a sense of anticipation, drawing the audience into the story as they wait for the inevitable release at the climax.

The rising action is also a space for reflection and exploration. As the protagonist faces external challenges, they should also be grappling with internal conflicts. What are they learning about themselves along the way? How are they changing in response to the events around them? By focusing on both external and internal growth, you create a richer, more layered narrative.

Conflict: The Catalyst for Growth

In Zen storytelling, conflict is not just about opposition or struggle—it is the catalyst for growth. Without conflict, there is no transformation, and without transformation, there is no story. The protagonist's journey is defined by the conflicts they face, both internal and external, and how they overcome them.

When building your plot, think carefully about the conflicts that arise. Are they meaningful? Do they challenge the protagonist in ways that force them to confront their own flaws, fears, or beliefs? The most impactful conflicts are those that push the protagonist toward change, forcing them to let go of old ways of thinking or to confront difficult truths.

Zen philosophy teaches that conflict is an opportunity for enlightenment. In storytelling, this means that every conflict should bring the protagonist closer to self-awareness or understanding. Whether it's a physical battle, an emotional confrontation, or a moral dilemma, the conflict should serve as a turning point in the character's arc.

The resolution of the conflict should also feel organic. Just as in life, not every conflict in a story will be resolved through force or aggression. Sometimes the resolution comes from acceptance, compromise, or a change in perspective. By embracing the Zen principle of balance, you can create conflicts that are resolved in ways that feel true to the character and the story's themes.

Falling Action and Resolution: Bringing the Story to Rest

After the climax, the story begins to wind down through the falling action and resolution. This is where the consequences of the protagonist's actions play out, and the story finds its conclusion. In Zen storytelling, the falling action is a moment of reflection—a chance for the characters and the audience to process the events of the climax and understand their impact.

The resolution should bring the story full circle, connecting back to the purpose or intention you set at the beginning. This doesn't mean every loose end needs to be tied up neatly, but the resolution should provide closure for the central conflict. Whether the protagonist achieves their goal or not, the resolution should reflect the growth and transformation they've experienced along the way.

In Zen philosophy, the resolution is often about acceptance—accepting the present moment, the lessons learned, and the impermanence of things. In storytelling, this can manifest in different ways, from a peaceful, reflective ending to a bittersweet or open-ended conclusion. The key is to allow the story to come to rest in a way that feels purposeful and meaningful.

Trusting the Process: Letting the Plot Evolve Naturally

One of the central teachings of Zen is to let go of control and trust the process. This applies to plot structure as well. While it's important to have a clear sense of direction and purpose, you don't need to plan every detail of the plot before you begin writing. Allow the plot to evolve naturally as you discover new aspects of the story and the characters.

Zen storytelling encourages you to embrace spontaneity and change. If the plot takes an unexpected turn, trust that this new direction might lead to something even more powerful than your original plan. By staying open to the possibilities that arise during the writing process, you create a plot that feels organic and alive, rather than forced or predetermined.

At the same time, stay grounded in your purpose. Every plot development should serve the larger narrative, pushing the protagonist toward their moment of transformation. By balancing structure and flexibility, you create a plot that is both intentional and dynamic.

Plot structure is the backbone of storytelling, but it doesn't need to be rigid or mechanical. By adopting a Zen approach to plot, you can build a narrative that flows naturally and with purpose, guiding the audience through a journey of growth, conflict, and resolution. The key is to find balance—between structure and spontaneity, between conflict and peace, between action and reflection. As you craft your plot, remember that the goal is not just to entertain but to create a meaningful experience for both your characters and your audience. By building a plot with purpose, you can guide your story toward a climax that resonates emotionally, and a resolution that offers both closure and reflection. The Zen of plot structure is about trusting the process, allowing the story to unfold with intention, and finding the deeper meaning in every step of the journey.

Themes and Zen Philosophy: Infusing Deeper Meaning into Stories

Themes are the underlying currents that give a story its deeper meaning. They are the messages, ideas, or questions that a story explores, resonating beyond the surface of plot and character. Zen philosophy, with its focus on mindfulness, impermanence, interconnectedness, and the search for inner truth, offers a rich foundation for developing themes that resonate deeply with audiences. When infused into stories, Zen-inspired themes can elevate a narrative, giving it emotional depth and universal relevance. In this chapter, we will explore how to weave Zen themes into storytelling to create a narrative that not only entertains but also invites reflection, introspection, and a sense of connection.

Understanding the Role of Themes in Storytelling

Themes are the heart of a story, the intangible ideas that thread through the narrative, giving it purpose and cohesion. While plot is about what happens and character is about who it happens to, theme is about why it matters. Whether you're writing about love, loss, fear, or courage, the theme is what transforms your story from a series of events into a meaningful exploration of human experience.

Themes help audiences connect to the emotional and philosophical core of the story. They offer insight into the human condition, asking questions or offering perspectives that resonate with readers or viewers on a deeper level. By grounding your story in a central theme, you give it a sense of purpose and direction, ensuring that each plot point and character decision reflects a larger idea.

When drawing on Zen philosophy, the themes you explore may revolve around concepts such as mindfulness, the nature of suffering, the acceptance of impermanence, the search for inner peace, or the interconnectedness of all things. These themes can bring a sense of calm reflection and wisdom to your story, while also adding layers of complexity and depth.

Exploring Zen Themes in Storytelling

Zen philosophy offers a wealth of themes that can enrich your storytelling. Here are some key Zen concepts that can be infused into your narrative to create deeper meaning:

Impermanence (Anicca): In Zen, impermanence is a fundamental truth—everything in life is transient, constantly changing. This theme can be explored through stories about loss, transformation, or the passage of time. Characters may struggle with letting go of the past or accepting that nothing remains the same. Stories infused with this theme often encourage reflection on the beauty of fleeting moments and the importance of embracing change rather than resisting it.

Mindfulness and Presence: Mindfulness, or being fully present in the moment, is central to Zen practice. This theme can be woven into stories where characters learn to let go of distractions, worries, or attachments, finding peace in the present. A narrative built around mindfulness might explore how characters shift their focus from external achievements to internal understanding, finding contentment not in what they have or do, but in simply being.

The Nature of Suffering (Dukkha): Zen acknowledges that suffering is a part of life, but it also teaches that suffering arises from attachment—our clinging to desires, fears, or expectations. A story centered around this theme might follow a character's journey toward understanding the roots of their suffering and learning to let go of the things causing them pain. This theme offers opportunities for exploring personal growth, healing, and the search for inner peace.

Non-Attachment: Non-attachment is a Zen principle that encourages letting go of material possessions, ego-driven desires, and the need for control. Characters driven by a desire for power, love, or success may learn that true peace comes from releasing their grip on these things. Stories exploring non-attachment often feature characters who must learn to accept life's uncertainties and embrace the freedom that comes from letting go.

Interconnectedness (Oneness): Zen teaches that everything is connected, and that separation is an illusion. This theme can be explored in stories that emphasize community, relationships, and the ways in which individual actions affect the whole. Characters may come to understand that their personal journey is intertwined with those of others, finding meaning in connection rather than isolation.

Acceptance: Acceptance is at the heart of Zen—the idea that peace comes not from changing the world, but from accepting it as it is. This theme can be explored through characters who struggle to control their environment or circumstances, only to realize that inner peace lies in acceptance, not resistance. Stories of acceptance often focus on reconciliation, forgiveness, and finding harmony with life's unpredictability.

Infusing Zen Themes into Plot and Character

To create a story that embodies Zen philosophy, it's important to weave your chosen themes into both the plot and the characters' development. The theme should not feel separate from the events of the story but should flow naturally from the characters' actions, decisions, and experiences.

Plot as a Reflection of Theme: The plot of your story should be structured in a way that reflects the central theme. For example, if you are exploring the theme of impermanence, your plot might revolve around a character coming to terms with loss or change. Each plot point can be designed to challenge the character's understanding of permanence, leading them toward greater acceptance of life's transience.

If your theme is mindfulness, the plot might show a character caught in the chaos of modern life, constantly distracted by external pressures. As the story progresses, the character learns to slow down, focus on the present moment, and find peace in simplicity. The events of the plot become a vehicle for the theme, allowing the audience to experience the message on both an emotional and intellectual level.

Character Development through Theme: Characters are the emotional anchors of your story, and their growth should reflect the central theme. In Zen storytelling, character arcs often involve inner transformation—a journey toward greater understanding, acceptance, or peace.

For example, a character grappling with the theme of non-attachment might start the story driven by ambition or desire, only to realize by the end that true fulfillment comes from letting go. Their decisions and interactions throughout the plot should reflect this evolving understanding, with each challenge bringing them closer to embracing the theme.

Similarly, a character exploring the theme of interconnectedness might begin the story feeling isolated or self-centered, but through their experiences, they come to understand the value of community and connection. The theme is woven into their relationships, decisions, and growth, making it an integral part of their journey.

Using Symbolism to Enhance Theme

Zen philosophy often expresses profound ideas through simple symbols—such as the circle (ensō) representing enlightenment, the lotus flower symbolizing purity and spiritual awakening, or the flowing river embodying impermanence. In storytelling, symbolism can be a powerful tool for conveying deeper meaning and reinforcing your theme.

When incorporating Zen themes into your story, think about how you can use symbols to enhance the narrative. These symbols don't need to be overt or heavy-handed; they can be subtle visual or metaphorical elements that resonate with the theme.

For example, a story about impermanence might include imagery of a withering flower, a crumbling building, or the changing of the seasons—each symbol reinforcing the idea that everything is transient. A story exploring mindfulness might feature moments of stillness, such as a character pausing to listen to the sound of the wind or the rhythm of their breath, subtly reminding the audience of the theme without explicitly stating it.

Symbolism allows you to communicate your theme on a subconscious level, adding layers of meaning to the story that the audience can interpret and reflect on.

The Power of Subtlety in Thematic Storytelling

One of the most important aspects of Zen storytelling is subtlety. Zen themes are often quiet and contemplative, inviting the audience to reflect on their own rather than delivering a direct message. When exploring deeper themes in your story, it's important to avoid heavy-handed exposition or overt moralizing. Instead, let the theme emerge naturally through the characters' actions, the plot's progression, and the overall tone of the narrative.

Subtlety invites the audience to engage with the story on a deeper level, drawing their own conclusions about the themes and messages. Rather than telling the audience what to think or feel, you allow them to experience the theme for themselves, creating a more intimate and personal connection to the story.

For example, a story about acceptance doesn't need to explicitly state that "acceptance leads to peace." Instead, you can show a character struggling with resistance, slowly learning to embrace their circumstances, and finding inner calm as a result. The theme is clear without being overt, allowing the audience to come to their own understanding.

Zen philosophy offers a profound well of themes that can infuse your stories with depth, purpose, and universal resonance. By exploring ideas such as impermanence, mindfulness, interconnectedness, and non-attachment, you create narratives that go beyond entertainment, inviting your audience to reflect on the deeper truths of life.

Infusing Zen themes into your plot, character development, and symbolism allows you to craft a story that feels purposeful and meaningful. Whether your story is a quiet meditation on life's transience or an epic journey of self-discovery, Zen themes bring a sense of calm, wisdom, and emotional depth to your storytelling.

Ultimately, the power of Zen-themed storytelling lies in its ability to connect the external events of the plot with the internal transformation of the characters, creating a harmonious balance between action and introspection, struggle and peace, conflict and resolution. Through this balance, you can create stories that not only entertain but also resonate on a deeper, more reflective level.

The Conflict Within: Exploring Inner and Outer Struggles

Conflict is the engine that drives any story forward. It creates tension, challenges characters, and keeps audiences engaged. While many stories focus on external struggles—battles against an antagonist, societal forces, or environmental obstacles—some of the most compelling narratives arise from internal conflict. The inner struggles of a character often mirror or influence their external battles, creating a rich, multilayered experience for the audience. In this chapter, we'll explore the balance between inner and outer conflicts, how they interact, and how to use these elements to craft stories that resonate deeply with readers or viewers.

Understanding the Nature of Conflict

Conflict, in its simplest form, is opposition. It's the force that stands between the protagonist and their goal. This opposition can be external, such as a villain trying to stop the hero, or it can be internal, such as a character grappling with their own fears, doubts, or desires.

In Zen philosophy, conflict is often seen as something that arises from attachment—our desire to control, achieve, or avoid certain outcomes. Internal conflict, therefore, is frequently tied to the character's attachment to specific ideas, beliefs, or emotions. External conflict, on the other hand, is shaped by the world around them, the obstacles they face, and the people who oppose them.

A compelling story balances both types of conflict, creating a narrative in which the protagonist's internal struggles influence how they face external challenges, and vice versa. By exploring this interplay, you can create a narrative that is emotionally complex and thematically rich, one where every battle—whether physical or emotional—reveals something deeper about the character and the human experience.

The Interplay between Inner and Outer Conflict

One of the most effective ways to create a dynamic story is to ensure that the inner and outer conflicts are interconnected. The outer conflict—the battles, confrontations, or obstacles the protagonist faces—should serve as a reflection of their internal struggle. Likewise, the character's internal conflict should influence how they approach and respond to external challenges.

For example, a protagonist who is internally struggling with self-doubt might face an external conflict that forces them to step into a leadership role. As they try to navigate the external challenge, their internal doubts and fears may cause them to make hesitant or reckless decisions, deepening the conflict on both levels. Eventually, as the protagonist grows and confronts their inner fears, they become more equipped to handle the external challenges with clarity and confidence.

By linking inner and outer conflicts, you create a story that is not only engaging on a plot level but also emotionally resonant. The external events of the story gain meaning because they are tied to the protagonist's internal journey. Similarly, the protagonist's growth and transformation feel earned because they have been shaped by both inner reflection and outer action.

Crafting Internal Conflict

Internal conflict arises from a character's inner struggles—often their fears, desires, flaws, or moral dilemmas. These conflicts are deeply personal and revolve around the character's emotions, thoughts, and beliefs. Crafting a compelling internal conflict involves digging into the psychology of the character and understanding what drives them, what they fear, and what they need to overcome within themselves.

To develop an internal conflict, start by asking key questions about your character:

- **What does the character desire most deeply?** Often, a character's desires create the foundation for internal conflict. Their longing for love, power, success, or redemption can shape their decisions and create tension when those desires are thwarted or complicated.

- **What are they afraid of?** Fear is a powerful source of internal conflict. A character's fear of failure, rejection, vulnerability, or loss can drive much of their behavior, often leading to self-sabotage, hesitation, or rash decisions.
- **What moral dilemmas do they face?** Characters often experience internal conflict when they are torn between competing values or goals. For example, a character might struggle between loyalty to a friend and their own personal ambition, or between doing what's right and doing what's easy.
- **What flaws or weaknesses do they need to confront?** Internal conflict can also stem from a character's flaws or shortcomings. Whether it's pride, jealousy, insecurity, or stubbornness, these traits can create obstacles that the character must overcome on their journey.

Internal conflict adds emotional depth to a story because it allows the audience to connect with the character on a more intimate level. We've all experienced doubt, fear, and inner turmoil, and when a character struggles with these emotions, it makes them more relatable and human.

Developing External Conflict

External conflict, by contrast, involves the forces outside of the protagonist that create obstacles or opposition. These can take the form of antagonists, environmental challenges, societal pressures, or even physical dangers. External conflict is often the more visible aspect of a story, providing the action, tension, and suspense that drive the plot forward.

However, external conflict should never feel arbitrary or disconnected from the protagonist's internal journey. Instead, the external conflict should challenge the character in ways that force them to confront their inner struggles. Each external obstacle becomes an opportunity for the protagonist to either grow or retreat further into their fears and doubts.

For example, in a story about a character struggling with guilt over a past mistake, the external conflict might involve someone from their past reentering their life and threatening to expose their secret. This external challenge forces the protagonist to grapple with their internal guilt and shame, creating a deeper and more layered conflict.

External conflict often falls into one of several categories:

- **Person vs. Person:** This type of conflict involves direct opposition between the protagonist and another character, often an antagonist. The antagonist may be a villain or simply someone whose goals are at odds with the protagonist's. The conflict can be physical, verbal, or psychological.
- **Person vs. Nature:** In this type of conflict, the protagonist is pitted against the forces of nature—such as a natural disaster, a dangerous wilderness, or a survival situation. The character's ability to overcome or adapt to these external challenges often parallels their internal journey.
- **Person vs. Society:** This conflict arises when the protagonist is in opposition to societal norms, laws, or expectations. The character may be fighting against injustice, corruption, or systemic oppression, and their external conflict reflects their internal struggle to assert their individuality or uphold their values.
- **Person vs. Self:** While this is often considered an internal conflict, it can also manifest externally when the character's inner turmoil causes them to create obstacles for themselves. A protagonist struggling with addiction, for example, may sabotage their own progress, creating external consequences that mirror their internal conflict.

The Moment of Convergence: Climax as the Intersection of Inner and Outer Conflict

In most stories, the climax represents the point where both the inner and outer conflicts reach their peak. It's the moment when the protagonist is forced to confront not only the external forces working against them but also the internal struggles that have been holding them back.

At the climax, the protagonist must make a critical choice or take decisive action that resolves both the outer conflict and the inner turmoil. This moment of convergence is what gives the climax its emotional weight. It's not just about whether the protagonist wins or loses the external battle—it's about whether they have grown enough internally to make the right decision or face their fears.

For example, in a story where the protagonist is afraid of vulnerability and has been pushing others away, the climax might involve a situation where they must choose between protecting themselves emotionally or risking vulnerability to save someone they care about. The external stakes (saving someone) are tied to the internal stakes (overcoming fear), creating a powerful moment of resolution.

• • • •

RESOLUTION AND GROWTH: After the Conflict

Once the inner and outer conflicts have reached their peak and been resolved, the resolution provides a space for reflection and growth. How has the protagonist changed as a result of the conflict? Have they gained new insights, let go of their fears, or achieved a sense of peace or understanding?

The resolution doesn't need to be a happy ending, but it should provide closure for both the internal and external conflicts. The protagonist should emerge from the conflict transformed in some way, having learned something important about themselves or the world.

For example, if the protagonist's internal conflict involved learning to trust others, the resolution might show them forming a new relationship or reconciling with someone from their past. The external conflict may be resolved (they've defeated the villain or overcome the obstacle), but the real victory lies in the protagonist's internal growth.

The most compelling stories are those that balance inner and outer conflict, using each to enhance and deepen the other. By exploring the internal struggles that drive your protagonist and linking them to the external challenges they face, you create a story that is both emotionally and narratively rich.

In Zen storytelling, conflict is not just about opposition—it's about transformation. Each challenge, whether internal or external, offers the protagonist an opportunity to grow, to let go of attachments, or to gain new understanding. The conflict within is as important as the conflict without, and together, they form the foundation of a story that resonates on multiple levels.

By weaving inner and outer struggles into your narrative, you craft a story that engages the audience both intellectually and emotionally, inviting them to reflect on their own conflicts and the ways in which their internal and external worlds are intertwined.

Balancing Action and Stillness: Crafting Dynamic Scenes

In storytelling, the rhythm of a narrative comes from the interplay between action and stillness. Action propels the plot forward, creating tension and excitement, while stillness offers moments of reflection, introspection, and emotional depth. The balance between these two elements is crucial for crafting dynamic scenes that engage the audience while providing room for character development and thematic exploration. In this chapter, we'll explore how to master the balance between action and stillness, using a Zen approach to create scenes that are both vibrant and meaningful.

The Purpose of Action in Storytelling

Action, in storytelling terms, refers to the events and physical movements that drive the plot. It encompasses everything from a high-stakes chase scene to a heated argument, to a character's decision to take a pivotal step in their journey. Action creates momentum, keeps the audience on the edge of their seat, and moves the story forward. It's essential for maintaining narrative tension and preventing the story from stagnating.

But action isn't just about spectacle. It's also about revealing character, advancing the plot, and deepening the themes of the story. Every action taken by a character should serve a purpose, whether it's demonstrating their emotional state, progressing their arc, or creating conflict with other characters or forces in the story.

In a Zen approach to storytelling, action is not about constant movement or overwhelming excitement. Instead, it's about intentional movement—action that is deliberate, meaningful, and rooted in the character's inner journey. The most impactful action scenes are those that resonate on both a physical and emotional level, reflecting the character's internal struggles and external goals.

The Power of Stillness: Creating Space for Reflection

Stillness, on the other hand, represents moments of quiet, introspection, or pause. These are the scenes where the action slows down, allowing the characters—and the audience—to reflect on what has happened and process the emotional or psychological impact. Stillness offers breathing room, giving the story time to settle and deepen.

In Zen, stillness is not just about the absence of movement; it's about presence. It's about being fully aware of the moment, embracing silence, and allowing space for contemplation. In storytelling, stillness can be just as powerful as action, if not more so. It's in these quiet moments that characters often experience growth, revelation, or connection.

For example, after a climactic battle or intense confrontation, a scene of stillness might show a character sitting alone, reflecting on the consequences of their actions or grappling with their emotions. These moments of quiet give the audience a chance to connect with the character on a deeper level, understanding their internal journey beyond the outward events of the plot.

The Dynamic Interplay between Action and Stillness

The most engaging stories are those that balance the pace of action with moments of stillness, creating a dynamic rhythm that ebbs and flows like a natural current. Too much action, and the story can feel relentless, leaving little room for emotional connection or thematic depth. Too much stillness, and the story can lose momentum, dragging in a way that diminishes tension.

In a Zen-inspired narrative, the interplay between action and stillness is seamless. Action and stillness flow into one another, creating a balanced rhythm that mirrors the natural cycles of life—movement followed by rest, conflict followed by reflection. By alternating between these two modes, you allow the audience to fully engage with both the physical and emotional aspects of the story.

Here are a few ways to strike the right balance between action and stillness in your scenes:

Use Action to Build Tension, Then Pause for Reflection: After an action-packed scene—whether it's a chase, a fight, or an emotional argument—follow it with a moment of stillness. This allows both the characters and the audience to process the events and feel the emotional weight of what has happened. The pause doesn't need to be long, but it should offer space for the characters to reflect or regroup, heightening the impact of the preceding action.

For example, after a protagonist narrowly escapes danger, a scene of stillness might show them catching their breath, nursing a wound, or sitting quietly as the adrenaline fades. This pause amplifies the intensity of the action by giving the audience a chance to absorb the consequences.

Let Stillness Set the Stage for Action: Stillness can also be used to build anticipation for action. A moment of quiet, where the characters are waiting or reflecting, can create a sense of tension that makes the subsequent action feel more explosive. This is particularly effective in scenes where characters are preparing for a significant event, such as a battle, a confrontation, or a critical decision.

The stillness before the storm gives the audience time to feel the weight of what's coming. It's in these quiet moments that the stakes are often most palpable, as the characters mentally and emotionally prepare for the action ahead.

Reveal Character Through Stillness: While action often reveals a character's choices and behavior under pressure, stillness can provide deeper insight into their emotional state, thoughts, and inner conflicts. Use stillness to explore the character's internal world—what are they thinking when they're not speaking or moving? How do they process their emotions when alone? These moments allow the audience to connect with the character on a more intimate level.

For instance, a character might sit in silence after receiving devastating news, their face showing only the slightest hints of emotion. The stillness allows the audience to project their own interpretations onto the scene, deepening the emotional resonance.

Let the Environment Reflect Action and Stillness: In many stories, the environment can play a key role in emphasizing the balance between action and stillness. For example, an action scene set during a thunderstorm, with loud crashes of lightning and wind, contrasts powerfully with a later scene of stillness in a quiet room lit by candlelight. The environment helps set the tone and mood for each mode, creating a natural rhythm within the story.

In Zen storytelling, nature is often used to mirror the internal state of the characters or the thematic elements of the plot. A moment of stillness might be accompanied by the sound of rain, the rustle of leaves, or the quiet flow of a river, grounding the character's emotional experience in the natural world.

Crafting Action with Purpose

When writing action scenes, it's important to remember that the purpose of action is not just to excite the audience but to reveal something deeper about the characters or the plot. Action should always serve a purpose in the larger narrative, whether it's advancing the story, creating tension, or developing character.

Here are some tips for crafting purposeful action scenes:

- **Make Action Reflect Internal Conflict:** The most impactful action scenes are those where the external events mirror the internal struggles of the character. A fight scene, for example, becomes more compelling when it's not just about physical combat but also about the character's inner battle—whether it's overcoming fear, dealing with anger, or proving their worth.
- **Use Action to Move the Plot Forward:** Every action scene should serve a specific narrative purpose. Whether it's moving the characters closer to their goal or introducing a new obstacle, action should never feel gratuitous. Ask yourself: What does this action scene accomplish in terms of plot, character development, or theme?
- **Keep Action Grounded in Emotion:** Even in the most intense action scenes, emotion should remain at the forefront. What are the characters feeling as they fight, flee, or confront each other? By grounding the action in the characters' emotional experience, you keep the audience invested in the outcome.

Crafting Stillness with Intention

Just as action should be purposeful, moments of stillness should also serve a clear narrative function. Stillness offers an opportunity for reflection, emotional release, and thematic exploration.

Here are some tips for creating meaningful stillness in your story:

- **Use Stillness to Explore Theme:** Stillness is the perfect time to reflect on the larger themes of your story. Whether it's a character contemplating their place in the world, struggling with the concept of impermanence, or seeking inner peace, these quiet moments allow you to delve into the philosophical underpinnings of your narrative.
- **Let Characters Breathe:** In moments of stillness, allow your characters to simply *be*. Rather than filling the scene with dialogue or exposition, let the silence speak for itself. These pauses can be incredibly powerful, giving the audience a chance to connect with the character's emotional state without needing everything spelled out.
- **Create Atmosphere:** Stillness doesn't mean the absence of movement or sound—it's about creating an atmosphere of calm, reflection, or tension. Use sensory details, such as the sound of wind, the flicker of candlelight, or the weight of silence, to create a mood that enhances the emotional tone of the scene.

The balance between action and stillness is what gives a story its rhythm, momentum, and emotional depth. By alternating between movement and pause, you create a dynamic narrative that engages the audience on multiple levels, from the physical excitement of action to the emotional resonance of quiet reflection.

In Zen storytelling, this balance mirrors the cycles of life—action followed by rest, tension followed by release, chaos followed by peace. By embracing both action and stillness, you craft scenes that not only move the plot forward but also give space for the characters and audience to reflect, grow, and connect with the deeper themes of the story.

Ultimately, the key to crafting dynamic scenes lies in intention. Whether your characters are running, fighting, reflecting, or simply sitting in silence, every moment should serve a purpose, contributing to the overall arc of the story and deepening the emotional impact.

The Harmony of Dialogue: Letting Words Flow Naturally

Dialogue is the heartbeat of a story. It breathes life into characters, reveals their thoughts, emotions, and relationships, and moves the plot forward. But crafting dialogue that feels authentic and impactful can be a delicate balance. Too much, and it can overwhelm the reader or viewer; too little, and the characters may feel distant or underdeveloped. In Zen storytelling, the key to creating compelling dialogue lies in finding harmony—allowing words to flow naturally, without forcing or overloading them, while ensuring that each line serves a purpose. In this chapter, we'll explore how to craft dialogue that is not only realistic but also resonates with meaning and flows effortlessly through the narrative.

The Zen of Less Is More

In Zen philosophy, simplicity is valued as a way to access deeper truths. This principle can be applied to dialogue, where less often reveals more. Rather than loading characters with heavy exposition or long-winded speeches, focus on what is essential. Let the dialogue emerge naturally, flowing from the character's emotional state and the needs of the moment. In Zen-inspired dialogue, silence can be just as powerful as speech, and a few well-chosen words can carry more weight than an entire paragraph of explanation.

Consider the power of understatement. In emotionally charged moments, characters don't need to say everything they feel. In fact, sometimes it's more impactful when they hold back, allowing the audience to read between the lines and feel the tension or emotion beneath the surface. A character who says, *"I'm fine,"* when clearly they're not, can convey far more complexity than a character who explicitly details their feelings.

Zen dialogue is about trusting the audience to understand what's unsaid as much as what is spoken. The harmony comes from knowing when to speak and when to let silence, body language, or the environment fill the gaps.

Letting Dialogue Arise from Character

Natural dialogue flows from the characters themselves. Each character should have their own voice, shaped by their personality, background, emotional state, and relationship with the other characters. When crafting dialogue, ask yourself: How would *this* character speak in this particular situation? Are they the type to be blunt and direct, or do they skirt around their emotions? Do they speak in long, eloquent sentences, or do they prefer short, clipped phrases?

By grounding dialogue in character, you ensure that every line feels authentic. Dialogue is not just about exchanging information—it's a reflection of who the characters are. Consider their motivations and emotional state when they speak. A character who is angry might speak in rapid, fragmented sentences, while someone who is calm or reflective might take their time, choosing their words carefully.

For example, imagine a tense scene where two characters are having an argument. Rather than both characters explaining their positions at length, one might lash out with sharp, cutting remarks, while the other responds with measured, restrained responses, hinting at an underlying tension. Their dialogue reveals not only the conflict but also their personalities and the nature of their relationship.

Subtext: What's Left Unsaid

Subtext is one of the most powerful tools in dialogue. It's the meaning beneath the words, the emotions and thoughts that the characters are not directly expressing but are still present in the conversation. In Zen storytelling, where subtlety is prized, subtext can create layers of meaning in dialogue, allowing the audience to engage more deeply with the characters and the story.

Subtext often arises from characters holding back their true feelings, either because they're afraid, uncomfortable, or trying to maintain control of the situation. For example, a character might say, *"I'm happy for you,"* but the way they say it—hesitant, with a forced smile—suggests the opposite. The real emotion is conveyed not through the words themselves, but through tone, body language, and context.

In Zen dialogue, subtext allows you to communicate complex emotions without being overt. By letting the audience infer what's going on beneath the surface, you invite them to engage more actively with the story. The tension between what's said and what's unsaid creates a dynamic flow in the conversation, making it feel more real and emotionally charged.

The Power of Silence

Silence is often undervalued in dialogue, but it can be one of the most powerful tools in storytelling. In Zen practice, silence is a form of mindfulness, a space for reflection, awareness, and connection. In dialogue, silence can create tension, highlight emotional weight, or simply allow characters (and the audience) to process what has been said.

Moments of silence between lines of dialogue can speak volumes. When a character pauses before responding, it invites the audience to reflect on what they might be thinking or feeling. Silence can suggest hesitation, discomfort, or an unspoken agreement between characters. It can also serve as a powerful contrast to action-heavy or emotionally intense scenes, giving the narrative room to breathe.

For example, imagine a scene where two characters are sitting together after a traumatic event. Instead of launching into a conversation about what happened, they might sit in silence for a few moments, processing their emotions. When they do speak, the words carry more weight because they emerge from that stillness, from a place of shared understanding.

Silence doesn't always have to be long or dramatic. Even a brief pause between lines of dialogue can shift the tone of a conversation, adding layers of meaning or creating suspense.

* * * *

AVOIDING EXPOSITION Dumps

One of the challenges of dialogue is balancing the need to convey information with the desire to keep the conversation natural. When characters explain too much or speak in ways that feel contrived, it disrupts the flow of the narrative and pulls the audience out of the story. These "exposition dumps" are moments where characters explain things to each other that they already know—often for the benefit of the audience.

In Zen-inspired storytelling, clarity comes from simplicity. Rather than having characters spell everything out, look for ways to reveal information naturally, through context, action, or subtext. Trust that the audience will pick up on the details without needing everything explained.

For example, instead of a character saying, *"As you know, we've been trapped on this island for three days without food or water,"* you could show the character's exhaustion, their cracked lips, the way they gaze longingly at the horizon, waiting for rescue. These visual or emotional cues convey the same information without forcing the dialogue to do all the work.

If you do need to convey important backstory or plot details through dialogue, try to weave it into the conversation in a way that feels natural. Characters can talk about their shared history or current situation, but it should feel like part of the flow of conversation, not a scripted explanation.

Letting Dialogue Serve the Story

While natural dialogue is important, every line should still serve the larger narrative. Dialogue should do one (or more) of the following:

- **Reveal character:** Dialogue is one of the primary ways we get to know characters. How they speak, what they choose to say (or not say), and how they interact with others all reveal important aspects of their personality, desires, and fears.

- **Advance the plot:** Dialogue can move the story forward by introducing new information, sparking conflict, or deepening relationships. It should never feel stagnant or unnecessary.
- **Create tension or conflict:** Conversations are rarely neutral. Even in peaceful or loving moments, there can be underlying tension or unresolved emotions. Dialogue can create conflict directly (through arguments or disagreements) or subtly (through miscommunication or unspoken feelings).
- **Explore themes:** Dialogue is a great way to subtly explore the themes of your story. Characters can express their views on the world, share their beliefs or philosophies, or challenge each other's perspectives, all of which can reflect the larger thematic concerns of the narrative.

In Zen storytelling, dialogue should always feel purposeful, but it shouldn't be forced or overly planned. Let the words flow naturally from the characters and the situation, but ensure that they contribute meaningfully to the story.

The Rhythm of Conversation

Dialogue has its own rhythm, a natural flow that mirrors real-life conversations. However, unlike in real life, where conversations can meander or include filler, dialogue in storytelling should feel sharp, purposeful, and rhythmically engaging.

Pay attention to the pacing of the conversation. In a heated argument, the dialogue might be fast, with characters interrupting each other, their words overlapping in frustration or passion. In a more reflective or intimate moment, the dialogue might slow down, with pauses between each line, giving space for the weight of the words to settle.

One of the best ways to get a feel for the rhythm of dialogue is to read it aloud. Hearing the words spoken can help you identify whether the conversation feels natural, whether it flows or drags, and whether the characters' voices are distinct.

The key to crafting effective dialogue lies in finding harmony—between what is said and what is left unsaid, between action and reflection, between natural flow and narrative purpose. In Zen storytelling, dialogue is not just about exchanging information or creating conflict—it's about revealing deeper truths, connecting characters, and exploring the themes that drive the story.

By letting words flow naturally from the characters and the situation, trusting the audience to pick up on subtext and silence, and avoiding unnecessary exposition, you create dialogue that feels authentic and emotionally resonant. In the end, the goal is not to force words onto the page, but to let them arise organically, creating conversations that feel alive, dynamic, and deeply connected to the heart of the story.

World-building is one of the most crucial aspects of storytelling, especially in genres such as fantasy, science fiction, or historical fiction, where the environment is as much a character as the people who inhabit it. A well-constructed world invites the audience to immerse themselves fully in the story, to lose themselves in its landscapes, cultures, and details. In Zen storytelling, world-building is not about overwhelming the audience with layers of intricate detail, but about creating an immersive setting that feels organic and harmonious. It's about building a world that serves the story and reflects its themes without unnecessary complexity. In this chapter, we'll explore how to use a Zen approach to create vivid, immersive settings that feel both real and purposeful.

The Zen of Simplicity in World-Building

In Zen philosophy, simplicity is not the absence of detail but the focus on what is essential. When it comes to world-building, the goal is not to overload the audience with an encyclopedia of facts about your world, but to offer just enough detail to spark the imagination and give the setting life. Simplicity allows room for the audience to engage, fill in the blanks, and experience the world more fully.

Rather than creating a complex system of politics, magic, or technology right from the start, begin by identifying the core elements that define your world. What are the key features that make this world unique? What aspects of the environment, culture, or history are essential to the story you want to tell?

For example, in a fantasy world, you don't need to describe the entire political structure of every kingdom or the detailed workings of every magical system in your universe. Instead, focus on the aspects that directly affect the story and the characters. What is the protagonist's relationship to the world? How does the environment shape their journey? By focusing on these core elements, you build a world that feels rich and lived-in without overwhelming the reader with unnecessary details.

Creating a World with Purpose

Every aspect of world-building should serve the larger story. In Zen storytelling, nothing exists without purpose. The world you create should be in harmony with the plot, characters, and themes of your story. Rather than world-building for its own sake, think about how each element contributes to the narrative.

For instance, if your story is about survival in a post-apocalyptic wasteland, the harshness of the environment should reflect the protagonist's inner struggle. The barren landscapes, lack of resources, and constant danger mirror the character's sense of isolation, fear, or desperation. The setting becomes a reflection of the protagonist's emotional journey, adding depth to both the world and the story.

Similarly, if your story explores themes of power, corruption, or inequality, the world should reflect these dynamics. A world where wealth is concentrated in the hands of a few while the majority suffer can create a backdrop that heightens the tension of the story and reinforces its themes.

By aligning your world with the themes and emotional tone of the story, you create a setting that feels cohesive and purposeful. Every mountain, city, and cultural norm should have a reason for existing, serving to enhance the narrative rather than distract from it.

Using the Five Senses to Build an Immersive World

Immersive world-building is not just about describing what a place looks like—it's about making the audience feel as though they are truly inside the world. One of the best ways to achieve this is by engaging the five senses: sight, sound, smell, taste, and touch. When you evoke the senses, you draw the audience deeper into the setting, making it feel real and tangible.

As you describe the world, think about how it would feel to walk through it. What does the air smell like in a bustling marketplace? What sounds fill the streets of a busy city or echo in the silence of a remote temple? How does the texture of the ground feel beneath a character's feet as they trek through a forest or climb a mountain?

For example, instead of simply saying, *"The market was crowded,"* you could write, *"The scent of spiced meats and sweet pastries filled the air as people jostled against one another, their voices rising in a constant hum of bargaining and chatter. The sun was hot overhead, and the worn cobblestones beneath her sandals were warm from the day's heat."* This description engages multiple senses—smell, sound, touch—and paints a vivid picture of the setting, making it come alive for the audience.

However, as with everything in Zen storytelling, balance is key. Avoid overwhelming the audience with too many sensory details at once. Focus on the essential sensations that will create the strongest impression of the world, leaving space for the reader's imagination to fill in the rest.

The Power of Suggestion in World-Building

One of the principles of Zen is to leave space for interpretation. In storytelling, this means trusting the audience to engage with your world and draw their own conclusions without over-explaining every detail. The power of suggestion allows you to imply aspects of the world rather than spelling them out directly.

For example, rather than giving a long description of the political situation in a kingdom, you might show a character nervously glancing at guards or overhearing a whispered conversation about unrest in the capital. These small details suggest a larger world in motion without interrupting the flow of the story with exposition.

By suggesting rather than explaining, you create a sense of mystery and depth in the world. The audience feels that there is more to the setting than what is immediately apparent, but they are not burdened with unnecessary information. This creates a world that feels lived-in and real, where not everything is laid bare at once.

Natural Elements and the Zen of Nature

In Zen philosophy, nature plays a central role, symbolizing harmony, simplicity, and interconnectedness. When building a world, consider how the natural environment shapes not only the physical landscape but also the culture, beliefs, and way of life of its inhabitants.

For example, in a world where towering mountains dominate the landscape, the people who live there might have a culture centered around altitude, revering the peaks as sacred or building their cities into the sides of cliffs. The natural world becomes an integral part of the setting, not just as a backdrop but as a force that influences how people live, think, and interact with each other.

Incorporating natural elements into world-building also allows for moments of stillness and reflection. A character pausing to listen to the sound of a river, feel the wind on their face, or watch the changing colors of the sky can create a sense of connection to the world and a deeper emotional resonance for the audience.

Balancing World-Building with Storytelling

One of the challenges of world-building is knowing how much detail to include and when to introduce it. A common pitfall is to overload the beginning of the story with world-building information, which can slow down the narrative and make it harder for the audience to become emotionally invested in the characters and plot.

In a Zen approach, world-building should be integrated naturally into the flow of the story. Introduce details gradually, allowing the audience to discover the world as the characters do. Show the world through the characters' interactions with it—how they navigate the terrain, engage with their culture, or respond to environmental challenges. This approach keeps the focus on the story while still creating a rich and immersive world.

For instance, instead of starting your story with a detailed explanation of how a city's water system works, you might have a character struggling to find clean water, revealing the scarcity and the social structures that control access to it through action and dialogue. The audience learns about the world in a way that feels organic and tied to the plot.

Cultural Depth in World-Building

A well-built world is not just a physical space—it is also shaped by the cultures, beliefs, and traditions of the people who live there. Creating cultures with depth can add richness and texture to your setting, making it feel more authentic and immersive.

When building cultures, think about their values, rituals, customs, and social hierarchies. What do these people believe about the world? How do they view life, death, love, and power? What are their myths, stories, and symbols? These cultural elements should be woven into the fabric of the story, influencing how characters think and act.

For example, in a world where honor is highly valued, a character's actions might be dictated by a strict code of conduct, leading to tension if they must choose between personal desire and societal expectations. The culture's beliefs about honor shape not only the character's internal conflict but also the larger social dynamics of the story.

Zen and the Art of Letting Go: Knowing When to Hold Back

In Zen storytelling, restraint is as important as creativity. When building a world, it can be tempting to include every detail you've imagined, but sometimes the most powerful world-building comes from knowing what to leave out. The art of letting go—of holding back information until the right moment, or allowing some details to remain unexplored—creates a sense of depth and mystery.

Just as Zen art often leaves parts of the canvas blank to let the mind wander and reflect, world-building can benefit from empty spaces. Not everything needs to be explained or fully fleshed out. Allowing certain aspects of the world to remain in the background can create intrigue and invite the audience to engage more deeply with the story.

For example, a character might mention an ancient, ruined city on the horizon, but the story never fully explains what happened there. The ruins become a symbol of a lost past, sparking the audience's imagination and adding depth to the world without needing a detailed backstory.

World-building, when done with care and intention, transforms a story from a series of events into an immersive, living experience. In Zen storytelling, world-building is not about complexity for its own sake—it's about creating a setting that feels harmonious, purposeful, and in service to the story. By focusing on what is essential, engaging the senses, and allowing the world to reflect the characters and themes, you can craft a setting that draws the audience in without overwhelming them.

The art of world-building is ultimately about balance—between detail and simplicity, between suggestion and explanation, between action and stillness. By following a Zen approach, you create a world that feels not only real but also deeply connected to the emotional and philosophical heart of the story.

The Power of Subtlety: Imbuing Stories with Nuanced Details

Subtlety is the art of conveying meaning without overtly stating it, allowing readers or viewers to engage with a story on a deeper, more personal level. It invites interpretation, reflection, and emotional resonance by weaving in layers of meaning through nuanced details. In storytelling, subtlety can create a rich and immersive experience, drawing the audience into the subtext of characters' actions, settings, dialogue, and themes. In Zen storytelling, where simplicity and mindfulness are key, subtlety plays an essential role in enhancing the narrative without overwhelming it. In this chapter, we'll explore how to use subtlety effectively to imbue stories with depth, complexity, and emotional power.

Understanding Subtlety in Storytelling

Subtlety allows the story to speak in whispers rather than shouts. It gives space for the audience to discover meaning on their own, fostering engagement and personal interpretation. This does not mean withholding information to the point of confusion but presenting details in a way that encourages the audience to read between the lines.

In Zen philosophy, subtlety is akin to the concept of *wabi-sabi*, which embraces imperfection and incompleteness, leaving space for reflection. In storytelling, this can manifest through hints, implications, and quiet moments that suggest more than they reveal. Subtlety trusts the audience to actively participate in the story, to notice the unspoken connections and underlying emotions.

Rather than explaining every detail or explicitly stating the theme, subtle storytelling allows characters, actions, and settings to carry layers of meaning. A glance, a pause, or an object placed carefully in the background can speak volumes, inviting the audience to immerse themselves more fully in the world you've created.

Using Subtlety in Character Development

Characters often reveal themselves not through grand speeches or overt declarations, but through small, seemingly insignificant details. Subtle character development allows the audience to get to know the characters gradually, discovering their motivations, fears, and desires through their actions, choices, and even what they choose to hide.

For example, a character's silence during a critical moment can be more telling than any outburst. The way they react to others, how they dress, or how they interact with their environment can all convey information about who they are. Perhaps a character compulsively checks their watch, hinting at underlying anxiety or impatience. Or maybe they carry an old, worn photo, silently signaling a deep emotional attachment or unresolved grief.

In Zen storytelling, this approach mirrors the idea that a person's true nature is revealed through small, everyday actions. By focusing on these details, you can craft characters that feel more authentic and complex. The audience doesn't need to know everything about a character upfront. Letting them discover the nuances over time, through subtle clues, keeps them engaged and invested.

Dialogue: Saying Less, Meaning More

Dialogue is one of the most effective tools for incorporating subtlety into storytelling. Rather than having characters say exactly what they feel or think, you can create more engaging and realistic conversations by allowing subtext to drive the interaction.

Subtext refers to the underlying meaning or emotion that is not explicitly stated in the dialogue but is implied through tone, body language, or context. Characters often speak indirectly about what's really on their minds, whether because of fear, social norms, or emotional complexity. Allowing the audience to pick up on this subtext creates a more dynamic and emotionally charged conversation.

For instance, instead of having a character say, *"I'm hurt that you didn't trust me,"* they might say something like, *"You didn't have to handle everything on your own."* The words are less direct, but the subtext—their hurt and disappointment—is clear. The audience understands the emotional depth without needing the character to spell it out.

By using subtext in dialogue, you create conversations that feel more realistic and nuanced. This approach mirrors real life, where people often speak indirectly about their true emotions or hide behind polite phrases. In Zen storytelling, this indirect approach aligns with the idea of *mujo* (impermanence)—the understanding that emotions, like words, are often fleeting, shifting, and difficult to pin down.

The Importance of Setting in Subtle Storytelling

Setting plays a key role in subtle storytelling. The world in which your characters live can carry symbolic meaning or reflect the emotional tone of the story without needing to be overtly explained. Just as a simple Zen garden can evoke tranquility and reflection through minimalism, your setting can suggest themes, moods, or character states with carefully chosen details.

For example, imagine a character returning to their childhood home. Instead of explicitly stating how they feel about being back, you might describe the peeling wallpaper, the way the air smells faintly of old wood, or the forgotten family photos gathering dust on a shelf. These subtle details create an atmosphere that reflects the character's emotions—perhaps a sense of nostalgia, loss, or discomfort.

In Zen-inspired storytelling, nature often serves as a metaphor for internal states. A quiet snowfall might represent peace or isolation, while a storm on the horizon could symbolize impending conflict. The setting, when used subtly, becomes an extension of the characters and themes, deepening the audience's connection to the story.

Symbolism and Metaphor: Layers of Meaning

Subtle storytelling often relies on symbolism and metaphor to convey deeper meaning without stating it directly. A well-placed object or recurring image can represent a character's inner struggle, a theme of the story, or a turning point in the plot. The key to using symbolism effectively is to make it feel organic, not forced or overly conspicuous.

For example, in a story about grief, a character might repeatedly encounter a broken object, such as a watch that no longer works. This object can symbolize the character's emotional state—time has stopped for them since their loss. The watch becomes a subtle reminder of the character's unresolved pain, without the need for dialogue or explanation.

Similarly, metaphors can add layers of meaning to the narrative. A river might serve as a metaphor for the passage of time or the flow of life, while a withering flower could represent the impermanence of beauty or the inevitability of death. These subtle elements encourage the audience to reflect on the deeper messages of the story, enriching their experience.

In Zen storytelling, symbolism often reflects the principles of nature, impermanence, and balance. The use of natural metaphors—such as the changing seasons or the growth of a tree—can evoke a sense of harmony between the characters and the world around them, adding depth to both the story and its themes.

The Role of Themes in Subtle Storytelling

Themes are the underlying ideas that give a story its meaning, and in subtle storytelling, these themes are often explored indirectly. Rather than explicitly stating the theme, the narrative allows it to emerge naturally through the actions, dialogue, and environment. This approach engages the audience on a deeper level, encouraging them to think about the story's larger message without being told what to feel or think.

For example, a story about redemption might not directly discuss the concept of forgiveness, but through the characters' actions, struggles, and choices, the theme gradually reveals itself. The protagonist's journey, the way they interact with others, and the consequences of their decisions all contribute to a nuanced exploration of the theme.

In Zen-inspired storytelling, themes often center around concepts such as impermanence, interconnectedness, acceptance, and inner peace. These themes are explored subtly through the characters' experiences and the natural world around them. For instance, a story about accepting the passage of time might unfold through quiet moments of reflection, where the changing seasons or the movement of clouds serve as metaphors for the character's internal journey.

• • • •

SILENCE AND PAUSES: Creating Space for Reflection

Just as in dialogue, where silence can be more powerful than words, moments of stillness and pauses in the narrative can enhance subtlety. These quiet moments allow the audience to absorb the emotional weight of the story, reflect on the characters' experiences, and connect with the deeper themes.

In Zen practice, silence is a form of mindfulness—a space where we can become aware of ourselves and the world around us. In storytelling, silence serves a similar purpose. It gives the audience room to breathe, to reflect on what has been said or left unsaid, and to engage more deeply with the characters and the story.

A character sitting in silence after a significant event, or a brief pause between two lines of dialogue, can carry immense emotional weight. These pauses create space for the audience to interpret the character's thoughts, emotions, or the significance of a moment without needing to spell it out.

Trusting the Audience

Perhaps the most important aspect of subtle storytelling is trust—trusting the audience to engage with the story, notice the details, and interpret the meaning for themselves. This doesn't mean making the story obscure or confusing, but rather giving the audience the opportunity to actively participate in the storytelling process.

By leaving room for interpretation, you allow the story to resonate in different ways for different people. Each audience member brings their own experiences, emotions, and perspectives to the story, and subtle storytelling invites them to find their own meaning within the narrative.

In Zen storytelling, this trust is central to creating a sense of harmony between the story and the audience. Just as a Zen garden invites contemplation through its simplicity, a subtle story invites reflection through its restraint and openness.

Conclusion: The Art of Subtlety in Storytelling

Subtlety is the art of saying more with less, of imbuing a story with layers of meaning through nuance, suggestion, and implication. In Zen-inspired storytelling, subtlety allows you to create a narrative that feels rich, authentic, and emotionally resonant without overwhelming the audience with overt explanations or heavy-handed themes.

By focusing on small details, subtext, symbolism, and moments of stillness, you can craft a story that invites the audience to engage deeply, reflect on the characters and themes, and find their own meaning within the narrative. The power of subtlety lies in its ability to create a sense of intimacy and connection between the story and the audience, allowing the story to unfold naturally and harmoniously. Ultimately, subtle storytelling is about trust—trusting the audience to explore the nuances of the story, and trusting the story itself to reveal its deeper truths in its own time. Through the careful balance of what is said and what is left unsaid, you can create a narrative that resonates long after the final word has been read or spoken.

The Zen of Emotional Beats: Writing with Sensitivity

Emotions are at the heart of storytelling. They connect readers and viewers to the characters and the journey, making the story resonate on a deeper, more personal level. But writing emotional moments requires more than just describing feelings—it involves crafting scenes with sensitivity, authenticity, and subtlety to create emotional beats that feel earned, powerful, and true to the story. In Zen-inspired storytelling, the emotional landscape of a story is handled with care and mindfulness, allowing moments of joy, sorrow, fear, or love to unfold naturally without being forced or overly dramatic. In this chapter, we'll explore how to write emotional beats with sensitivity, balance, and depth, ensuring that they resonate with the audience and enhance the narrative.

What Are Emotional Beats?

Emotional beats are moments in the story when the emotional intensity shifts or deepens. These are the points when characters experience significant emotional changes—whether it's a moment of realization, connection, conflict, or loss. Emotional beats are often turning points in a character's journey, marking key moments of growth, decision, or transformation.

In Zen storytelling, emotional beats are treated with care. Rather than overwhelming the audience with intense emotions, these beats unfold with a sense of balance and restraint, allowing the emotions to feel authentic and true to the characters' experiences. The goal is to evoke emotion without manipulating it, to guide the audience into feeling rather than telling them how to feel.

Creating Emotional Authenticity

One of the most important aspects of writing emotional beats is ensuring that they feel authentic. Forced or melodramatic emotions can quickly alienate the audience, making the moment feel contrived. Instead, emotional beats should arise naturally from the characters' experiences, choices, and the overall flow of the story.

To create emotional authenticity, it's essential to understand your characters deeply. What are their fears, desires, and vulnerabilities? How do they process emotions? Not every character will express their feelings in the same way, and understanding how your characters react to emotional situations helps ensure that their responses feel real and believable.

For example, a character who is naturally stoic might not cry during a moment of loss, but their grief could be shown through small, subtle actions—such as the way they linger at the site of the loss, or how they quietly distance themselves from others. This kind of nuanced, restrained emotional beat feels more authentic because it aligns with the character's personality and emotional state.

In Zen practice, there is an emphasis on accepting emotions as they come without clinging to or resisting them. This can be reflected in storytelling by allowing emotions to unfold naturally, without forcing a specific outcome. Characters experience emotions as part of their journey, not as moments to be exaggerated or overly dramatized.

Building Emotional Beats Gradually

In Zen storytelling, just as in meditation or mindfulness, emotional clarity often comes through patience and gradual unfolding. The most impactful emotional beats are not rushed or thrown at the audience all at once. Instead, they are built slowly, allowing tension or emotional complexity to accumulate until the right moment of release.

For example, a powerful emotional beat might come after several smaller moments of emotional buildup. A character who has been silently enduring hardship throughout the story may finally break down in a quiet, personal moment, offering a cathartic release not just for the character but for the audience as well. The emotional impact is heightened because the audience has witnessed the character's journey over time, creating an emotional payoff that feels earned.

This gradual buildup mirrors the Zen approach of staying present and aware, allowing emotions to develop naturally over time. Emotional beats that emerge too quickly or without proper buildup can feel shallow or unearned, but when allowed to grow organically, they become deeply resonant and meaningful.

The Power of Subtle Emotional Beats

In Zen-inspired storytelling, subtlety is key. Emotional beats don't always need to be grand or intense to be effective. Sometimes, the most powerful emotional moments are the quiet ones—the small gestures, the lingering silences, the unspoken emotions that ripple beneath the surface.

For example, instead of a dramatic confession of love, a subtle emotional beat might be conveyed through a shared glance or a quiet gesture—a character brushing their hand against another's, or offering support without saying a word. These small, understated moments can carry immense emotional weight because they feel real and grounded in the characters' relationship.

By trusting the audience to pick up on these subtleties, you allow them to engage more deeply with the story. Instead of relying on overt emotional cues, you can create an atmosphere where emotions are felt rather than explicitly stated. In Zen, this idea aligns with the principle of *ma*—the space between things, where silence and stillness hold meaning. In emotional storytelling, this space allows the audience to interpret and connect with the characters on a more intimate level.

Using Environment to Enhance Emotional Beats

The environment, or setting, can play a significant role in amplifying the emotional beats of a story. By carefully choosing or describing the setting, you can enhance the emotional tone of a scene without needing to spell out the characters' feelings.

For example, a character's emotional isolation might be emphasized by placing them in a vast, empty landscape, where the silence and emptiness around them mirror their internal state. Similarly, a moment of emotional tension might be heightened by the sound of rain tapping against the window, adding a sense of melancholy or unresolved tension to the scene.

In Zen storytelling, nature and the environment are often used as metaphors for the characters' emotional journey. A sunrise might symbolize hope or renewal, while a dying tree could represent loss or decay. These natural elements, when woven into the emotional beats of the story, create a sense of harmony between the internal and external worlds, deepening the audience's connection to the characters' emotions.

The Importance of Pacing in Emotional Beats

Pacing is crucial when it comes to emotional beats. Too many emotional highs and lows can exhaust the audience, while too few can leave the story feeling flat. In Zen-inspired storytelling, emotional pacing is about finding balance—allowing moments of intensity to flow naturally between periods of stillness or calm.

After an emotionally charged scene, it's often helpful to give both the characters and the audience time to breathe. This allows the emotions to settle and gives space for reflection. Just as in meditation, where moments of stillness allow for deeper awareness, moments of emotional quiet can create a deeper understanding of the characters and their journey.

For example, after a heated argument or a dramatic revelation, you might include a scene where the character is alone, reflecting on what happened. This moment of stillness helps process the emotional beat and provides a sense of balance before the story moves forward.

Letting Characters Process Emotions in Their Own Way

Every character processes emotions differently, and this diversity should be reflected in the emotional beats of your story. Some characters might react immediately and intensely, while others may take time to reflect or suppress their emotions until they can no longer hold them in.

In Zen practice, there is an understanding that emotions are fleeting, and that acceptance of emotions, rather than resistance, leads to greater clarity. Applying this to storytelling, characters should be allowed to experience and process their emotions in a way that feels true to who they are, without forcing a particular reaction.

For example, a character who values control might initially suppress their grief after a loss, only to let it spill out later in a private moment. Another character might express their emotions through actions rather than words—offering a gift, performing an act of kindness, or making a sacrifice that reveals their feelings without needing to articulate them.

By allowing characters to process emotions in their own way, you create emotional beats that feel authentic and nuanced, making the characters' emotional journeys more relatable and believable.

• • • •

TRUSTING THE AUDIENCE with Emotional Beats

Finally, trust is a vital component of writing emotional beats with sensitivity. Trust that the audience will connect with the emotional undercurrents of your story without needing everything spelled out. Emotional beats don't need to be loud or obvious to be impactful. By letting emotions emerge naturally through subtle details, meaningful interactions, and well-placed silences, you give the audience the opportunity to engage more deeply with the story.

Zen storytelling emphasizes the importance of presence and mindfulness—of being fully aware of the moment without trying to control it. In the same way, trust the emotional beats of your story to unfold at their own pace, allowing the audience to experience them in their own time and in their own way.

Emotional beats are the moments in a story that connect us to the characters and their journey on a profound level. In Zen-inspired storytelling, these beats are written with sensitivity, authenticity, and subtlety, allowing emotions to flow naturally without being forced or overly dramatic. By focusing on emotional authenticity, gradual buildup, subtlety, pacing, and the characters' individual ways of processing emotions, you can create emotional moments that resonate deeply with the audience.

The key to writing powerful emotional beats lies in balance. Just as in Zen practice, where stillness and movement exist in harmony, emotional storytelling should flow between intensity and quiet, allowing both the characters and the audience space to process and reflect. By trusting the story, the characters, and the audience, you can create emotional beats that feel earned, impactful, and true to the heart of the narrative.

Meditation Techniques for Writers: Focusing the Mind

Writing requires focus, clarity, and creativity, but the modern world is filled with distractions and mental clutter that can make it difficult to enter a flow state. Meditation, a practice rooted in Zen philosophy, offers a powerful way to quiet the mind, sharpen concentration, and unlock deeper levels of creativity. For writers, meditation can be a tool not only for relaxation but also for enhancing the writing process by helping you stay present, channel ideas more freely, and connect with your creative intuition. In this chapter, we'll explore meditation techniques tailored specifically for writers, guiding you to focus the mind and tap into your creative potential.

The Benefits of Meditation for Writers

Before diving into specific techniques, it's important to understand how meditation benefits the writing process. By practicing mindfulness and stillness, you can:

1. **Improve Focus and Concentration:** Meditation helps train the mind to stay focused on the task at hand, reducing mental wandering and increasing your ability to concentrate on your writing without distraction.
2. **Enhance Creativity:** Meditation quiets the analytical, overactive mind, allowing creative ideas to flow more freely. By accessing deeper levels of awareness, you can unlock new perspectives, ideas, and insights that may have been buried beneath the surface.
3. **Reduce Stress and Anxiety:** Writing can be an emotionally demanding process, especially when dealing with deadlines, creative blocks, or self-doubt. Meditation calms the nervous system, helping you manage stress and maintain a sense of calm, even in the face of challenges.
4. **Cultivate Presence and Mindfulness:** Meditation teaches you to be fully present in the moment, which is essential for writing. When you are truly present, you connect more deeply with your characters, your story, and your creative vision.
5. **Increase Self-Awareness:** Meditation helps you become more aware of your thoughts and emotions, making it easier to identify patterns of self-doubt, fear, or procrastination. With this awareness, you can consciously redirect your energy toward writing rather than getting lost in mental distractions.

Now, let's explore some specific meditation techniques that can help you cultivate focus, creativity, and mindfulness in your writing practice.

1. Mindful Breathing Meditation

Mindful breathing is one of the simplest and most effective meditation techniques for writers. By focusing on the breath, you train the mind to stay anchored in the present moment, reducing mental chatter and enhancing concentration.

How to Practice:

1. Find a comfortable, quiet place to sit. Close your eyes and take a deep breath in, then exhale slowly.
2. Begin to focus your attention on your breath. Notice the sensation of the air entering and leaving your nostrils, or the rise and fall of your chest or abdomen.
3. As thoughts arise (and they will), gently acknowledge them without judgment, and then return your focus to the breath. The goal is not to stop thinking but to practice bringing your attention back to the breath whenever you become distracted.
4. Continue this practice for 5-10 minutes, or longer if you feel comfortable.

How It Helps Writers: Mindful breathing helps you develop focus and train your attention. By practicing this meditation regularly, you'll find it easier to maintain concentration while writing, and you'll be better equipped to bring your mind back to the task at hand whenever distractions arise.

2. Visualization Meditation for Creativity

Visualization meditation taps into the power of imagination, allowing you to see your story, characters, or settings clearly in your mind's eye. This technique can be especially helpful when you're stuck or struggling to visualize a scene.

How to Practice:

1. Sit in a comfortable position, close your eyes, and take a few deep breaths to relax.
2. Choose a specific aspect of your story to focus on—this could be a character, a setting, or a key scene.
3. Begin to visualize this aspect of your story in as much detail as possible. If you're visualizing a character, imagine their appearance, clothing, mannerisms, and voice. If you're visualizing a scene, picture the setting, the atmosphere, and any sensory details (smells, sounds, textures).
4. Allow your mind to explore this visualization without forcing it. Let the details unfold naturally, and if new ideas or insights arise, take note of them.
5. After a few minutes, gently open your eyes and write down any details or ideas that emerged during the meditation.

How It Helps Writers: Visualization meditation enhances your ability to see your story vividly in your mind, making it easier to bring those images to life on the page. It also unlocks new creative possibilities by allowing your mind to wander and discover fresh details or ideas you may not have considered before.

3. Focused Attention Meditation for Clarity

This meditation technique is designed to help you focus on a single idea or concept, such as the theme of your story, the emotional journey of a character, or the structure of a scene. By focusing your attention on one thing, you clear away mental distractions and gain clarity.

How to Practice:

1. Sit comfortably and close your eyes. Take a few deep breaths to center yourself.
2. Choose a specific aspect of your writing to focus on. This could be a character's motivation, a scene's structure, or a thematic element of your story.

3. Hold this idea gently in your mind. Don't try to analyze or overthink it—simply focus your attention on it and observe what thoughts or insights arise naturally.

4. If your mind starts to wander, gently bring your focus back to the chosen idea. Stay with it for 5-10 minutes, allowing your mind to explore without forcing conclusions.

5. When you're finished, open your eyes and jot down any thoughts or discoveries that came to you during the meditation.

How It Helps Writers: Focused attention meditation helps you gain clarity on specific elements of your story. By focusing on one idea at a time, you clear away distractions and allow your mind to work through creative challenges with greater focus and insight.

4. Loving-Kindness Meditation for Self-Compassion

Writing can be a difficult and vulnerable process, and it's easy to fall into patterns of self-criticism or doubt. Loving-kindness meditation (also known as *metta* meditation) helps you cultivate compassion for yourself, reducing the mental pressure you may place on yourself as a writer.

How to Practice:

Sit comfortably, close your eyes, and take a few deep breaths.

Begin by focusing on yourself. Silently repeat phrases of loving-kindness, such as: *"May I be happy. May I be healthy. May I be at peace. May I be free from suffering."* As you say these phrases, try to genuinely feel compassion and kindness for yourself.

After a few minutes, expand your meditation to include others. You might silently offer loving-kindness to a friend, family member, or even all beings. Repeat phrases like: *"May they be happy. May they be healthy. May they be at peace."*

Continue this practice for 5-10 minutes, allowing feelings of compassion and kindness to fill your mind.

How It Helps Writers: Loving-kindness meditation helps you let go of self-criticism and cultivate a sense of compassion for yourself as a writer. It can reduce the stress and pressure of the writing process, allowing you to approach your work with a greater sense of ease and acceptance.

5. Walking Meditation for Creative Flow

Walking meditation is a dynamic practice that combines mindfulness with movement. It's an excellent way to clear mental blockages, refresh your mind, and stimulate creative thinking.

How to Practice:

1. Find a quiet place to walk, whether it's outside in nature or in a peaceful indoor space.
2. As you walk, focus your attention on the sensation of your feet touching the ground, the rhythm of your steps, and the movement of your body. Walk slowly and mindfully, paying attention to each step.
3. As thoughts arise, acknowledge them and gently return your focus to the act of walking. Allow yourself to relax into the rhythm of the movement.
4. After a few minutes, you may find that creative ideas begin to flow naturally. If so, let your mind wander gently, exploring any thoughts or ideas that arise.
5. Continue walking for 10-20 minutes, or until you feel refreshed and inspired.

How It Helps Writers: Walking meditation helps clear mental blockages and encourages creative flow. The rhythmic movement and mindfulness of walking can stimulate new ideas, solutions, or breakthroughs, making it a great practice for overcoming writer's block or generating fresh creative energy.

Meditation offers writers a powerful tool for focusing the mind, reducing distractions, and tapping into creative intuition. By incorporating meditation techniques such as mindful breathing, visualization, focused attention, loving-kindness, and walking meditation into your writing routine, you can enhance your focus, creativity, and emotional resilience.

The key to using meditation effectively as a writer is consistency. Just as you practice writing regularly, practicing meditation—even for just a few minutes each day—can lead to significant improvements in your mental clarity, emotional well-being, and creative flow. By approaching writing with a calm, centered mind, you can connect more deeply with your stories and bring your creative vision to life with greater ease and authenticity.

The Resolution: Visualizing the Ending with Serenity

Endings are one of the most critical parts of any story, whether you're writing a novel, a screenplay, or a short story. A well-crafted ending leaves a lasting impression, offering a sense of closure or reflection that resonates with the audience long after the final page or scene. But achieving the right resolution can be challenging. How do you bring your story to a satisfying close while staying true to the themes, characters, and emotions you've woven throughout the narrative? In Zen storytelling, the key to a meaningful ending lies in visualizing the resolution with serenity—allowing the story to end naturally, with purpose and grace, rather than forcing a conclusion. In this chapter, we'll explore how to visualize the ending of your story with a calm and focused mind, embracing the principles of Zen to create a resolution that feels organic, balanced, and deeply resonant.

The Importance of a Resonant Ending

Before diving into the practice of visualizing the ending, it's important to understand what makes an ending resonate with an audience. A powerful ending doesn't necessarily mean a happy one or a neatly tied-up resolution. Instead, it's about emotional and thematic closure—giving the characters, and the audience, a sense that the journey has come full circle, or that a meaningful transformation has taken place.

A resonant ending aligns with the themes of the story, reinforces the character's arc, and often leaves the audience with something to think about or feel long after the story ends. It invites reflection, just as meditation invites us to sit with our thoughts and emotions.

In Zen-inspired storytelling, the resolution is often peaceful, reflective, and purposeful. The story doesn't need to end with a grand revelation or dramatic twist; instead, it can conclude with a quiet, meaningful moment that encapsulates the essence of the journey. By visualizing the ending with serenity, you allow the story to resolve naturally, without rushing or forcing it into a particular outcome.

Step 1: Cultivate Stillness before Writing the Ending

The first step in visualizing the resolution is to cultivate stillness in your mind. Writing an ending from a place of calm and clarity allows you to approach the conclusion with focus and sensitivity. Meditation or mindful breathing can help you center yourself before you begin crafting the final scenes.

How to Practice:

1. Find a quiet space where you won't be disturbed. Sit comfortably and close your eyes.
2. Take a few deep breaths, focusing on the sensation of the air entering and leaving your lungs. Allow any mental distractions or worries to fade into the background.
3. Once you feel centered, bring your story to mind. Visualize the characters and the journey they've been on up to this point.
4. Sit with the story for a few moments, reflecting on the themes, emotional beats, and key moments that have shaped the narrative.

By creating stillness, you clear away mental clutter and open yourself to the possibilities of how the story might naturally conclude. This moment of calm also allows you to connect more deeply with the emotions of the characters and the thematic currents running through the narrative.

Step 2: Visualize the Ending with Intention

With your mind quiet and focused, begin to visualize the ending of your story. Don't rush or force it—let the resolution unfold naturally, guided by the themes and emotions that have been present throughout the narrative.

Questions to Ask:

- **What emotional state do I want the audience to be left in?** Do you want them to feel peaceful, contemplative, bittersweet, or inspired? Understanding the emotional tone of the ending will guide the way you approach it.
- **How has the protagonist changed?** The resolution should reflect the character's growth or transformation. What has the protagonist learned, and how does this knowledge affect their final actions or decisions?
- **What message or theme should resonate in the final moments?** Think about the central themes of your story. Whether it's about love, loss, redemption, or inner peace, the resolution should reinforce these themes in a subtle yet meaningful way.

As you visualize the ending, try to see it as a complete moment. Imagine the final scene in detail: where it takes place, how the characters are positioned, what they say (if anything), and what the environment around them conveys. The ending doesn't need to be dramatic; even a quiet gesture, a shared look, or a moment of stillness can carry profound emotional weight when written with intention.

Step 3: Embrace a Sense of Impermanence

Zen philosophy embraces the idea of impermanence—the understanding that all things change and nothing lasts forever. This concept can be a powerful guide when crafting an ending, as it reminds us that not everything needs to be resolved perfectly or tied up neatly. The story, like life, can end with a sense of openness or ambiguity.

Consider endings that reflect the impermanence of life—where characters part ways, where time moves forward, or where things are left unsaid but deeply felt. These endings resonate because they feel true to the ebb and flow of existence, allowing the audience to reflect on the passage of time, the nature of change, and the cycles of life.

An ending that embraces impermanence might involve a character coming to terms with loss, accepting a difficult truth, or moving forward despite uncertainty. This kind of resolution offers a quiet, profound sense of closure while acknowledging that life, like the story, continues beyond the final page.

Step 4: Use Symbolism to Strengthen the Ending

Symbolism is a powerful tool in crafting an ending with emotional and thematic depth. By incorporating subtle symbols or metaphors into the final scene, you can enhance the resonance of the resolution without overtly stating the story's message.

For example, a sunrise might symbolize new beginnings or hope, while a closing door could represent the end of a chapter in the character's life. Natural elements, such as the changing of seasons or the movement of water, often work well as symbols of transition, growth, or impermanence.

In Zen storytelling, symbols are often quiet, understated, and open to interpretation. Rather than using heavy-handed imagery, allow the symbolism to emerge organically from the story. The audience may not consciously recognize every symbol, but they will feel its emotional impact on a deeper level.

Step 5: Trust the Ending to Unfold Naturally

One of the central teachings of Zen is to let go of control and trust the process. This applies to writing the ending as well. Once you've visualized the resolution and allowed it to take shape in your mind, trust that the ending will unfold naturally on the page.

Avoid the temptation to force a particular outcome or tie up every loose end. Instead, let the story guide you to its conclusion. Sometimes the most powerful endings are those that feel organic and true to the emotional journey of the characters, even if they leave certain questions unanswered.

By trusting the process, you allow the ending to retain a sense of openness, inviting the audience to continue reflecting on the story long after it's over. This sense of openness creates a lasting emotional connection, as the resolution resonates with the complexities of life itself.

Step 6: Find Peace in the Ending

As you write the final scenes, focus on finding peace in the resolution. Whether your story ends with triumph, loss, or quiet reflection, aim to create a sense of emotional balance. Even in stories with darker or more ambiguous endings, there should be a feeling that the narrative has reached a natural resting place—a moment where the characters, and the audience, can find stillness.

Finding peace in the ending doesn't mean everything must be resolved perfectly, but it does mean that the story has reached a state of acceptance. The characters have come to terms with their journey, the themes have been fully explored, and the emotional beats have been given the space they need to resonate.

In Zen practice, peace is often found in acceptance of the present moment, no matter how imperfect it may be. In storytelling, peace comes from knowing that the story has unfolded as it was meant to, and that the ending reflects the truth of the journey.

The resolution is the final gift you give to your audience, and it deserves to be crafted with care, mindfulness, and serenity. By visualizing the ending with a calm, focused mind, you can create a conclusion that feels true to the characters, the themes, and the emotional core of the story.

In Zen-inspired storytelling, the ending is not about grand gestures or forced resolutions. Instead, it's about finding balance, accepting impermanence, and allowing the story to end naturally, with purpose and grace. By trusting the process and embracing stillness, you can write an ending that resonates deeply, leaving the audience with a sense of closure, reflection, and peace.

Remember, a powerful ending doesn't need to be loud or dramatic. Sometimes, the quietest moments carry the greatest emotional weight. By writing the resolution with serenity, you invite your audience to sit with the story, to reflect on its meaning, and to carry its lessons with them long after the final word.

Conflict Resolution: Achieving Balance in Storytelling

Conflict is the driving force behind any compelling narrative, providing tension, stakes, and opportunities for character development. It keeps readers or viewers engaged by presenting obstacles that challenge the protagonist, forcing them to grow, change, or confront difficult truths. However, just as important as creating conflict is resolving it. The resolution of conflict can make or break a story—bringing satisfaction, meaning, and closure to the narrative or leaving the audience feeling unsatisfied. Achieving balance in conflict resolution is a delicate process, and Zen storytelling provides a framework for resolving conflicts in a way that feels harmonious, natural, and true to the story's deeper themes.

In this chapter, we'll explore how to resolve conflicts in a way that brings balance, ensuring that the resolution aligns with the emotional and thematic arcs of the story, while avoiding forced or contrived endings. By approaching conflict resolution through a Zen-inspired lens, you'll be able to craft endings that resonate with authenticity and leave a lasting impression.

The Purpose of Conflict in Storytelling

Before diving into how to resolve conflict, it's essential to understand the role conflict plays in a story. Conflict is what propels the narrative forward—it creates tension, presents challenges, and forces the protagonist to make difficult decisions. Without conflict, there is no journey or growth, as the character would have no reason to evolve or change.

There are two primary types of conflict in storytelling:

- **External Conflict:** This is the outward struggle between the protagonist and external forces, such as antagonists, nature, society, or fate. External conflict presents obstacles that the protagonist must overcome to achieve their goal.
- **Internal Conflict:** This refers to the psychological or emotional struggle within the protagonist. It might involve conflicting desires, fears, moral dilemmas, or unresolved trauma. Internal conflict is often more nuanced and complex, driving character development and emotional depth.

In Zen storytelling, both external and internal conflicts are essential, but their resolution is approached with a sense of balance and acceptance. Instead of simply "winning" or "losing," the resolution of conflict is often about finding harmony, understanding, or personal growth.

Step 1: Understanding the Nature of Conflict Resolution

Conflict resolution in storytelling doesn't always mean that the protagonist achieves victory over their obstacles. Sometimes, resolution comes from acceptance, compromise, or personal transformation. The way a conflict is resolved should feel true to the story and the characters, rather than adhering to formulaic expectations of triumph or defeat.

A balanced conflict resolution should address both the external and internal aspects of the protagonist's journey. Often, the resolution of the external conflict mirrors the resolution of the internal one. For example, a protagonist who has been battling external forces might find that their true challenge is within themselves—resolving their inner conflict allows them to approach the external conflict with newfound clarity or strength.

Zen philosophy teaches that peace and harmony come from accepting life's impermanence and the natural flow of events. Applying this idea to conflict resolution means that the ending doesn't need to be perfect or tied up neatly. It should reflect the character's growth and the thematic depth of the story, even if not all external challenges are fully resolved.

Step 2: Resolving External Conflict with Meaning

External conflict often drives the plot, but its resolution should be more than just a simple "win" or "lose." A balanced resolution of external conflict considers the emotional and thematic journey of the characters, ensuring that the outcome resonates on a deeper level.

When resolving external conflict, consider the following:

- **What has the protagonist learned from this conflict?** The resolution should reflect the growth or transformation of the protagonist. Have they become more courageous, compassionate, or self-aware? The external victory or loss should mirror the internal change they've undergone.
- **Is the resolution too easy?** Be mindful of avoiding resolutions that feel too convenient or contrived. If the external conflict is resolved too quickly or without effort, it can undercut the stakes and emotional investment. A balanced resolution should feel earned, with the protagonist confronting real challenges before achieving resolution.
- **How does the resolution align with the story's themes?** The external conflict should tie into the story's larger themes. For example, if the theme of the story is about letting go of control, the resolution might involve the protagonist realizing that they can't control everything and learning to accept uncertainty.

A Zen-inspired resolution often involves harmony, but this doesn't necessarily mean a "happy" or "perfect" ending. Instead, it means finding a natural conclusion that feels true to the story and its characters. For example, a story about survival in the wilderness might end not with the protagonist defeating nature, but with them learning to live in harmony with it.

Step 3: Resolving Internal Conflict with Grace

Internal conflict is often the heart of a story, and its resolution is key to creating emotional resonance. While external conflict drives the action, internal conflict drives the character's emotional journey. Resolving internal conflict with grace requires understanding the protagonist's psychological or emotional struggles and allowing them to come to a place of acceptance, transformation, or understanding.

To resolve internal conflict:

- **Focus on the character's growth:** The resolution of internal conflict should reflect the emotional or psychological growth of the protagonist. Have they overcome a deep-seated fear, reconciled with a part of themselves, or found inner peace? The resolution doesn't need to be dramatic—it can be a quiet moment of acceptance or realization.

- **Embrace complexity:** Internal conflict resolution is often more nuanced than external conflict. It's rarely a clear-cut "win." Instead, it might involve accepting difficult truths, finding balance between conflicting desires, or letting go of past wounds. This complexity makes the resolution feel more realistic and emotionally resonant.
- **Avoid rushing the resolution:** Internal conflict should be given time to unfold naturally. A rushed resolution can feel superficial or unearned. Allow the character to wrestle with their emotions, reflect on their experiences, and reach a resolution that feels genuine.

In Zen storytelling, internal conflict resolution often involves embracing impermanence, accepting the present moment, or finding inner peace despite external challenges. This aligns with the Zen concept of *mujo*, the idea that all things change and that peace comes from accepting the ebb and flow of life.

Step 4: Finding Balance in the Resolution

A balanced resolution addresses both the external and internal conflicts in a way that feels cohesive and meaningful. The resolution should tie together the character's personal journey and the plot's events, creating a sense of harmony between the two.

In Zen practice, balance is key—neither extremes of control nor complete detachment are ideal. Instead, balance is found by navigating the middle path. In storytelling, this balance means finding a resolution that honors both the emotional and thematic arcs of the story while avoiding easy answers or contrived conclusions.

Some ways to achieve balance in conflict resolution include:

Blending external and internal resolutions: The external conflict may resolve in a way that mirrors the protagonist's internal growth. For example, a character who learns to trust others might finally accept help to overcome an external obstacle. This creates a sense of balance between the internal and external worlds.

Creating space for ambiguity: Not all conflicts need to be fully resolved. In fact, leaving certain questions or conflicts open can create a sense of realism and depth. A character might resolve their internal conflict, but the external world may remain complex or unresolved. This type of ending can reflect the Zen principle of *mujo*—that life is ever-changing and not everything can be neatly tied up.

Reflecting on the journey, not just the outcome: A balanced resolution doesn't focus solely on whether the protagonist wins or loses. Instead, it reflects on the journey they've taken, the lessons they've learned, and how they've changed. In Zen storytelling, the journey itself is often more important than the final destination.

Step 5: Letting Go of the Need for Perfection

In Zen philosophy, there is an understanding that perfection is an illusion. Instead of striving for a "perfect" resolution, focus on a resolution that feels true to the story. This might mean embracing imperfection, complexity, or ambiguity in the ending. Just as a Zen garden is beautiful in its simplicity and natural imperfections, a story's resolution can be powerful when it feels authentic, even if it's not perfectly wrapped up.

For example, a protagonist may not achieve their goal in the way they originally intended, but they might find peace or acceptance in the process. A romantic relationship might not be fully reconciled, but there may be a moment of understanding or connection that brings emotional closure. These endings feel real because they reflect the complexities of life and human emotion.

In Zen storytelling, the act of letting go—of control, of expectations, of perfection—is essential. By letting go of the need for a perfect or "happy" ending, you allow the story to resolve in a way that feels true to its emotional and thematic core.

Conclusion: Achieving Balance in Conflict Resolution

Conflict resolution is one of the most critical elements of storytelling, offering closure, transformation, and meaning to both the characters and the audience. By approaching conflict resolution through a Zen-inspired lens, you can achieve balance in your story's ending—resolving external and internal conflicts in a way that feels natural, meaningful, and emotionally resonant.

A balanced resolution reflects the character's growth, aligns with the themes of the story, and embraces the complexities of life. Whether the ending is triumphant, bittersweet, or open-ended, the key is to create a resolution that feels true to the journey and leaves the audience with a sense of closure, reflection, and peace.

In the end, conflict resolution in storytelling is about more than just tying up loose ends—it's about honoring the emotional and thematic depth of the story, finding harmony between the character's internal and external worlds, and allowing the story to come to a natural and satisfying close.

The Creative Void: Embracing Emptiness to Spark Ideas

Creativity is often seen as a process of constant output—generating ideas, solving problems, and shaping concepts into something tangible. But what if the secret to sparking new ideas lies not in the act of creation, but in embracing emptiness? In Zen philosophy, emptiness, or *shunyata*, is not a void of nothingness but a space of potential, where infinite possibilities exist. By allowing yourself to enter this creative void—where the mind is free from distractions, expectations, and preconceived notions—you open yourself up to new insights, fresh ideas, and deeper creative flow.

In this chapter, we'll explore the concept of the creative void and how embracing emptiness can help you spark new ideas, break through creative blocks, and connect with your intuition. By quieting the mind and letting go of the need to constantly produce, you create space for inspiration to arise naturally, in its own time and form.

The Power of Emptiness in Creativity

At first glance, the idea of embracing emptiness may seem counterintuitive to creativity. After all, isn't creativity about filling the blank page or screen with words, images, or ideas? But in Zen, emptiness is not a barren void. It is a fertile space from which all things emerge. The absence of noise and mental clutter creates room for new ideas to surface—ideas that may have been drowned out by the constant push to create or think.

In the creative process, emptiness offers several key benefits:

- **Clearing Mental Clutter:** Embracing emptiness allows you to release the mental chatter, self-doubt, and overthinking that often block creativity. In this quiet space, you can connect with your deeper thoughts and creative intuition.
- **Creating Space for New Ideas:** When the mind is constantly full of distractions or preconceived ideas, there's little room for fresh inspiration. Emptiness creates space for new ideas to arise, often in unexpected ways.
- **Reducing Pressure to Produce:** Many writers and creators feel pressure to constantly generate content or ideas, leading to burnout or creative blocks. Embracing emptiness removes this pressure, allowing creativity to flow naturally, without forcing it.
- **Tapping into Intuition:** In the quiet of emptiness, you become more attuned to subtle insights and gut feelings. These intuitive sparks can lead to breakthroughs in your writing or creative work.

In Zen practice, sitting in stillness and embracing the emptiness of the present moment is a pathway to enlightenment and clarity. In the same way, allowing yourself to sit in the creative void can lead to moments of profound inspiration and insight.

Step 1: Letting Go of Expectations

The first step to embracing the creative void is letting go of expectations—expectations about what your creative process should look like, how quickly ideas should come, or what form they should take. Often, these expectations create mental tension, blocking the natural flow of creativity.

How to Practice:

1. **Release the Need for Immediate Results:** Enter the creative process without expecting to come up with the "perfect" idea right away. Instead, allow yourself to sit in the unknown, trusting that ideas will come in their own time.
2. **Avoid Overplanning:** While it's important to have goals or intentions, overplanning or trying to control

every aspect of your creative process can stifle spontaneity. Embrace the uncertainty and unpredictability of creativity.

3. **Embrace Failure as Part of the Process:** Let go of the fear of making mistakes or failing. The creative void is a space where you can explore without judgment or pressure. Failure is not an endpoint but a stepping stone toward new ideas.

In Zen, the practice of *mushin*—"no mind"—encourages a state of being free from distractions, ego, and preconceived notions. By practicing *mushin* in your creative work, you clear the mental space needed for true inspiration to arise.

Step 2: Quieting the Mind through Meditation

One of the most effective ways to enter the creative void is through meditation. Meditation helps quiet the mind, creating a sense of stillness and openness where new ideas can surface. By focusing on the present moment and letting go of mental distractions, you create the conditions for creativity to flow.

How to Practice:

1. **Sit in a Comfortable Position:** Find a quiet place where you won't be disturbed. Sit in a comfortable position, close your eyes, and take a few deep breaths.
2. **Focus on Your Breath:** Begin by focusing on the sensation of your breath entering and leaving your body. If your mind starts to wander (which it will), gently bring your focus back to your breath. The goal is not to stop thinking but to cultivate a sense of calm awareness.
3. **Allow Thoughts to Come and Go:** As you meditate, thoughts may arise. Rather than trying to push them away, simply observe them without judgment, then let them pass. Over time, your mind will quiet, creating space for new ideas to emerge.
4. **Stay Open to Insights:** After meditating for 10-15 minutes, you may notice that ideas or insights begin to arise naturally. These moments of clarity are often subtle, so stay open to whatever thoughts or feelings come up.

By incorporating meditation into your creative practice, you create a regular space for emptiness—a fertile ground where ideas can take root and grow.

Step 3: Embracing Stillness and Boredom

In today's fast-paced world, we're often conditioned to avoid stillness or boredom. We fill every spare moment with distractions—scrolling through social media, checking emails, or watching TV. But stillness and even boredom are fertile grounds for creativity. When you allow yourself to sit with boredom, without seeking to fill the void, your mind begins to wander in creative ways.

How to Practice:

1. **Take Breaks Without Distractions:** Instead of filling every break with distractions, try taking moments of stillness throughout your day. Whether it's sitting quietly with a cup of tea or walking without your phone, give yourself space to be present with your thoughts.
2. **Allow Yourself to Be Bored:** Boredom can be uncomfortable, but it's also a gateway to creativity. When the mind isn't constantly stimulated, it starts to generate its own ideas and entertain itself in new ways.
3. **Observe Your Thoughts:** In moments of stillness or boredom, pay attention to where your mind naturally drifts. These moments of mental wandering can lead to unexpected ideas or creative breakthroughs.

In Zen practice, stillness is a pathway to deeper awareness. By embracing stillness in your creative process, you invite new ideas to emerge from the quiet spaces of your mind.

Step 4: Freewriting and Stream of Consciousness

Freewriting is a powerful technique that allows you to enter the creative void by letting go of control and allowing your thoughts to flow freely onto the page. In freewriting, there are no rules, no pressure to write something "good," and no need to stick to a specific structure or idea.

How to Practice:

Set a Timer: Start by setting a timer for 10-15 minutes. During this time, your goal is to write continuously without stopping.

Write Without Judgment: Let your thoughts flow freely onto the page, without worrying about grammar, coherence, or structure. The key is to keep writing, even if it feels like nonsense. You can write about anything—ideas for your story, your current mood, or random thoughts that pop into your head.

. . . .

DON'T EDIT: Resist the urge to edit or correct yourself. Freewriting is about letting go of control and allowing ideas to emerge without judgment.

Review Later: After the timer goes off, take a break before reviewing what you've written. You may find that hidden within the stream of consciousness are sparks of ideas, phrases, or concepts that you can later develop into something more refined.

Freewriting is a way to embrace the creative void by bypassing the analytical mind and tapping into the subconscious. It allows ideas to flow freely, often leading to surprising and original insights.

Step 5: Trusting the Process

Perhaps the most important aspect of embracing the creative void is trusting the process. Creativity doesn't always work on demand, and sometimes the best ideas come when you least expect them—after you've given yourself time to step away, clear your mind, and return with fresh eyes.

How to Practice:

1. **Be Patient with Yourself:** Creativity isn't always a linear process, and it's normal to experience periods of stagnation or uncertainty. Trust that by creating space for emptiness, new ideas will come when the time is right.
2. **Let Go of the Need for Immediate Solutions:** Sometimes the most powerful ideas arise when you're not actively searching for them. Trust that the creative void will yield inspiration in its own time, and avoid the temptation to force an idea to emerge.
3. **Return to the Void When Needed:** When you feel stuck, overwhelmed, or uninspired, return to the creative void. Whether through meditation, stillness, or freewriting, allow yourself to re-enter that space of potential and possibility.

In Zen practice, trust is an essential part of the journey. Just as you trust the present moment to unfold as it should, trust that your creative process will lead you where you need to go—even if the path isn't always clear right away.

The creative void is not a space of nothingness but a fertile ground where new ideas can take root and flourish. By embracing emptiness—whether through meditation, stillness, freewriting, or letting go of expectations—you create space for creativity to flow naturally and intuitively. In Zen-inspired storytelling, the creative void is a source of inspiration, offering clarity, insight, and fresh perspectives.

Rather than fearing the blank page or the unknown, learn to welcome it as part of the creative process. By entering the creative void with an open mind and a sense of curiosity, you allow ideas to emerge in their own time, leading to deeper, more authentic creativity. Trust that in the quiet spaces of the mind, the seeds of your next great idea are already waiting to be discovered.

Writing with Clarity and Purpose: A Mindful Approach

Clarity and purpose are two essential elements of powerful storytelling. When writing is clear, it resonates with the reader, cutting through confusion and distraction. When writing has purpose, every sentence, scene, and character serves a specific role in the narrative, guiding the reader toward the heart of the story. In Zen philosophy, mindfulness—being fully present and aware of your actions—plays a central role in achieving clarity and purpose. By approaching writing with mindfulness, you can hone your craft, ensuring that every word on the page is intentional and impactful.

In this chapter, we'll explore how to bring a mindful approach to your writing practice, allowing clarity and purpose to guide your storytelling. Whether you're working on a novel, screenplay, or short story, applying mindfulness techniques can help you stay focused, avoid distractions, and ensure that your writing remains purposeful and effective.

The Importance of Clarity in Storytelling

Clarity in writing is about more than just avoiding complex language or confusing sentence structures. It's about ensuring that your ideas are communicated clearly and that your readers or viewers can follow the narrative without getting lost. Clear writing eliminates unnecessary distractions, allowing the audience to connect with the emotions, themes, and characters at the heart of the story.

Clarity is essential in:

1. **Character Development:** Clear character motivations, emotions, and actions help the audience understand why a character behaves in certain ways. When motivations are unclear or inconsistent, the character's journey can feel muddled or unsatisfying.
2. **Plot Progression:** A clear plot ensures that the audience knows where the story is going, even if there are surprises or twists along the way. If the plot becomes convoluted or overly complex, it can confuse and disengage the audience.
3. **Themes and Messages:** Clarity helps ensure that the themes of your story come through without being heavy-handed or obscure. Your audience should be able to grasp the underlying messages of your work without feeling lost in ambiguity.

To write with clarity, you must first achieve clarity of thought. This is where mindfulness comes in—by practicing mindful writing, you can focus on the essence of what you want to communicate and strip away anything unnecessary or distracting.

Step 1: Cultivating Mindfulness in Writing

Mindfulness is the practice of being fully present in the moment, observing your thoughts, emotions, and actions without judgment. When applied to writing, mindfulness helps you become more aware of the choices you make—what words you use, how you structure sentences, and what details you include or omit. This awareness allows you to write with greater focus and clarity.

How to Practice:

1. **Set an Intention Before Writing:** Before you begin a writing session, take a moment to set a clear intention. What do you want to accomplish in this session? Are you focusing on a specific scene, character, or theme? Setting an intention helps you stay mindful of your purpose throughout the writing process.
2. **Write with Presence:** As you write, bring your full attention to the page. Avoid distractions, and if you find your mind wandering, gently bring it back to the task at hand. Be aware of each word you choose and how it contributes to the overall narrative.
3. **Observe Your Thoughts Without Judgment:** During the writing process, you may experience self-doubt, frustration, or creative blocks. Instead of reacting to these emotions, observe them with curiosity. Acknowledge the thoughts and feelings without judgment, and return your focus to the present moment.
4. **Take Breaks for Reflection:** Writing with clarity doesn't mean forcing words onto the page. Take regular breaks to step back and reflect on what you've written. This gives you time to gain perspective and ensure that your writing remains aligned with your original intention.

By cultivating mindfulness in your writing practice, you become more aware of the choices you make and more attuned to the clarity of your narrative.

Step 2: Writing with Purpose

Purposeful writing means that every sentence, scene, and character serves a function in the story. There is no filler, no wasted words—everything is intentional, contributing to the plot, theme, or character development. Writing with purpose keeps your story focused and coherent, ensuring that the reader remains engaged and that the narrative moves forward with momentum.

How to Practice:

Identify the Core Message or Theme: Before you begin writing, identify the core message or theme you want to explore. What is the underlying purpose of your story? Whether it's about love, loss, redemption, or personal growth, knowing your theme helps you stay focused and ensures that every scene supports the larger narrative.

Ensure Every Scene Has a Function: As you write each scene, ask yourself: What purpose does this scene serve? Does it advance the plot, develop a character, or reinforce the theme? If a scene feels like filler or doesn't serve a clear purpose, consider cutting or revising it.

Be Intentional with Details: Purposeful writing involves being selective with the details you include. Instead of overwhelming the reader with unnecessary information, focus on the details that enhance the story. For example, if you're describing a character's room, choose a few key items that reveal something about their personality or emotional state, rather than describing every object in the room.

Stay Focused on the Story's Arc: Every story has a narrative arc, and purposeful writing ensures that each scene moves the story forward along this arc. Be mindful of pacing, and avoid tangents that pull the story away from its central path.

By writing with purpose, you maintain a sense of direction and focus, ensuring that your story remains engaging and impactful.

Step 3: Simplifying for Clarity

Simplicity is at the heart of clarity. In Zen philosophy, simplicity is not about removing complexity, but about stripping away what is unnecessary to reveal the essence of something. In writing, simplicity means distilling your ideas and language to their purest forms, ensuring that your message comes through without confusion or clutter.

How to Practice:

1. **Use Clear, Direct Language:** Avoid overly complex or flowery language. While it's tempting to use elaborate descriptions or complicated sentence structures, simplicity often leads to greater impact. Focus on writing sentences that are clear and easy to understand.
2. **Eliminate Redundancies:** Be mindful of repetition or unnecessary words. For example, instead of saying, "She nodded her head in agreement," you can simply write, "She nodded." Small changes like this can make your writing more concise and efficient.
3. **Cut Unnecessary Scenes or Characters:** If a scene or character doesn't contribute to the overall narrative, consider cutting it. Simplifying your story in this way helps maintain clarity and keeps the reader focused on the essential elements of the plot.
4. **Revise with an Eye for Clarity:** After completing a draft, revise with the goal of clarifying your ideas. Are there any sections that feel confusing or unclear? Are your character motivations and plot points easy to follow? Revision is an opportunity to refine your story and ensure that your message comes through clearly.

By simplifying your writing, you remove distractions and allow the heart of the story to shine through.

Step 4: Staying True to the Story's Intent

Writing with clarity and purpose also means staying true to the story's intent. As you develop characters, plotlines, and themes, it's important to remain grounded in the original intention of the story. While creativity often leads you in new directions, maintaining an understanding of the story's core purpose ensures that you don't lose focus or drift away from the central message.

How to Practice:

1. **Return to Your Original Intention:** Periodically revisit the intention you set at the beginning of the writing process. Are you still aligned with the core themes and messages you wanted to explore? If you've drifted, consider how to bring the story back on course.
2. **Be Open to Evolution:** While it's important to stay true to your original intent, be open to the natural evolution of your story. Characters and themes may develop in unexpected ways. Stay mindful of how these changes affect the overall purpose of the narrative, and make adjustments as needed.
3. **Focus on the Essential Questions:** What is the heart of your story? What emotional journey are the characters undergoing? Staying focused on these essential questions ensures that your writing remains purposeful and aligned with the story's intent.

By staying true to the story's core purpose, you create a narrative that feels cohesive and meaningful, offering a deeper connection to the audience.

Step 5: Practicing Patience and Presence

Writing with clarity and purpose requires patience. Creativity can't be rushed, and clarity often comes through the process of revision, reflection, and refinement. By practicing presence and mindfulness, you allow yourself to engage fully with the writing process, without feeling pressured to achieve perfection immediately.

How to Practice:

1. **Be Patient with the Process:** Understand that writing with clarity takes time. It's normal for your first drafts to be messy or unclear—this is part of the process. Be patient with yourself as you refine your ideas.
2. **Embrace the Journey of Writing:** Writing is not just about the end product; it's about the journey of discovery, reflection, and growth. Stay present with each writing session, focusing on the small steps that move you toward clarity.
3. **Revise with Mindfulness:** When revising your work, approach it mindfully. Read through your writing with fresh eyes, looking for places where clarity can be improved or purpose can be strengthened. Take your time to ensure that each revision brings you closer to your ultimate goal.

By practicing patience and staying present, you allow clarity and purpose to emerge naturally, creating a narrative that feels intentional and impactful.

Writing with clarity and purpose is not just about crafting well-structured sentences or delivering a coherent plot—it's about creating a story that resonates deeply with the audience. By approaching your writing mindfully, you ensure that every word, scene, and character serves a meaningful role in the narrative. You simplify your ideas, stay true to the story's intent, and focus on the essence of what you want to communicate.

A mindful approach to writing helps you stay present, engaged, and aligned with the core message of your story. It encourages you to write with intention, stripping away unnecessary distractions and allowing your narrative to shine with clarity and purpose. Through mindfulness, you connect more deeply with your creative process, ensuring that your writing is not only clear and purposeful but also deeply impactful and resonant.

Action is the heartbeat of storytelling. It propels the narrative forward, reveals character traits, and heightens emotional stakes. While dialogue and description are vital tools for expressing a story's themes and emotions, movement and action bring the story to life. In storytelling, movement isn't just about physical gestures or fights—it's about how characters' actions, body language, and environments convey meaning and move the plot forward. In Zen philosophy, flow and movement are often viewed as natural, continuous processes, much like the flow of water. When applied to storytelling, movement becomes not just a tool for action but a way to guide the narrative with fluidity and purpose.

In this chapter, we'll explore how to use movement and action effectively in your storytelling. Whether you're writing an intense fight scene, a quiet moment of reflection, or a dynamic sequence of events, understanding how to harness the flow of action will help you create stories that engage and captivate the audience on both a visual and emotional level.

The Role of Movement in Storytelling

Movement is more than just physical action—it reflects the inner world of characters, the rhythm of the plot, and the overall pacing of the story. In storytelling, movement serves several key functions:

1. **Revealing Character:** A character's movements, gestures, and physicality can reveal important aspects of their personality. Are they calm and deliberate in their actions, or do they move with nervous energy? A character's body language can convey their emotional state or intentions without a single word of dialogue.
2. **Driving Plot:** Action sequences, whether they involve physical conflict or a character's decision-making, push the plot forward. Every movement has a consequence, and each action shapes the story's direction.
3. **Building Tension and Suspense:** Action, especially when combined with well-paced movement, is a powerful tool for creating tension and suspense. The speed or slowness of movement can intensify emotions, whether it's the fast-paced action of a chase scene or the slow, deliberate movements of a character on the verge of making a life-changing decision.
4. **Enhancing Atmosphere:** The way characters move through space can contribute to the atmosphere of the story. A character walking slowly through a dimly lit corridor, pausing to listen for sounds, creates a mood of suspense and uncertainty. Conversely, a bustling city scene filled with rapid movements and constant activity conveys a sense of chaos and energy.

Understanding the role of movement allows you to craft scenes that are visually and emotionally engaging, ensuring that every action serves a narrative purpose.

· · · ·

STEP 1: CHARACTERIZING Movement

The way a character moves tells us as much about them as their words. A confident character might walk with a straight back and purposeful strides, while an anxious character might fidget, hesitate, or avoid eye contact. Characterizing movement helps to reveal the internal state of the character and adds depth to their personality.

How to Practice:

1. **Observe Body Language:** In real life, pay attention to how people move in different situations. Notice how their body language changes depending on their mood or interactions. Apply these observations to

your characters, ensuring that their physical actions align with their emotional states.

2. **Match Movement to Motivation:** Consider your character's motivations when describing their movements. For example, a character with a goal or plan will likely move with intention, while a character facing fear or doubt may move more cautiously. Matching movement to motivation deepens the reader's understanding of the character's internal conflict.

3. **Use Gestures to Convey Emotion:** Small gestures can carry significant emotional weight. A character who clenches their fists might be expressing anger or frustration, while a character who repeatedly checks their watch could indicate anxiety or impatience. Use these subtle movements to add layers to your characters' emotions without needing to state them explicitly.

Example: Instead of writing, "She was nervous," show the reader through movement: *"Her fingers trembled as she fumbled with the papers, glancing over her shoulder at the door. She tapped her foot, unable to sit still, her eyes darting across the room, searching for something—anything—to distract her racing thoughts."*

Through movement, the character's nervous energy becomes palpable, adding tension to the scene without explicitly stating her emotions.

Step 2: Pacing Action for Impact

The pacing of action is crucial in determining how a scene unfolds emotionally and narratively. Fast-paced action often creates excitement, chaos, or tension, while slower-paced movement allows for reflection, suspense, or emotional depth. To maintain balance in storytelling, it's important to vary the pacing of action, allowing moments of intensity to be followed by moments of calm.

How to Practice:

Vary the Speed of Action: In scenes of high intensity (like a chase or fight), quick, sharp movements can create a sense of urgency and tension. Conversely, slowing down the action at key moments can build suspense or allow for introspection. Use pacing to control the emotional flow of the scene.

Build Momentum Gradually: Don't rush into high-action scenes too quickly. Allow tension to build slowly, with movements that grow in intensity over time. This gradual escalation makes the climactic action more impactful and satisfying for the audience.

Pause for Reflection: After a moment of intense action, give the characters—and the reader—a chance to reflect on what has happened. This moment of stillness provides emotional depth and highlights the consequences of the action.

Example: Imagine a fast-paced chase scene where a character is running through a crowded marketplace. The action is frenetic, with the character dodging obstacles, pushing through crowds, and breathing heavily. But after the chase, the scene slows: *"He leaned against the brick wall, gasping for air, his pulse racing in his ears. The world around him seemed to blur as he struggled to catch his breath, his hand shaking as he wiped the sweat from his brow. For a brief moment, the chaos stilled, leaving only the pounding of his heartbeat and the weight of what he'd just escaped."*

The pause after the action adds emotional weight to the scene, allowing the audience to feel the character's relief and exhaustion.

Step 3: Movement as Metaphor

In storytelling, movement can be symbolic, representing internal struggles, themes, or transformations. A character's physical journey might mirror their emotional journey, and their movements through space can serve as metaphors for the challenges they face. By using movement symbolically, you can add layers of meaning to your story.

How to Practice:

1. **Mirror Internal Conflict with Physical Movement:** A character's movement can reflect their inner

conflict. For example, a character grappling with indecision might pace back and forth, while a character experiencing emotional growth might move more confidently or freely as the story progresses.

2. **Use Movement to Represent Themes:** Movement can symbolize larger themes in your story, such as freedom, entrapment, or change. A character breaking free from physical restraints might symbolize breaking free from emotional constraints, while a journey across a vast landscape could represent a search for identity or meaning.

3. **Incorporate Natural Elements:** The natural world often reflects the emotional or thematic flow of a story. Characters moving through changing weather, seasons, or landscapes can evoke a sense of transition or transformation. A storm might represent internal turmoil, while a character walking through a serene forest could symbolize inner peace or clarity.

Example: In a story about personal transformation, a character who has spent most of the narrative feeling trapped and uncertain might experience a shift in movement: *"For the first time in weeks, she stood tall, her shoulders no longer hunched with the weight of self-doubt. She walked with purpose now, each step lighter than the last, as if the ground beneath her feet no longer pulled her down but propelled her forward."*

The character's physical movement reflects her emotional journey, symbolizing newfound strength and confidence.

Step 4: Choreographing Action Scenes

When writing action-heavy scenes, such as fight sequences, chases, or battles, it's important to choreograph the action clearly and logically. Readers need to be able to follow the sequence of events, visualizing the movements without becoming confused or disoriented. A well-choreographed action scene immerses the reader in the moment, making them feel the intensity of the conflict.

How to Practice:

1. **Plan the Action Logically:** Map out the sequence of events in an action scene before writing it. Consider the physical space, the characters involved, and how their movements interact. Make sure the action flows naturally from one moment to the next.

2. **Use Short, Punchy Sentences for Fast-Paced Action:** When writing fast-paced action scenes, shorter sentences can create a sense of urgency and excitement. Quick, sharp descriptions mimic the rapid movements of the characters, pulling the reader into the intensity of the moment.

3. **Be Clear and Precise:** Avoid overly complex descriptions that might confuse the reader. Keep the action clear and focused, using precise language to describe each movement. The reader should always be able to visualize where the characters are and what they're doing.

Example: In a fight scene, instead of writing: *"He quickly punched the man and then kicked him in the stomach, making him fall backward as he groaned in pain."*

Try: *"His fist shot forward, landing hard against the man's jaw. A swift kick to the gut sent him stumbling back, gasping for air."*

The shorter sentences and vivid verbs create a more immediate, intense action sequence, drawing the reader into the scene.

Step 5: Using Stillness for Emotional Depth

While movement is key to action, stillness can be just as powerful. Moments of stillness create contrast, allowing for emotional reflection and deepening the impact of the story's action. In Zen storytelling, stillness often represents mindfulness, presence, and awareness—qualities that can enrich your characters' internal journeys.

How to Practice:

Pause for Emotional Impact: After a significant action sequence, use moments of stillness to allow the characters (and the reader) to process the emotional weight of what has happened. Stillness creates space for reflection, grief, relief, or revelation.

Contrast Movement with Stillness: The contrast between movement and stillness heightens the emotional intensity of both. A character moving rapidly through a chaotic environment may suddenly stop, the stillness amplifying the emotional stakes of the moment.

Use Stillness as Resolution: Stillness can serve as a powerful resolution to conflict. A character who has been in constant motion may find peace in a moment of stillness, signifying the end of a journey or an emotional breakthrough.

Example: After an intense argument between two characters, stillness can emphasize the emotional fallout: *"The room fell silent. She stood motionless, the echoes of their words hanging in the air like a thick fog. Her hands, which had trembled with rage moments before, now lay limp at her sides. She didn't move—couldn't move—as the weight of what had been said settled over her like a stone."*

The stillness here creates emotional depth, allowing the reader to feel the aftermath of the conflict.

Storytelling through movement is about more than just writing action scenes—it's about understanding how physical actions, body language, and the rhythm of motion shape the emotional and narrative flow of your story. By using movement with intention, you can reveal character, drive the plot, and build tension, all while creating a dynamic, immersive experience for your audience.

In Zen-inspired storytelling, movement is a natural flow, much like the movement of water. It can be fast or slow, intense or calm, but it is always purposeful. Whether you're writing a high-stakes chase, a quiet moment of reflection, or a symbolic journey, the flow of action helps guide the reader through the story with clarity, emotion, and meaning. By balancing movement and stillness, pacing action for impact, and using movement as metaphor, you can create a narrative that feels alive, resonant, and deeply engaging.

Writing for Visual Effects: Imagining the Unseen

In modern storytelling, especially in film, television, and even novels, visual effects (VFX) have become an integral tool for bringing imaginative worlds, extraordinary characters, and impossible scenarios to life. As a writer, you may not be directly involved in creating these effects, but you are responsible for crafting the blueprints that inspire them. Writing for visual effects requires a delicate balance of vivid description and creative restraint. You need to describe the unseen—the things that don't exist yet—but you must also leave room for collaboration with visual artists who will bring your ideas to life.

In Zen philosophy, there is a concept called *kū* (emptiness or potential), which suggests that emptiness is not devoid of meaning but is full of potential waiting to be realized. When writing for visual effects, you're often working within this space of potential, describing things that exist only in your imagination and trusting others to shape them into something tangible. This chapter explores how to approach writing for visual effects, focusing on imagining the unseen while keeping the balance between clear descriptions and creative flexibility.

The Role of Visual Effects in Storytelling

Visual effects serve multiple purposes in storytelling. They can create entire worlds, enhance action sequences, bring mythical creatures or impossible phenomena to life, or subtly enhance the atmosphere of a scene. Writing with VFX in mind means envisioning these extraordinary elements while keeping the story grounded in its emotional and narrative core.

Here are some key roles visual effects play in storytelling:

1. **World-Building:** In science fiction, fantasy, and other speculative genres, VFX can create entirely new worlds, from vast alien landscapes to futuristic cities. These visual elements often shape the tone and mood of the story.
2. **Enhancing Action:** VFX can amplify the intensity of action sequences, making the impossible seem real—whether it's superheroes flying, cars flipping in mid-air, or magical duels unfolding in elaborate ways.
3. **Symbolism and Metaphor:** VFX can also be used symbolically, representing abstract ideas or internal character experiences. For example, a character's inner turmoil might be visually represented by a storm raging outside.
4. **Seamless Storytelling:** Not all visual effects are flashy. Many are invisible to the audience but crucial to the storytelling, such as digitally removing modern objects in a period film or enhancing natural landscapes.

As a writer, your job is to communicate the idea and emotion behind these effects in a way that inspires the visual artists to bring your vision to life while leaving enough creative space for interpretation.

Step 1: Imagining the Unseen

When writing for visual effects, your first task is to imagine what doesn't exist yet. This is where your creativity comes into play—your words are the bridge between concept and visual realization. To inspire the VFX team, you must provide enough detail to convey the essence of what you envision without micromanaging the specifics.

How to Practice:

1. **Start with the Emotion or Theme:** Before diving into the technical description of the visual effect, think about the emotional or thematic impact you want the effect to have. How does the visual effect enhance the emotional tone of the scene? For example, if a character is experiencing awe and wonder at a vast alien landscape, describe how the environment makes them feel, not just what it looks like.

2. **Use Vivid Descriptions without Overloading Detail:** Be specific enough to paint a picture, but avoid overly detailed or technical descriptions. Trust that the visual effects team will handle the fine details. Instead of saying, *"A spaceship hovers exactly 100 feet above the city, emitting a blue light that oscillates at 15 Hz,"* focus on the impact of the spaceship's presence: *"A massive spaceship looms over the city, its eerie blue light casting long shadows across the skyline, filling the air with a low hum that vibrates in the chest."*

3. **Draw from Real-Life Visuals:** Even though you're imagining the unseen, it helps to ground your descriptions in real-world phenomena. Use metaphors or analogies to compare the visual effect to something familiar. For instance, *"The cloud of dust spread like smoke from an ancient volcano, rising slowly before dissipating into the still air."* This creates a vivid image while allowing room for interpretation.

4. **Leave Room for Collaboration:** Remember, the visual effects artists are part of the storytelling team. They bring their expertise to the table, so leave space for them to interpret and expand upon your ideas. Don't feel the need to describe every pixel—focus on the overall effect and mood you want to convey.

Example: Instead of writing, *"A swirling vortex opens, with colors of red and black mixing together in tight spirals,"* you might say: *"A violent vortex rips open in the sky, swirling with dark clouds and crimson light. The ground trembles beneath it, and the air feels charged with danger, as if reality itself is being torn apart."*

This description communicates the emotion and impact of the visual effect, while giving the VFX team room to interpret and expand on the details.

• • • •

STEP 2: INTEGRATING VFX with Story and Character

Visual effects are most powerful when they serve the story, not just as spectacle but as a means to explore themes and character arcs. When writing for VFX, think about how the effects are integrated into the emotional and narrative beats of the story.

How to Practice:

1. **Align VFX with Character Emotion:** Visual effects can be used to externalize a character's internal state. For example, a character's fear might be mirrored by an environment becoming increasingly dark and hostile, or their moment of triumph might be accompanied by the clearing of storm clouds.

2. **Make VFX Story-Driven:** Every visual effect should have a purpose in advancing the plot or developing characters. Ask yourself how the effect adds to the story. Is it creating a sense of wonder, danger, or mystery? Does it reveal something new about the world or the characters? Effects that don't serve the story can end up feeling like empty spectacle.

3. **Use VFX as a Metaphor:** In some stories, VFX can represent abstract ideas or themes. For instance, a scene where reality warps and bends could symbolize a character's loss of control or descent into madness. The visual effect becomes a storytelling tool rather than just a visual spectacle.

Example: Imagine a character who is trapped in a dream world, struggling to break free. Instead of simply describing the visual effect of the dream breaking apart, you could tie it to the character's emotional state: *"As he reached for the door, the dream began to fracture, jagged cracks spreading through the air like shattered glass. His heart raced—he could feel the weight of reality slipping away. The walls rippled, melting into darkness, as the familiar world dissolved, leaving him suspended in a void."*

Here, the visual effects of the dream fracturing and the world dissolving reflect the character's emotional journey, heightening the tension and urgency of the scene.

Step 3: Collaborating with Visual Artists

Writing for visual effects is inherently collaborative. As a writer, your role is to provide the foundation for the VFX artists, who will interpret and expand upon your ideas. Clear communication and a willingness to be flexible are essential.

How to Practice:

Use the Script as a Blueprint: When writing visual effects into your script, think of it as a blueprint, not a finished product. The VFX team will take your ideas and work with the director to bring them to life. Be descriptive but not prescriptive, focusing on what the effect is meant to accomplish rather than exactly how it should look.

Be Open to Feedback and Changes: Visual effects can be costly and time-consuming, so be open to adjustments based on technical limitations or budget constraints. Flexibility is key in ensuring that your vision can be realized effectively.

Collaborate early in the Process: If possible, collaborate with the visual effects team early in the development process. Their insights can help you understand what's feasible and how certain effects can be achieved. This early collaboration ensures that the VFX align with the story from the beginning.

Trust the Creative Process: VFX artists bring their expertise and creativity to the table. Trust them to interpret your vision and enhance it in ways you might not have expected. The best visual effects often come from a synergy between the writer's ideas and the artist's execution.

Step 4: Balancing Detail with Imagination

While it's important to be vivid in your descriptions, balance is crucial. You want to give enough detail to inspire the visual effects team without boxing them in or overwhelming the reader with technical jargon. The goal is to ignite imagination, not burden the script with excessive detail.

How to Practice:

1. **Prioritize the Emotion and Impact of the Scene:** Focus on how the visual effect feels rather than how it works. Describe the emotional impact on the characters and the atmosphere it creates.
2. **Avoid Over-Explaining the Technicalities:** It's not your job to explain how the visual effect will be executed (unless it's integral to the story mechanics). Leave the technical execution to the experts. Instead, describe the effect in terms of its narrative and emotional significance.
3. **Leave Gaps for Interpretation:** Like a Zen garden, where empty spaces allow for reflection, leaving some aspects of your visual effects description open-ended can spark creativity in the visual effects team. Provide the key elements and mood, and allow the artists to fill in the gaps.

Example: Instead of writing, *"The time portal opens, emitting a white light and sending particles spiraling outward in concentric circles,"* you could write: *"A rip in time unfolds before them, glowing with an otherworldly light. The air shimmers, as if reality itself is being pulled apart, revealing a glimpse of something beyond the present—something both ancient and infinite."*

This description focuses on the feeling and impact of the portal opening rather than dictating exactly how the effect should look.

Step 5: Creating Moments of Awe and Wonder

One of the greatest strengths of visual effects is their ability to create moments of awe and wonder—scenes that transport the audience to places they've never imagined or that make the impossible seem real. Writing these moments requires tapping into the sense of wonder you want the audience to feel and conveying that in your descriptions.

How to Practice:

1. **Think Big, but Stay Grounded in Emotion:** When writing awe-inspiring moments, such as a character seeing an alien world for the first time, focus not just on the spectacle but on the emotional response it evokes in the character. Their reaction can serve as a guide for the audience's emotional experience.
2. **Use VFX to Heighten Emotional Stakes:** Awe and wonder aren't just about scale—they're about the emotional stakes attached to the moment. A character standing on the edge of a cliff, overlooking a vast, alien landscape, is more powerful if that moment is tied to their personal journey, such as facing the unknown or discovering something about themselves.
3. **Let the Visuals Speak for Themselves:** Sometimes, less is more. Trust that the visual effects team will bring the sense of wonder to life without needing every detail spelled out. Focus on what the moment represents and how it advances the story.

Example: *"As the ship emerged from the nebula, the view stretched before them—a sprawling galaxy, each star glimmering with ancient light. For a moment, time seemed to stand still, the vastness of the universe pressing down on him. He had never felt so small, yet so connected to something far greater than himself."*

This description captures the awe of the moment while leaving the specific visuals open to interpretation, allowing the VFX team to create something breathtaking.

Writing for visual effects requires you to step into the realm of imagination, envisioning the unseen and bringing it to life on the page. It's a delicate balance of vivid description and creative restraint—providing enough detail to inspire the visual effects team without dictating every aspect of how it should be realized.

By focusing on the emotion, symbolism, and narrative purpose behind the visual effects, you ensure that they serve the story rather than overshadow it. The most effective visual effects are those that enhance the audience's connection to the characters, the world, and the themes of the story. Through collaboration with visual artists and by leaving room for interpretation, you can create a seamless integration of visual effects that brings your imaginative worlds to life in ways that captivate, move, and inspire. Ultimately, writing for visual effects is about embracing the potential of the unseen—allowing your creativity to flow and trusting in the process of collaboration to turn your words into something extraordinary.

Zen and the Power of Silence: Knowing When to Pause in a Story

In the art of storytelling, silence is often overlooked but can be as powerful as action or dialogue. Much like the concept of *ma* in Zen philosophy—the space between things—silence in storytelling allows for reflection, emotional depth, and meaning to emerge from the spaces left unsaid. These moments of pause can be pivotal in giving the audience time to process and absorb the narrative's emotional undercurrents. Pauses, when used effectively, create contrast, heighten tension, and deepen the story's impact.

In this chapter, we will explore the power of silence and pauses in storytelling, understanding how these quiet moments can bring clarity, emotional resonance, and balance to your narrative. By incorporating moments of stillness, you allow your story to breathe, creating a rhythm that resonates with the audience on a deeper level.

The Role of Silence in Storytelling

Silence, whether it is a literal absence of sound or a figurative pause in the narrative, serves multiple purposes in storytelling. It can create tension, allow for emotional reflection, or emphasize a moment's significance. Just as in Zen practice, where silence and stillness lead to greater awareness and insight, silence in a story opens a space for the audience to engage more deeply with the characters, themes, and emotional beats.

Here are some key ways silence functions in storytelling:

1. **Creating Emotional Weight:** Pauses can make significant emotional moments hit harder. Rather than rushing from one scene to the next, silence gives the audience time to feel the weight of what has happened.
2. **Building Suspense:** Silence before or during a tense moment can amplify suspense. In horror or thriller stories, a quiet moment before a sudden shock heightens the sense of fear or unease.
3. **Giving Space for Reflection:** Pauses between intense action or dialogue scenes allow the audience—and the characters—to process what has happened. These moments of quiet reflection often lead to emotional growth or deeper character understanding.
4. **Heightening Contrast:** Silence creates contrast in pacing. After a high-stakes or action-heavy scene, a moment of stillness can offer relief, making the next burst of activity or dialogue more impactful.

By understanding when to pause and how to use silence effectively, you create a dynamic rhythm in your storytelling, where action, dialogue, and stillness work together to deliver emotional depth and narrative clarity.

• • • •

STEP 1: RECOGNIZING Moments that Need a Pause

The first step to using silence in your story is recognizing when to pause. Not every moment requires a dramatic break or quiet reflection, but certain key points in the narrative benefit from stillness.

How to Practice:

1. **Identify Emotional Peaks:** Moments of high emotional intensity—whether they involve joy, sorrow, fear, or anger—often require pauses to allow the audience to fully experience the emotion. After a character experiences a major loss or revelation, giving the scene room to breathe ensures that the emotional impact sinks in.
2. **Highlight Important Decisions:** When a character faces a difficult choice, a pause before they act can emphasize the gravity of the moment. Allowing silence before the decision creates tension and gives weight to the character's internal conflict.

3. **Build Tension Before Action:** In action or suspense-driven stories, a moment of silence before a major event or confrontation can amplify the tension. Silence before a jump-scare in horror or a pause before a character makes a risky move in an action sequence intensifies the stakes.
4. **Reflect After Intense Action:** After a fast-paced or chaotic scene, a moment of stillness helps the audience and the characters recover. It gives space for emotional processing and sets up the next sequence with greater clarity and balance.

Example: After a climactic argument between two characters, a pause can give the audience time to feel the weight of their words: *"He stared at her, his chest heaving, the words hanging between them like broken glass. For a long moment, neither of them moved. The silence stretched, thick and suffocating, as the reality of what they had said began to settle in."*

This pause allows the audience to absorb the emotional intensity of the scene, creating space for reflection before the story moves forward.

Step 2: Using Silence to Reveal Character

Silence can often reveal more about a character than dialogue or action. In moments of stillness, a character's body language, facial expressions, or even their refusal to speak can convey deep emotional truths or inner conflict. This is particularly powerful in moments of grief, fear, contemplation, or uncertainty.

How to Practice:

Show Emotions Through Body Language: When a character is silent, their body language can speak volumes. A character who turns away, clenches their fists, or drops their gaze can communicate as much (or more) than words.

Use Pauses for Internal Conflict: If a character is wrestling with a difficult decision or grappling with conflicting emotions, a pause can show the complexity of their internal struggle. Rather than telling the audience what the character is thinking, show it through their stillness.

Silence as a Defense Mechanism: A character might use silence as a form of self-protection, avoiding vulnerability or hiding their true feelings. This kind of silence can create tension between characters, leaving things unsaid while the audience senses the underlying emotional currents.

Example: Instead of writing, *"She was too sad to respond,"* you can show the character's silence: *"Her lips parted, but no words came. She closed her mouth again, her hands tightening around the edges of the chair. In the quiet that followed, her eyes glistened, but she refused to let the tears fall."*

This silence conveys the character's emotional state without explicitly stating it, allowing the audience to connect more deeply with her feelings.

Step 3: Creating Suspense with Silence

Silence is one of the most effective tools for building suspense. By slowing down the action and withholding information, you create anticipation, making the audience lean in, waiting for what comes next. In thriller, horror, or mystery stories, silence can stretch a moment, intensifying the audience's sense of fear or anxiety.

How to Practice:

1. **Slow Down Before Key Moments:** Before revealing something shocking or pivotal, create a pause. This silence heightens the audience's anticipation, drawing out the tension before the moment of action.
2. **Withhold Information:** Let silence create suspense by leaving things unsaid. A character's refusal to answer a question, or a pause before revealing crucial information, can create a sense of unease and tension.
3. **Use Environment to Amplify Silence:** In suspenseful moments, the surrounding environment can contribute to the feeling of stillness. The absence of sound—such as a character holding their breath in a silent room—intensifies the audience's focus on what will happen next.

Example: In a suspenseful scene, silence before an attack or confrontation can heighten the tension: *"The hallway was empty. Too empty. She held her breath, straining to hear something—anything—but the silence pressed down on her like a weight. Her fingers tightened around the handle of the door. One step closer, and then another. The silence stretched, almost unbearable, until—"*

This pause creates a sense of impending danger, drawing out the suspense before the next action.

· · · ·

STEP 4: LETTING SILENCE Serve as Resolution

Not every story or scene requires a loud or climactic resolution. Sometimes, the most powerful way to end a conflict or emotional arc is through silence. When words have been exhausted, and there's nothing left to say, silence can serve as a peaceful, contemplative resolution.

How to Practice:

1. **Use Silence after Emotional Climax:** After an emotional high point, such as a confrontation, revelation, or loss, silence allows both the characters and the audience to process what has happened. It signals that the emotional journey has reached a natural conclusion, even if not every question has been answered.

2. **End a Scene on Silence:** Not every scene needs to end with dialogue or action. A quiet moment, where characters reflect in silence, can be a poignant way to close a chapter or sequence. It gives weight to the preceding events and lets the audience sit with the emotional resonance.

3. **Let the Audience Reflect:** Silence at the end of a scene or story invites the audience to reflect on what they've just experienced. Rather than wrapping everything up neatly, a pause allows the reader or viewer to contemplate the deeper meaning or implications of the story.

Example: After a climactic event, silence can bring closure: *"The wind had died down. They stood on the edge of the field, watching the sun sink below the horizon. Neither of them spoke. There were no words left, and none were needed. In the stillness, they both understood—this was the end."*

This moment of silence serves as a peaceful resolution, offering emotional closure without the need for additional dialogue.

Step 5: Finding Balance Between Silence and Action

As with all aspects of storytelling, balance is key. Too much silence can slow down the pacing, while too little can leave the story feeling rushed or overwhelming. By varying moments of silence with action, dialogue, or tension, you create a dynamic rhythm that keeps the audience engaged.

How to Practice:

Alternate between Silence and Movement: Silence is most effective when contrasted with action or dialogue. Use moments of stillness after high-intensity scenes to give the audience space to breathe and reflect, then return to action when the story demands it.

Use Silence Sparingly for Impact: Too much silence can dilute its effect. Reserve pauses for moments that truly need emotional weight or reflection. When used sparingly, silence carries more power.

Pace Your Story Thoughtfully: Consider the pacing of your overall narrative. Fast-paced scenes might need brief pauses for reflection, while slower scenes may benefit from moments of action to keep the momentum going. The ebb and flow of silence and action create a more engaging story.

Example: After an intense battle, a moment of silence can emphasize the emotional toll: *"The battlefield was quiet now, save for the wind stirring the dust. He stood alone, sword still in hand, but it felt heavy, like the weight of everything* *he had lost. For a moment, he just stood there, staring at the ruins around him. Then, with a slow breath, he sheathed the sword and turned away."*

This pause allows the character to process the aftermath of the battle, creating emotional depth and contrast after the action.

Conclusion: The Power of Silence in Storytelling

Silence is a powerful tool in storytelling, offering moments of reflection, tension, and emotional resonance. In Zen philosophy, silence is often seen as a pathway to deeper awareness and understanding, and in storytelling, it serves a similar role—allowing the audience to connect more deeply with the characters and the narrative.

By recognizing when to pause, using silence to reveal character emotions, creating suspense, and letting silence serve as a resolution, you enhance the emotional depth and meaning of your story. Balance is key—knowing when to pause and when to let action or dialogue drive the scene creates a dynamic rhythm that keeps the audience engaged while giving space for reflection.

In the end, silence speaks volumes. When used effectively, it allows your story to breathe, letting emotions and meaning unfold naturally in the spaces between words. Trust in the power of stillness, and your storytelling will resonate with a quiet strength that lingers long after the final word.

The Writer's Journey: Achieving Creative Enlightenment

Writing is not just an act of putting words on a page—it's a journey of discovery, growth, and transformation. For many, the creative process mirrors a personal journey, filled with challenges, breakthroughs, frustrations, and moments of clarity. Much like the path to enlightenment in Zen philosophy, the writer's journey is one of self-awareness, perseverance, and mindful practice. Achieving creative enlightenment doesn't mean finding perfection; it means reaching a place of balance, peace, and understanding within your creative process. In this chapter, we'll explore the concept of the writer's journey, drawing parallels between the pursuit of creative fulfillment and the principles of Zen enlightenment. We'll focus on how mindfulness, acceptance, and continuous growth can lead to creative breakthroughs and a deeper connection with your writing. By embracing the challenges and joys of the journey, you can cultivate a sense of creative enlightenment that transcends the outcome and lives in the process itself.

The Parallels between Zen and the Writer's Journey

The path to Zen enlightenment is often described as a journey of self-realization, where the individual seeks to transcend the ego, cultivate mindfulness, and embrace the present moment. The writer's journey, in many ways, follows a similar path—writers strive to overcome self-doubt, silence the inner critic, and connect deeply with their ideas and the world they are creating. Just as the Zen practitioner learns to let go of attachment to outcomes, the enlightened writer learns to trust the process rather than fixate on perfection.

Here are some key parallels between Zen practice and the writer's journey:

Letting Go of Perfection: Zen teaches that striving for perfection leads to suffering because perfection is an illusion. Similarly, writers often fall into the trap of seeking perfection in their work, which can lead to frustration and creative blocks. Achieving creative enlightenment means accepting imperfection as part of the process.

Embracing the Present Moment: Zen emphasizes mindfulness and being fully present in each moment. In writing, this translates to focusing on the work at hand without worrying about the future (whether the piece will be successful or published) or the past (mistakes or previous failures). Creative enlightenment comes from immersing yourself in the act of writing.

Continuous Growth: The Zen journey is not about reaching a final destination but about continuous self-growth and discovery. In writing, this means recognizing that the journey never truly ends—there is always more to learn, explore, and create. Every project, draft, and revision is part of the ongoing process of growth.

Silencing the Ego: In Zen, enlightenment involves transcending the ego, freeing oneself from self-centered thoughts and desires. In writing, this can mean letting go of the need for external validation and writing from a place of authenticity. Creative enlightenment arises when you write for the love of the craft, not for the approval of others.

Step 1: Letting Go of Perfection

One of the greatest obstacles on the writer's journey is the pursuit of perfection. Many writers hold themselves to impossibly high standards, expecting their first drafts to be flawless or comparing their work to that of other authors. This mindset leads to frustration, self-doubt, and creative paralysis. In Zen practice, the concept of *wabi-sabi*—the acceptance of imperfection and impermanence—is central to finding peace. In the same way, letting go of perfection in writing allows you to embrace the beauty of the process, flaws and all.

How to Practice:

1. **Allow First Drafts to Be Messy:** Accept that your first draft will not be perfect—and it doesn't need to be. Instead of aiming for perfection, focus on getting your ideas down on paper. Revisions will come later, but the initial act of creation should be free from the pressure to get everything right.

2. **Reframe Mistakes as Opportunities:** In Zen, mistakes are viewed not as failures but as opportunities for learning and growth. Apply this mindset to your writing. If something doesn't work, don't see it as a failure—see it as an opportunity to explore a new direction or deepen your understanding of the story.

3. **Focus on Progress, Not Perfection:** Celebrate your progress, no matter how small. Each word written, each scene revised, is a step forward on your creative journey. Instead of striving for a perfect end result, focus on the satisfaction of continuous improvement.

Example: Instead of fixating on perfecting the opening sentence of your novel, allow yourself to write it as it comes, knowing you can return to it later. The act of moving forward is more important than getting it "right" in the first draft: *"The sky was the color of old bruises, the wind biting at her cheeks as she walked through the empty streets. It wasn't how she had imagined this day would end, but then again, nothing had gone as planned."*

This draft may not be perfect, but it's a starting point. Trust that clarity and refinement will come in the revision process.

Step 2: Writing in the Present Moment

Mindfulness is central to the Zen journey. It involves being fully present in whatever you are doing—whether it's breathing, walking, or writing—without distractions or judgments. For writers, being present means immersing yourself in the story, focusing on the act of writing without worrying about the outcome or comparing yourself to others. When you write mindfully, you are more attuned to your creative instincts, and the writing process becomes a form of meditation.

How to Practice:

Set Aside Time for Focused Writing: Create a space where you can write without distractions. Set a timer for 20-30 minutes and commit to being fully present with your writing during that time. Don't check your phone, don't worry about editing—just focus on the words as they flow.

Let Go of Judgment: As you write, let go of the need to evaluate every sentence or idea. Write freely, allowing the words to come without overanalyzing or critiquing them. Judgment can come later, during revision.

Practice Breathing Exercises Before Writing: Before you begin your writing session, take a few deep breaths to center yourself. This simple practice helps clear your mind of distractions and brings you into the present moment, ready to focus on your creative work.

Example: When sitting down to write a difficult scene, focus on the present moment. Instead of worrying about whether the scene is "good enough" or if it will resonate with readers, simply immerse yourself in the experience of the characters: *"She stood at the edge of the cliff, the wind whipping through her hair, her heart pounding in her chest. Below, the waves crashed against the rocks, relentless and wild. For a moment, she felt like she was part of the sea—untethered, powerful, and free."*

By focusing on the sensory details and emotions of the scene, you remain present in the story, allowing it to unfold naturally.

Step 3: Embracing the Process of Growth

Just as Zen enlightenment is an ongoing process rather than a final destination, so too is the writer's journey one of continuous growth. Every project, every draft, and every revision teaches you something new. Achieving creative enlightenment means recognizing that the journey never truly ends—there is always more to explore and discover in your writing.

How to Practice:

1. **View Each Project as a Learning Experience:** Whether you're working on a short story, novel, or screenplay, approach each project as an opportunity to learn and grow. Embrace the challenges, knowing that every struggle is helping you become a better writer.
2. **Revise with a Growth Mindset:** Instead of dreading revisions or seeing them as a sign of failure, approach them with curiosity. Revisions are an opportunity to refine your work, explore new ideas, and deepen your understanding of your story.
3. **Celebrate Your Progress:** Take time to reflect on how far you've come as a writer. Celebrate the small victories—whether it's completing a chapter, finding a breakthrough in a plot problem, or simply writing regularly. Acknowledge your growth and use it as motivation to keep moving forward.

Example: When revising your manuscript, instead of focusing on what didn't work, approach the revision process with excitement about the possibilities for improvement. Look for opportunities to deepen characters, clarify themes, or enhance pacing. This mindset allows you to see revision as a creative opportunity rather than a chore.

Step 4: Silencing the Inner Critic

One of the biggest obstacles to creative enlightenment is the inner critic—the voice inside your head that doubts your abilities, questions your worth as a writer, and criticizes every sentence you write. In Zen practice, the goal is to transcend the ego and quiet the mind's chatter. For writers, achieving creative enlightenment means learning to silence the inner critic so you can write from a place of authenticity and freedom.

How to Practice:

Acknowledge the Critic, Then Let It Go: When the inner critic starts to speak, acknowledge its presence but don't engage with it. Treat it like a cloud passing by—acknowledge it, then let it drift away without giving it power over your creative process.

Write Freely Without Editing: Silence the inner critic by committing to freewriting. Set a timer for 10-15 minutes and write without stopping or editing. This exercise helps quiet the critical voice and allows your creativity to flow unimpeded.

Replace Criticism with Curiosity: When self-doubt creeps in, replace critical thoughts with curiosity. Instead of thinking, *"This idea is terrible,"* ask yourself, *"What could I explore here? What potential does this idea have?"* Shifting to a mindset of curiosity keeps you open to possibilities rather than shutting down your creativity. **Example:** During a writing session, if you find yourself thinking, *"I'm not sure this scene works,"* reframe the thought: *"I wonder how I can make this scene more emotionally impactful? What's at the heart of this moment?"* This shift from criticism to curiosity keeps you engaged with the creative process rather than stalling your progress.

Step 5: Trusting the Journey

Perhaps the most important element of achieving creative enlightenment is trust—trusting yourself, trusting your process, and trusting the journey. Writing is filled with uncertainty, but by embracing the unknown and letting go of the need for control, you free yourself to create authentically. Trust that every challenge is part of the path and that every step forward brings you closer to your creative potential.

How to Practice:

1. **Let Go of the Need for Control:** Writing can be unpredictable, and sometimes your story may take unexpected turns. Trust the process, even when it feels uncertain. Let go of the need to control every aspect of the story, and allow it to unfold naturally.
2. **Trust your Instincts:** You know your story better than anyone. Trust your creative instincts, even if they lead you in unexpected directions. Writing from a place of intuition often results in more authentic and impactful storytelling.
3. **Embrace Uncertainty:** Writing is a journey filled with unknowns. Instead of fearing uncertainty, embrace it as part of the creative process. Trust that you will find your way, even if the path isn't always clear.

Example: If you find yourself uncertain about where your story is heading, instead of trying to force a resolution, allow yourself to explore different possibilities. Trust that the right path will reveal itself in time, and continue writing with an open mind.

The writer's journey is one of continuous discovery, growth, and transformation. Achieving creative enlightenment doesn't mean reaching a point of perfection—it means embracing the process, letting go of self-doubt and the need for control, and finding joy in the act of creation itself. By letting go of perfection, practicing mindfulness, embracing growth, silencing the inner critic, and trusting the journey, you can cultivate a sense of creative enlightenment that allows you to write with clarity, freedom, and purpose. Just as in Zen practice, the journey is not about the destination but about being fully present in the process, learning from each experience, and finding peace in the act of writing.

The Zen of Pacing: Knowing When to Slow Down or Speed Up

Pacing is one of the most important yet subtle aspects of storytelling. It's the rhythm of your narrative—the ebb and flow of action, emotion, and suspense that keeps readers or viewers engaged. Just as Zen philosophy emphasizes balance and flow, so too must a story find its natural pace, moving seamlessly between moments of intensity and stillness. Knowing when to slow down and when to speed up can be the difference between a story that captivates its audience and one that loses their interest.

In this chapter, we'll explore the Zen of pacing—how to mindfully control the speed of your story to create emotional resonance, build tension, and maintain engagement. Like a master of martial arts, who moves fluidly between fast strikes and slow, deliberate movements, a skilled storyteller understands the importance of both rapid action and quiet moments of reflection. By tuning into the natural rhythm of your story, you can create a dynamic and balanced narrative that guides the audience on a compelling journey.

The Importance of Pacing in Storytelling

Pacing is not just about how fast or slow your story moves; it's about how the flow of events, dialogue, and description affects the audience's emotional engagement. A well-paced story keeps readers or viewers interested, creating moments of excitement, tension, or emotional depth at just the right time. When pacing is off—too fast or too slow—audiences may feel disconnected, confused, or overwhelmed.

Here's why pacing matters:

1. **Building Emotional Depth:** Slowing down the pace allows time for characters to develop, relationships to grow, and themes to be explored. It creates space for emotional beats to resonate with the audience.
2. **Increasing Tension and Suspense:** Faster pacing accelerates action and raises stakes, pulling the audience to the edge of their seats. Quick pacing works especially well in scenes of danger, conflict, or revelation.
3. **Creating Contrast and Variety:** Alternating between fast and slow pacing keeps the story dynamic. Just as a song builds energy and then returns to quieter moments, pacing variation keeps the audience engaged and prevents monotony.
4. **Controlling the Reader's Experience:** Pacing dictates how quickly the audience absorbs information. Slowing down can draw attention to significant details, while speeding up can rush the reader or viewer toward an anticipated climax.

By understanding the ebb and flow of pacing, you can guide your audience through the story with ease, ensuring that each moment feels intentional and impactful.

· · · ·

STEP 1: RECOGNIZING When to Slow Down

Slowing down in a story allows space for deeper emotional exploration, world-building, and character development. These quieter moments can be just as engaging as action scenes, offering the audience time to connect with the story on a more intimate level.

How to Practice:

1. **Slow Down for Emotional Beats:** When a character experiences a significant emotional moment—such as grief, joy, or realization—take your time. Let the audience feel the weight of the moment by lingering on the character's thoughts, body language, and sensory experiences. This allows the emotional impact to sink

in.

2. **Pause to Explore Character Relationships:** If your story focuses on relationships—whether romantic, familial, or friendship-based—slow pacing is essential for building authentic connections. Give characters time to interact, reflect, and grow. Dialogue, shared experiences, and quiet moments between characters can create emotional depth and believability.

3. **Build Atmosphere and Setting:** In stories where world-building or atmosphere is important (such as fantasy, science fiction, or historical fiction), slower pacing allows the audience to immerse themselves in the setting. Take time to describe the environment, the culture, or the small details that make your world feel real.

4. **Give Time for Reflection:** After moments of intense action or conflict, slowing down allows the characters—and the audience—to process what has happened. Reflection gives emotional weight to the events of the story and prevents the pacing from becoming exhausting.

Example: Imagine a scene where a character has just learned devastating news. Instead of rushing through their reaction, slow the pace: *"She stood motionless, her breath catching in her throat. The letter in her hands trembled, the words blurring as her vision clouded with unshed tears. For a long moment, she simply stared at the page, the weight of the truth sinking deeper with each passing second. Her chest felt tight, as if the room itself was closing in around her."*

By focusing on the character's internal experience and slowing down the description, the emotional impact is heightened.

Step 2: Knowing When to Speed Up

While slow pacing is essential for emotional depth and world-building, faster pacing brings excitement, tension, and forward momentum. Knowing when to speed up your narrative can create urgency and keep the audience on the edge of their seat.

How to Practice:

1. **Accelerate During Action Scenes:** In moments of action—such as a fight, chase, or intense confrontation—faster pacing keeps the tension high. Use short, punchy sentences to convey the quick movements and rapid decision-making involved in the scene. Speeding up during action makes the audience feel as though they're right there with the characters.
2. **Drive the Story Forward in High-Stakes Moments:** When the stakes are high and the characters are racing against time or facing an imminent threat, faster pacing reflects the urgency of the situation. This keeps the audience engaged and creates a sense of anticipation.
3. **Use Pacing to Build Suspense:** In thrillers or mysteries, speeding up the pacing as characters uncover clues or approach a dangerous situation can build suspense. The quicker pace pulls the audience along, making them eager to discover what happens next.
4. **Avoid Overloading with Detail in Fast Scenes:** During fast-paced moments, avoid slowing down with unnecessary description or lengthy internal monologues. Keep the focus on action and forward momentum. You can return to emotional reflection or detail once the intensity has passed.

Example: In an action-packed scene, speeding up the pacing enhances the urgency: *"The explosion rocked the building, sending shards of glass raining down. She ducked, sprinting toward the exit as the walls groaned, threatening to collapse. Her heart pounded, each second stretching thin as she pushed herself harder, faster—her breath ragged, her legs burning. The door was just ahead, but the fire was closing in."*

The shorter sentences and rapid description create a sense of speed and danger, pulling the reader into the action.

Step 3: Balancing Fast and Slow Pacing

A well-paced story knows when to slow down and when to speed up, creating a dynamic rhythm that engages the audience and keeps the story fresh. Alternating between fast and slow pacing prevents the narrative from becoming monotonous and allows both the quiet moments and the action-packed scenes to shine.

How to Practice:

Alternate between Action and Reflection: After a fast-paced scene, give the characters (and the audience) time to reflect. This creates a natural ebb and flow, allowing moments of high tension to be balanced with introspection or emotional depth.

Use Pacing to Reflect the Character's Journey: A character's internal journey often mirrors the pacing of the story. When a character is experiencing emotional turmoil or growth, the pacing may slow to give time for reflection. During moments of clarity or action, the pacing may speed up to reflect their sense of purpose.

Create Contrast for Maximum Impact: Fast-paced scenes feel more intense when they're contrasted with slower, quieter moments. Likewise, a slow, emotional scene feels more poignant when it follows a burst of action or excitement. Use this contrast to your advantage by carefully balancing fast and slow pacing throughout the narrative.

Example: In a story with a fast-paced chase scene followed by a moment of quiet reflection, the contrast heightens both the intensity of the action and the emotional depth of the quiet moment: *"He raced through the narrow streets, the sound of footsteps pounding behind him. His lungs burned, but he couldn't stop. Not now. Not when he was so close. The alley twisted ahead, and he ducked into the shadows, heart hammering in his chest. Silence. Finally, he let himself breathe. Leaning against the cold stone wall, he wiped the sweat from his brow and closed his eyes, the adrenaline slowly fading."*

The fast-paced chase builds tension, while the slower, reflective moment afterward provides a sense of relief and emotional grounding.

Step 4: Pacing Dialogue

Dialogue is another key area where pacing plays a significant role. Quick, back-and-forth exchanges can create energy, tension, or a sense of urgency, while slower, more deliberate conversations can build emotional depth or highlight important themes.

How to Practice:

Use Quick Dialogue for Tension or Humor: Rapid-fire dialogue works well in moments of tension, conflict, or humor. Characters interrupting each other or speaking in short, clipped sentences can reflect heightened emotions or quick thinking.

Slow Dialogue for Emotional Depth: In more emotional or reflective scenes, allow the dialogue to slow down. Characters might pause between lines, speak in longer sentences, or leave room for silence between responses. This pacing gives the audience time to absorb the emotional weight of the conversation.

Break Up Dialogue with Action: To control pacing, intersperse dialogue with brief moments of action or description. This helps prevent dialogue-heavy scenes from feeling stagnant and maintains the rhythm of the story.

Example: In a tense conversation, quick dialogue heightens the tension: *"'You can't be serious,' she snapped.*
'I am. We don't have time.'
'But—'
'No buts. We're doing this.'
She clenched her fists, biting back the words that rose to her lips. 'Fine. But don't say I didn't warn you.'"
The short, rapid exchanges create a sense of urgency, reflecting the tension between the characters.

Step 5: Trusting the Natural Rhythm of Your Story

In Zen philosophy, flow is central to achieving harmony. The same is true for storytelling. By tuning into the natural rhythm of your narrative, you can find the right balance between fast and slow pacing. Trust your instincts—if a scene feels like it needs more time to breathe, slow down. If the story feels like it's dragging, speed it up. Finding this balance is an intuitive process, and with practice, you'll develop a sense for when to shift the pace.

How to Practice:

1. **Listen to Your Story's Flow:** Pay attention to how your story feels as you write. Does a scene feel rushed? Does another feel like it's lingering too long? Trust your instincts to adjust the pacing as needed.
2. **Consider the Emotional Journey:** Think about the emotional journey of your characters and how the pacing reflects their inner experiences. Faster pacing may reflect urgency, while slower pacing gives time for introspection or emotional weight.
3. **Revise for Pacing:** During revisions, read your story aloud to get a sense of its rhythm. If a scene feels too slow or too fast, adjust accordingly. The revision process is where pacing can be fine-tuned to create a balanced, engaging narrative.

Example: As you write or revise, ask yourself whether the pacing serves the emotional arc of the story. If a climactic moment feels rushed, consider slowing it down to give the characters and the audience time to process: *"She opened the letter with trembling hands, the paper rustling in the stillness. Her eyes moved over the words, and her breath caught in her throat. She read it again. Slowly. The meaning sinking in like a stone, pulling her deeper into the silence."*

Pacing is the rhythm that guides your story, controlling the speed at which events unfold and emotions resonate. By mastering the art of pacing, you create a dynamic narrative that flows naturally between fast-paced action and slow, reflective moments. The Zen of pacing lies in finding balance—knowing when to slow down to allow for emotional depth and when to speed up to build tension or excitement. Just as a Zen practitioner moves with the natural flow of life, a skilled storyteller moves with the flow of the narrative, trusting their instincts to guide the pace. Whether you're writing an action-packed thriller or a quiet, introspective drama, understanding the power of pacing allows you to engage your audience fully and create a story that lingers long after the final page is turned. By paying attention to the natural rhythm of your story and balancing fast and slow pacing, you'll achieve harmony in your storytelling, creating a narrative that feels both dynamic and deeply resonant.

Breathing Life into Secondary Characters: The Balance of Ensemble

Every great story is not only about the protagonist but also about the world they inhabit. This world is often populated by secondary characters who bring depth, nuance, and dimension to the narrative. These characters can be mentors, sidekicks, antagonists, or confidants, and while they may not be the central focus, they play a crucial role in shaping the story. Much like an ensemble cast in a performance, these secondary characters provide balance, contrast, and support, making the protagonist's journey feel more complex and interconnected.

In Zen philosophy, balance is key—everything must exist in harmony with its surroundings. This concept of harmony is essential when creating an ensemble of characters that feel alive, purposeful, and relevant. While the protagonist's journey may be the heart of the story, secondary characters are the veins that help circulate the energy of the narrative. By giving each secondary character purpose, depth, and life, you ensure that they contribute meaningfully to the story without overshadowing the main character or becoming mere plot devices.

In this chapter, we'll explore how to breathe life into secondary characters, finding the right balance between their roles and the protagonist's journey, and creating an ensemble that enhances your story's emotional and narrative depth.

The Importance of Secondary Characters

Secondary characters play vital roles in a story's ecosystem. They provide emotional support, challenge the protagonist, reveal important information, and enrich the world of the narrative. Without a well-developed supporting cast, the protagonist's journey can feel one-dimensional, as if they're navigating a world that only revolves around them.

Here are key roles secondary characters fulfill in storytelling:

1. **Reflecting or Contrasting the Protagonist:** Secondary characters often mirror or contrast the protagonist, highlighting key aspects of their personality or journey. A mentor might reflect the protagonist's future self, while a foil could expose their flaws or weaknesses.
2. **Advancing the Plot:** While secondary characters shouldn't exist solely for the plot, their actions often play a role in moving the story forward. They may introduce new conflicts, offer solutions, or help the protagonist overcome obstacles.
3. **Providing Different Perspectives:** Secondary characters bring unique viewpoints, adding complexity to the narrative. Their beliefs, motivations, and experiences offer contrast to the protagonist's perspective, enriching the story's themes and emotional layers.
4. **Enhancing World-Building:** Through secondary characters, you can expand the world of your story. Whether it's a best friend who provides insight into the protagonist's past or a mysterious antagonist who reveals hidden facets of the setting, secondary characters help flesh out the world and make it feel lived-in.

By investing time and attention into secondary characters, you create a fuller, more immersive narrative, where every character has their own purpose and place within the story's ecosystem.

Step 1: Giving Each Character a Purpose

A strong ensemble of secondary characters begins with giving each character a distinct purpose within the story. Rather than existing merely to serve the protagonist's needs or advance the plot, secondary characters should have their own motivations, desires, and arcs. Their purpose doesn't need to be grand, but it should feel authentic and relevant to the larger narrative.

How to Practice:

1. **Ask What the Character Wants:** Every character, no matter how minor, should have their own desires and motivations. Even if their goal isn't central to the story, knowing what drives them helps create a sense of realism and depth. Ask yourself: What does this character want? How does it align with or conflict with the protagonist's goals?
2. **Define Their Role in the Protagonist's Journey:** Consider how each secondary character contributes to the protagonist's journey. Do they provide support, challenge, or wisdom? Do they complicate the protagonist's decisions or offer a new perspective? Defining this role helps ensure that the character feels integral to the story.
3. **Avoid One-Dimensional Roles:** While some secondary characters may serve specific functions (like a mentor, sidekick, or love interest), avoid reducing them to one-dimensional archetypes. Give them complexity by exploring their backstory, flaws, and contradictions.

Example: Instead of having a mentor who exists solely to guide the protagonist, give them their own motivations and struggles: *"Jiro had spent years honing his craft, but now, as the new generation of warriors rose, he wondered if his wisdom had any place in this world. Training Kai wasn't just about passing on skills—it was about proving, to himself, that he still mattered."*

By giving the mentor a personal stake in the relationship, you add depth to both the mentor and the protagonist's journey.

Step 2: Crafting Distinct Voices and Personalities

Secondary characters become memorable when they have distinct voices, personalities, and quirks that differentiate them from the protagonist and from one another. These unique traits not only make the characters feel more real but also add texture and variety to the narrative.

How to Practice:

Develop Unique Speech Patterns: Pay attention to how each character speaks. Do they use formal or casual language? Are they verbose or concise? Do they have specific phrases or mannerisms? Giving each character a distinct voice makes them stand out in dialogue and helps the audience connect with them.

Highlight Contrasting Traits: When creating an ensemble, think about how each secondary character contrasts with the others. For example, one character might be stoic and serious, while another is light-hearted and impulsive. These contrasts create interesting dynamics and prevent characters from blending together.

Use Quirks to Add Depth: Quirks—whether it's a peculiar habit, a strange hobby, or a particular way of thinking—can make secondary characters more memorable. These quirks should feel organic to the character and reveal something deeper about their personality or past.

Example: Imagine a scene where the protagonist's sidekick has a unique quirk that contrasts with the protagonist's serious demeanor: *"Rena couldn't resist the urge to narrate her every move, no matter how mundane. 'And now,' she whispered theatrically, 'I'll open the door with the stealth of a cat...'*

'Rena,' I hissed, 'it's just a door.'

She winked. 'No detail is too small for the great detective.'"

Rena's quirky, playful nature contrasts with the protagonist's more serious approach, making their interactions more dynamic.

Step 3: Balancing Screen Time

One of the challenges in writing secondary characters is finding the right balance of screen time. Too much focus on secondary characters can detract from the protagonist's journey, while too little can leave them feeling underdeveloped. The key is to give each character just enough attention to serve their role in the story without overwhelming the narrative.

How to Practice:

1. **Prioritize Key Moments:** Focus on the moments where secondary characters can shine or where their role in the protagonist's journey is most significant. These key moments allow secondary characters to leave a lasting impression without taking over the narrative.
2. **Weave Characters into the Protagonist's Arc:** Instead of giving secondary characters isolated scenes that don't contribute to the larger story, weave their interactions with the protagonist into the central arc. This ensures that every scene moves the story forward, even when the focus shifts to a secondary character.
3. **Avoid Overcrowding:** Be mindful of how many secondary characters you introduce. While an ensemble can add richness, too many characters can overwhelm the reader or viewer. Ensure that each character has a clear purpose and avoid unnecessary side plots that detract from the main narrative.

Example: A scene where a secondary character's role is highlighted without overshadowing the protagonist: *"As we set up camp, Leila moved silently beside me, her hands deftly knotting the ropes. She glanced up, catching my eye. 'You think we'll make it tomorrow?'*

I hesitated, unsure how to answer. Leila didn't press. She never did. But in the quiet of her question, I felt the weight of her belief in me—steady, unwavering, even when I doubted myself."

Leila's presence adds emotional depth and insight into the protagonist's inner conflict, but the scene remains focused on the protagonist's journey.

Step 4: Giving Secondary Characters Their Own Arcs

While the protagonist's journey may be the central focus, secondary characters often have their own mini-arcs—personal growth, conflicts, or challenges that run parallel to the main story. These arcs don't need to be as fully developed as the protagonist's, but they add depth and dimension to the characters, making them feel like real people with their own lives.

How to Practice:

1. **Create Parallel Journeys:** Consider how a secondary character's arc might mirror or contrast with the protagonist's. For example, a sidekick might start out as a skeptic, only to become a true believer by the end of the story. These parallel journeys can add emotional complexity and reinforce the story's themes.
2. **Resolve or Acknowledge Their Arc:** While secondary characters' arcs don't need to take center stage, it's important to acknowledge their growth or resolution by the end of the story. This gives the audience closure and reinforces the idea that the secondary characters are fully realized individuals.
3. **Don't Force Unnecessary Arcs:** Not every secondary character needs a complete arc. Some characters serve their purpose without undergoing significant change, and that's okay. Focus on giving arcs to the secondary characters who have the most emotional or narrative relevance.

Example: A secondary character with their own arc might be a mentor who struggles with letting go of their role: *"Master Liang watched as his student executed the final move, the precision in her form unmistakable. Pride swelled in his chest, but so did a deep, quiet sadness. She no longer needed him. He had done his part. Now, all that remained was to step aside. 'Well done,' he said softly, his voice carrying both admiration and farewell."*

Master Liang's arc is subtle but clear—he has completed his journey as a mentor, and now his role in the protagonist's life must come to an end.

Step 5: Creating Interactions That Deepen the Story

The interactions between the protagonist and secondary characters—and between the secondary characters themselves—are what breathe life into the ensemble. These interactions should feel authentic, complex, and emotionally resonant, revealing new facets of the characters and pushing the story forward.

How to Practice:

Explore Different Types of Relationships: Not all secondary characters need to have positive or supportive relationships with the protagonist. Rivalries, conflicts, and misunderstandings between characters can add tension and complexity, making their interactions more engaging.

Use Conflict to Reveal Character: Conflict, whether it's external or internal, can reveal a great deal about a character. Use disagreements, challenges, or differing viewpoints to deepen relationships and add nuance to the story.

Highlight Moments of Connection: While conflict can drive the story, moments of connection between characters are equally important. These quiet, intimate exchanges can reveal vulnerability, strengthen bonds, or provide emotional support.

Example: In a scene where two secondary characters interact, their conversation deepens both their relationship and the overall story: *"'You don't always have to carry the weight alone, you know,' Tomas said, his voice softer than usual.*

Rosa didn't look up from the map. 'I'm fine.'

He shook his head, stepping closer. 'No, you're not. And it's okay to admit that.'

For a moment, she stayed silent, her fingers tracing the worn edges of the paper. Then, finally, she spoke, her voice barely a whisper. 'I don't know how.'

Tomas placed a hand on her shoulder. 'You don't have to know. That's why I'm here.'"

This interaction not only reveals Rosa's inner struggle but also strengthens her relationship with Tomas, adding emotional depth to both characters.

In storytelling, secondary characters are not mere accessories to the protagonist's journey—they are integral to the richness and complexity of the narrative. By giving each secondary character a purpose, distinct personality, and meaningful role in the story, you create an ensemble that enhances the emotional and thematic layers of your work.

The Zen of ensemble writing lies in balance—knowing how to give secondary characters enough depth and attention to make them feel real without overshadowing the protagonist. By crafting a well-rounded cast of characters, you bring your story to life, creating a world where every character, no matter how minor, feels purposeful and alive. Ultimately, the balance of ensemble is about harmony—each character, like a note in a symphony, contributes to the overall sound of the story, adding richness, complexity, and meaning. By mastering this balance, you'll create a narrative that feels dynamic, interconnected, and deeply resonant.

Special effects (SFX) allow writers and filmmakers to break the boundaries of reality, bringing fantastical elements, impossible feats, and larger-than-life moments to the screen or page. From otherworldly environments to jaw-dropping action sequences, special effects open the door to visual storytelling that pushes the limits of the imagination. However, for all their power, special effects are not just about spectacle—they must serve the story, enhance emotional beats, and elevate the narrative experience.

In this chapter, we will explore how to effectively script special effects, focusing on how to visualize the impossible in a way that is clear, compelling, and rooted in the story. Just like in Zen philosophy, where the balance between the seen and unseen brings harmony, special effects must strike a balance between spectacle and substance, ensuring they support the narrative rather than overshadowing it. Whether you are writing for film, television, or even novels, understanding how to conceptualize and integrate special effects can elevate your storytelling to new heights.

The Role of Special Effects in Storytelling

Special effects play a variety of roles in storytelling, from creating immersive worlds to enabling visually stunning action sequences. However, the most important role of special effects is to serve the narrative. They should enhance the emotional weight of a scene, clarify abstract concepts, or make the impossible feel real and believable.

Here are key ways special effects enhance storytelling:

1. **World-Building:** In science fiction, fantasy, and other speculative genres, special effects help create entire worlds that are visually distinct and rich with detail. These worlds immerse the audience in environments that would be impossible to depict otherwise, from futuristic cities to alien planets.
2. **Enhancing Action:** Special effects allow for incredible action sequences that go beyond the limitations of real-world physics. Whether it's superheroes battling in mid-air or spaceships engaging in intergalactic dogfights, special effects make these extraordinary moments possible.
3. **Conveying the Abstract or Supernatural:** Special effects can visually represent concepts that are otherwise difficult to describe—such as magic, time travel, or the inner workings of the mind. They offer a way to externalize abstract or invisible elements, making them tangible for the audience.
4. **Amplifying Emotional Beats:** Well-placed special effects can heighten the emotional stakes of a scene, whether it's through a visually stunning transformation, a climactic explosion, or a moment of eerie silence where the environment itself seems to react to a character's emotions.

While special effects can dazzle and amaze, their true power lies in their ability to enhance the emotional and thematic depth of a story. A well-executed special effect not only looks impressive but also serves a purpose within the narrative.

Step 1: Visualizing the Impossible

The first step to scripting special effects is to visualize the impossible. As a writer, you're tasked with imagining things that don't yet exist—whether it's a portal to another dimension, a character undergoing a physical transformation, or a battle between mythical creatures. To bring these elements to life, you must be able to clearly describe what they look like, how they function, and how they impact the world and characters.

How to Practice:

1. **Start with the Emotional Core:** Before diving into the technical details of the effect, consider the emotional or narrative impact it needs to have. Is this effect meant to awe, terrify, or mystify the audience?

Understanding the emotional core of the effect will help guide how you describe it.

2. **Use Real-World Analogies:** Even when visualizing the impossible, grounding your descriptions in real-world comparisons can make the effect more relatable and understandable. For example, describing a portal as having "rippling edges like water disturbed by a stone" gives the reader or production team a visual anchor to build from.

3. **Focus on Key Visual Details:** When scripting special effects, you don't need to describe every single detail—leave room for the visual effects team to bring their expertise. Instead, focus on the key elements that define the effect, such as its color, shape, movement, or the way it interacts with the environment. These details will provide enough information to spark the imagination of the VFX team.

4. **Consider the Physicality:** If the special effect involves characters or objects, think about how the effect interacts with them physically. Does it change their appearance, movement, or surroundings? Does it alter the way they perceive the world around them? These considerations help ground the effect in the story's reality.

Example: Instead of writing, *"A magical shield appears around the hero,"* you might describe it with more visual clarity and emotional resonance: *"A shimmering shield of light flared into existence, wrapping itself around her like the wings of a phoenix. The air around it hummed with energy, crackling like the first sparks of a storm, as her enemies recoiled, their weapons useless against its golden glow."*

This description provides the emotional weight of the shield's appearance while giving enough visual detail to guide the VFX team.

Step 2: Integrating Special Effects into the Story

Special effects should never exist in isolation—they need to be seamlessly integrated into the story. This means thinking about how the effect impacts the characters, the environment, and the narrative as a whole. A good special effect enhances the tension, stakes, or emotional depth of the scene, rather than distracting from it.

How to Practice:

1. **Align Effects with Story Arcs:** Ensure that special effects are not just random spectacles but are tied to the story's progression. For example, if a character unlocks a new power, the visual effects should reflect the significance of this moment in their arc. Similarly, if an effect occurs during a pivotal battle, it should escalate the stakes of that conflict.

2. **Use Special Effects to Reveal Character:** Special effects can be a tool to show how a character is changing or responding to a situation. For example, if a character's emotions are tied to their powers, the visual effects could fluctuate based on their emotional state. This connection between effect and character deepens the audience's understanding of both.

3. **Consider Environmental Impact:** Special effects often have a ripple effect on the surrounding environment. A massive explosion might send debris flying, alter the landscape, or plunge the characters into darkness. Think about how the effect changes the physical world of the story and how characters must adapt in response.

4. **Don't Overload the Scene:** Too many special effects in a single scene can become overwhelming and dilute the impact of each one. Choose key moments to highlight with special effects and let them shine. Remember, less is often more when it comes to creating an emotional impact.

Example: Instead of describing an isolated visual of a spaceship crash, integrate the effect into the larger narrative: *"The ship plummeted from the sky, trailing a plume of fire and smoke. It smashed into the mountainside, sending a shockwave that rippled through the valley. The ground shook beneath their feet, the roar of the impact still echoing in their ears as dust and debris rained down like ash. But there was no time to stand in awe—the enemy was already advancing, undeterred by the chaos."*

This description integrates the crash into the environment and the action, making it a pivotal moment in the story rather than a standalone visual.

Step 3: Making the Impossible Feel Real

One of the biggest challenges in scripting special effects is making the impossible feel real. Even the most fantastical elements need to have some grounding in reality, otherwise, they can feel disconnected from the world of the story. Creating a sense of believability, even in the midst of the extraordinary, helps the audience stay emotionally engaged.

How to Practice:

1. **Incorporate Sensory Details:** Ground special effects by including sensory details that go beyond just visual description. How does the effect sound, smell, or feel to the characters? Including these sensory elements makes the effect more tangible for the audience.
2. **Show Characters Reacting Realistically:** The way characters respond to the special effects can make a huge difference in how believable they feel. If something extraordinary happens, characters should react in ways that feel authentic to their personalities and the stakes of the scene. Whether it's awe, fear, or confusion, their reactions help anchor the effect in the reality of the story.
3. **Respect the Laws of Physics (When Necessary):** Even in a fantastical world, respecting basic laws of physics can help ground the special effects. For example, if an explosion occurs, characters might be knocked back by the force, or a magical portal might require energy to sustain. These small details create a sense of realism even in the midst of the impossible.
4. **Add Weight and Consequence:** Special effects should have real consequences on the characters and world. If a building is destroyed, how do the characters navigate the wreckage? If a character uses a powerful magical ability, what physical toll does it take on them? Adding weight and consequence makes the effects feel integral to the story, rather than just visual flourishes.

Example: Instead of simply describing a dragon breathing fire, ground the effect in sensory and physical reality: *"The dragon's maw opened wide, a roar echoing through the valley as flames erupted from its throat. The heat hit them first, a wave of blistering air that singed their clothes and scorched the earth beneath their feet. The smell of burning wood and charred stone filled the air, and for a moment, all sound was drowned out by the crackling inferno."*

By including sensory details and describing the physical impact of the fire, the effect feels more real and immersive.

Step 4: Collaborating with Visual Effects Teams

Scripting special effects is a collaborative process. As a writer, your job is to provide a clear vision of the effect while leaving room for the expertise and creativity of the visual effects (VFX) team. Clear communication and collaboration are essential for ensuring that your vision comes to life on screen in a way that serves the story.

How to Practice:

1. **Provide a Strong Blueprint:** Your script should provide a clear description of the special effect, focusing on its key elements and its role in the story. However, avoid micromanaging the details—trust the VFX team to bring their technical expertise to the table.

2. **Be Open to Adjustments:** Budget, time, or technical limitations may require adjustments to your original vision. Be flexible and open to changes that maintain the spirit of the effect while accommodating practical constraints.

3. **Collaborate Early in the Process:** Whenever possible, collaborate with the VFX team early in the development process. Their insights can help shape the way special effects are integrated into the story and ensure that your vision is feasible within the scope of the project.

4. **Trust the Creative Process:** The VFX team will likely bring their own creative ideas and innovations to the table. Trust in their expertise and be open to their suggestions. Often, their interpretations of your ideas can enhance the story in ways you hadn't anticipated.

Example: In your script, you might describe a portal opening: *"A swirling vortex of light and shadow appears in the center of the room, its edges flickering like the surface of water disturbed by a breeze. The air hums with energy, and objects around the room begin to tremble as the portal grows larger, distorting everything in its wake."*

This description provides enough detail to convey the key elements and emotional tone of the effect while allowing the VFX team the freedom to interpret and expand upon the vision.

Step 5: Knowing When to Hold Back

While special effects can elevate a story, knowing when to hold back is equally important. Overloading a scene with too many effects can overwhelm the audience and detract from the emotional or narrative focus. Like in Zen philosophy, where simplicity often leads to greater clarity, sometimes the most powerful moments come from restraint.

How to Practice:

Choose Key Moments for Effects: Not every scene needs to be visually spectacular. Reserve special effects for key moments in the story where they will have the greatest emotional or narrative impact.

Let the Story Lead: Special effects should always serve the story, not the other way around. If a scene works without an elaborate effect, it's often better to let the emotional or character-driven elements take the spotlight.

Create Contrast: Special effects are most impactful when contrasted with quieter, more grounded moments. This balance creates a dynamic narrative rhythm, where moments of awe or spectacle are interspersed with more intimate or reflective scenes.

Example: If the story is building toward a climactic battle, you might choose to save the most dramatic special effects for the peak of that battle, using smaller, subtler effects in earlier scenes to build anticipation. This contrast makes the final explosion of effects feel more powerful.

Scripting special effects is about more than just creating visually stunning moments—it's about using the impossible to enhance the emotional and narrative depth of your story. By visualizing the impossible in a way that serves the story, grounding it in sensory and physical reality, and collaborating with your visual effects team, you can bring your vision to life in a way that feels both believable and awe-inspiring.

The key to mastering special effects lies in balance—knowing when to amplify the visual spectacle and when to hold back, allowing the emotional core of the story to shine. By integrating special effects with purpose, you create a narrative where the impossible feels real and the extraordinary becomes an essential part of the storytelling experience.

Ultimately, special effects are a powerful tool in the storyteller's arsenal, and when used effectively, they can elevate your story, making the impossible not only possible but unforgettable.

Finding the Story's Core: Simplifying the Complex

Every story, no matter how intricate or expansive, has a central theme, message, or emotional truth that forms its foundation. This is the story's core—the essence that connects with the audience on a deep, emotional level. However, in the process of writing, it's easy to get lost in subplots, world-building, or complex character arcs, causing the core message to become muddled or obscured. Much like Zen philosophy, which seeks to strip away the unnecessary to reveal truth in its simplest form, storytelling requires a process of distillation to uncover and highlight what truly matters.

In this chapter, we will explore the art of simplifying complexity, focusing on how to identify and maintain the story's core. Simplifying doesn't mean losing depth or nuance—it means refining the narrative to its essential components, so that every scene, character, and plot point serves the story's central purpose. By finding the core of your story, you create a narrative that resonates deeply, feels cohesive, and delivers an emotional impact that stays with the audience.

The Importance of the Story's Core

The core of a story is its beating heart—the central theme or emotional truth that drives the entire narrative. Everything else—whether it's character development, plot twists, or setting—exists to serve this core. When the core of a story is strong, the audience can feel it in every scene. But when the core is lost amid unnecessary complexity, the story can feel disjointed or confusing.

Here's why the story's core matters:

1. **Creating Emotional Resonance:** A strong core creates a clear emotional throughline that allows the audience to connect with the story on a personal level. Whether it's a theme of love, loss, redemption, or identity, the core grounds the story in universal human experiences.
2. **Guiding Narrative Structure:** The core acts as a guide for your narrative decisions. When you know the story's central message or theme, it becomes easier to make choices about which scenes, characters, or subplots to include or cut.
3. **Maintaining Focus:** Stories can become complex, especially when dealing with multiple characters, timelines, or plotlines. A clear core helps maintain focus, ensuring that all the narrative elements work in harmony rather than competing for attention.
4. **Amplifying Impact:** When everything in the story aligns with its core, the emotional and thematic impact is amplified. The audience walks away with a clear understanding of what the story was about and why it mattered.

• • • •

STEP 1: IDENTIFYING the Story's Core

The first step to simplifying complexity is to identify the core of your story. This involves distilling your narrative down to its most essential elements: What is the heart of your story? What is the message or emotional truth you want to communicate? Finding this core provides clarity and direction, allowing you to shape the rest of the story around it.

How to Practice:

1. **Ask What the Story Is About at Its Deepest Level:** Strip away the plot details, subplots, and secondary characters, and ask yourself: What is this story truly about? This could be a theme, such as "the importance

of family," or an emotional journey, such as "a character's struggle to find their identity."

2. **Define the Emotional Through-line:** Every story has an emotional arc, even if it's subtle. Ask yourself what emotional journey the protagonist (or other central characters) undergoes. What do they feel at the beginning of the story, and how does that change by the end? This emotional through-line often reflects the core of the story.

3. **Boil It Down to a Single Sentence:** Try to summarize the core of your story in one sentence. This exercise forces you to distill your narrative to its essence. For example: *"This is a story about a father's journey to reconnect with his estranged daughter."* This sentence acts as a guiding light, ensuring that all elements of the story serve this central idea.

4. **Look for the Universal Truth:** The best stories tap into universal truths or experiences. Ask yourself: What is the larger truth or message that this story is exploring? Whether it's about love, loss, fear, or hope, this truth forms the foundation of your story's core.

Example: If your story is about a group of survivors in a post-apocalyptic world, the core might not be just about survival, but about the characters rediscovering what it means to be human in the face of destruction: *"At its heart, this is a story about resilience and the enduring power of hope, even in the darkest times."*

This core provides emotional and thematic guidance, helping to focus the story on what truly matters.

Step 2: Stripping Away the Unnecessary

Once you've identified the story's core, the next step is to simplify by stripping away anything that doesn't directly serve that core. This process of elimination can be challenging, especially if you've grown attached to certain scenes or subplots, but it's essential for creating a cohesive, focused narrative.

How to Practice:

Examine Each Scene's Purpose: Go through your story scene by scene and ask yourself: Does this scene contribute to the core of the story? If it doesn't advance the emotional or narrative through line, consider cutting or revising it.

Streamline Subplots: Subplots can add depth to a story, but too many can dilute the impact of the main narrative. Ensure that each subplot aligns with the core theme or message. If a subplot feels tangential or distracting, simplify or remove it.

Focus on Essential Characters: Secondary characters can enrich a story, but too many can clutter it. Focus on the characters who play a key role in advancing the core of the story. If a character isn't contributing to the protagonist's journey or the main theme, consider combining them with another character or cutting their role.

Simplify World-Building: In genres like fantasy or science fiction, world-building is crucial, but it can also overwhelm the core message if not carefully managed. Focus on the aspects of the world that directly support the story's themes or character arcs. Avoid excessive detail or lore that doesn't serve the core.

Example: In a story about a character's search for self-identity, a subplot about a rival character's business dealings might detract from the central journey. By stripping away that subplot and focusing on interactions that challenge the protagonist's sense of self, the story becomes clearer and more emotionally focused.

Step 3: Strengthening the Emotional Through line

To ensure that your story's core resonates with the audience, you need to strengthen the emotional through line. This involves weaving the emotional journey of your characters into every scene, creating a sense of cohesion and momentum that builds toward an emotionally satisfying conclusion.

How to Practice:

Keep the Protagonist's Emotional Arc Central: No matter how complex your plot, the protagonist's emotional journey should remain the focal point. Revisit the character's emotional arc frequently to ensure that each scene contributes to their growth, challenges, or transformation.

Use Symbolism and Metaphor: One way to strengthen the emotional core of your story is to use symbolism or metaphor to reflect the characters' internal struggles. For example, a storm could symbolize a character's inner turmoil, or a broken mirror could represent fractured self-identity. These elements add emotional depth without complicating the plot.

Create Emotional Echoes: Repetition of emotional beats or themes throughout the story creates a sense of cohesion. These emotional echoes remind the audience of the central theme and reinforce the story's core. For example, if your story is about redemption, key moments of forgiveness or guilt might echo throughout the narrative.

Ensure the Climax Reflects the Core: The emotional climax of the story should directly relate to the core theme or message. This is the moment when the protagonist's internal journey comes to a head, and the audience should feel that the story has been building toward this point all along.

Example: In a story about a character learning to forgive themselves, the emotional throughline might involve moments where they face their past mistakes, encounter forgiveness from others, and ultimately learn to extend that forgiveness to themselves. Each of these moments strengthens the core theme of self-acceptance.

Step 4: Trusting Simplicity

Simplicity is often more powerful than complexity. When you trust the core of your story and allow it to guide your narrative choices, you create a story that feels focused, emotionally resonant, and impactful. The challenge lies in trusting that simplicity doesn't mean a lack of depth—it means clarity of purpose.

How to Practice:

1. **Embrace Minimalism in Description:** When writing scenes, focus on what is essential. Avoid overloading the reader with unnecessary details or descriptions. Trust that the emotional weight of the scene will carry through, even with fewer words.
2. **Use Dialogue with Purpose:** In dialogue, aim for simplicity and clarity. Every line should serve a purpose, whether it's revealing character, advancing the plot, or reinforcing the core theme. Avoid conversations that don't add to the emotional or narrative progression.
3. **Let Silence and Stillness Speak:** Sometimes, what's left unsaid can be more powerful than dialogue or action. Trust in the power of silence, stillness, and subtext to convey the deeper emotional truths of your story. Let the audience fill in the gaps with their own interpretations.
4. **Resist the Urge to Over-Explain:** Allow your audience to engage with the story on their own terms. Avoid over-explaining themes, messages, or character motivations. Simplicity often means trusting that your audience will pick up on the subtleties and deeper meanings without being told outright.

Example: In a scene where a character reconciles with a long-lost sibling, rather than using lengthy dialogue to explain their feelings, you might opt for a simpler, more emotionally charged moment: *"They stood in silence for a long time, the years of distance hanging between them like smoke. Then, without a word, he stepped forward and embraced her, his arms trembling as if the weight of every missed opportunity had just lifted."*

This simplicity allows the audience to feel the emotional depth of the moment without being overwhelmed by words.

Step 5: Maintaining Clarity through Revision

Finding the core of your story often involves multiple rounds of revision. As you revise, continually ask yourself whether each element of the story serves the core message. Be willing to make changes that clarify the story's purpose, even if it means cutting scenes, characters, or subplots that you initially thought were essential.

How to Practice:

1. **Revisit the Core during Revisions:** As you revise, keep the core of the story in mind. Re-evaluate scenes, subplots, and characters to ensure they align with the central theme or emotional journey. If something feels off, it may be because it strays too far from the core.
2. **Streamline the Plot:** Look for opportunities to simplify the plot without losing depth. Are there scenes or sequences that can be combined? Can certain plot points be clarified or tightened? Simplifying the plot allows the core message to shine through more clearly.
3. **Listen to Feedback:** Feedback from others can help you identify areas where the core of your story may be getting lost. Pay attention to moments where readers or viewers seem confused, disengaged, or overwhelmed, and use their insights to simplify and refocus the narrative.
4. **Trust Your Instincts:** Ultimately, you know the heart of your story better than anyone else. Trust your instincts about what feels true to the core and what may be pulling the story off course. Simplicity doesn't mean dumbing down the narrative—it means distilling it to its most powerful, essential form.

Example: During revision, you might realize that a subplot about a character's career struggles detracts from the main story about their relationship with their estranged parent. By cutting or streamlining the subplot, you bring the focus back to the emotional core of the story.

Simplifying the complex isn't about removing depth or nuance from your story—it's about refining your narrative so that every element serves the core message or emotional truth. By identifying the heart of your story and stripping away the unnecessary, you create a narrative that feels cohesive, focused, and resonant.

In Zen philosophy, simplicity is seen as a path to enlightenment—a way of seeing the world in its purest, most truthful form. In storytelling, simplicity allows the audience to engage with the emotional and thematic core of the narrative without being distracted by unnecessary complexity. By trusting simplicity and embracing clarity, you create a story that speaks to the universal human experience in a way that is both powerful and unforgettable.

At the end of the day, the core of your story is what lingers in the hearts and minds of the audience. It's the truth that resonates beyond the plot twists, special effects, or world-building. By finding and focusing on that core, you ensure that your story leaves a lasting impact, reaching the audience on a deeper, more meaningful level.

Writing in a state of deep focus, often referred to as "flow," is a powerful experience for any writer. It's the moment when words seem to pour effortlessly from your mind onto the page, when time disappears, and you become completely immersed in your story. This flow state is often elusive, but when it's achieved, it can lead to some of your most inspired and effective writing.

Zen practice teaches the importance of mindfulness, being fully present in the moment, and letting go of distractions to find a state of calm and clarity. This state of Zen focus aligns closely with the flow state in writing. By approaching writing with mindfulness and intention, you can cultivate the conditions that allow flow to occur, leading to more productive and fulfilling writing sessions.

In this chapter, we will explore the connection between Zen focus and writing in a flow state. You'll learn how to cultivate the mental clarity and emotional balance necessary to enter this state more regularly, and how to create an environment that supports deep, uninterrupted focus.

Understanding Flow State in Writing

Flow is a mental state in which a person is fully immersed in an activity, with a feeling of energized focus and complete involvement. Psychologist Mihaly Csikszentmihalyi, who popularized the concept of flow, described it as a state where a person is so absorbed in what they are doing that nothing else seems to matter. In writing, this often translates to a sense of effortless creativity and deep connection with your story.

Here are some key characteristics of the flow state:

1. **Complete Focus:** In a flow state, distractions fade away, and your attention is fully directed toward the task at hand. You are not thinking about external concerns or self-doubt—your mind is entirely in the moment.
2. **Effortlessness:** Writing in flow feels easy. Ideas and words come naturally, and you don't struggle to find the right phrasing or structure. It feels as though the story is unfolding on its own, with you simply guiding it.
3. **Timelessness:** When you are in flow, you lose track of time. Hours can pass without you realizing it because you are so deeply engaged in the writing process.
4. **Joy and Satisfaction:** Writing in flow is often accompanied by a sense of joy and fulfillment. The act of creation becomes intrinsically rewarding, and you feel deeply satisfied with the progress you are making.
5. **Heightened Creativity:** Flow often brings about a surge of creativity. You may find that you're coming up with new ideas, plot twists, or character developments that surprise even you.

While flow can't be forced, there are ways to create the conditions that make it more likely to occur. By adopting a mindful approach to your writing, you can tap into the Zen-like focus that allows you to enter this state more frequently.

Step 1: Preparing the Mind for Focus

Flow begins with mental clarity. Just as Zen practice involves clearing the mind through meditation and mindfulness, writing in flow requires a state of mental calm and focus. Before diving into a writing session, it's important to prepare your mind, releasing distractions and setting your intention.

How to Practice:

1. **Begin with Mindful Breathing:** Take a few minutes before you start writing to engage in mindful breathing. Focus on your breath as it moves in and out of your body, allowing your thoughts to settle. This

simple exercise helps center your mind and brings you into the present moment, ready to focus on your writing.

2. **Set an Intention for Your Writing Session:** Before you start, take a moment to set an intention. What are you hoping to achieve in this session? Whether it's completing a chapter, exploring a new character's backstory, or simply enjoying the creative process, setting an intention helps clarify your focus.

3. **Let Go of Perfectionism:** One of the biggest obstacles to flow is the inner critic—the voice that questions every word and doubts every idea. Before you begin, consciously let go of the need to write perfectly. Remind yourself that the first draft doesn't need to be flawless—it just needs to exist. By releasing the pressure of perfection, you free yourself to write more fluidly.

4. **Create a Mental Trigger:** Many Zen practices use rituals or triggers to signal the start of meditation. You can create a similar ritual for your writing. It might be lighting a candle, playing a specific type of music, or simply sitting in a particular chair. This trigger helps signal to your brain that it's time to enter a focused, creative state.

Example: Before starting your writing session, sit quietly with your eyes closed. Take five deep breaths, focusing on the sensation of air entering and leaving your body. As you breathe, mentally release any distractions or worries. When you feel ready, set a simple intention for your writing session: *"I will focus on exploring my protagonist's emotional arc in this chapter."* When you open your eyes, begin writing with a calm, clear mind.

Step 2: Creating an Environment for Flow

Your environment plays a key role in fostering flow. Zen practice emphasizes the importance of a serene, uncluttered space that promotes focus and calm. Similarly, a well-prepared writing environment can help eliminate distractions and allow you to fully immerse yourself in your work.

How to Practice:

1. **Eliminate Distractions:** The modern world is full of distractions, from social media to noisy environments. Before you begin writing, take steps to minimize distractions. Turn off notifications, close unnecessary tabs on your computer, and put your phone on silent or airplane mode. If possible, write in a quiet space where you won't be interrupted.
2. **Declutter Your Space:** A cluttered environment can lead to a cluttered mind. Clear your workspace of unnecessary items, keeping only what you need for your writing session. A clean, minimalist space can help create a sense of calm and focus, allowing you to more easily enter a state of flow.
3. **Use Sensory Cues:** Sensory cues, such as calming music, lighting, or even scent, can help signal to your brain that it's time to focus. Soft background music, white noise, or nature sounds can enhance concentration for some writers. Similarly, lighting a candle or using essential oils with calming scents like lavender can create a peaceful atmosphere.
4. **Make Your Writing Tools Comfortable:** Whether you write on a computer, in a notebook, or with a typewriter, ensure that your writing tools are comfortable and conducive to flow. A well-lit, ergonomic space, a comfortable chair, and writing tools that you enjoy using can make a big difference in maintaining focus during long writing sessions.

Example: Before you begin writing, take five minutes to tidy your workspace. Remove any unnecessary items, and organize your desk so that only your writing materials are in front of you. Light a candle or play soft instrumental music in the background to create a peaceful, focused atmosphere. With distractions minimized and your environment set, you are now ready to enter a flow state.

Step 3: Writing Without Distraction

Once you've prepared your mind and environment, it's time to start writing. The key to flow is uninterrupted focus. When distractions or interruptions pull you out of the moment, it can take a long time to get back into that focused state. Learning to maintain a single-pointed focus on your writing is essential for sustaining flow.

. . . .

HOW TO PRACTICE:

Set a Timer for Focused Writing: One effective way to sustain focus is to write in timed intervals, such as the Pomodoro Technique. Set a timer for 25 or 30 minutes and commit to writing without stopping during that time. After the timer goes off, take a short break. This method helps keep you focused and reduces the urge to check your phone or engage in other distractions.

Keep Writing, Even When You Feel Stuck: Flow often comes in waves—there may be moments when you feel stuck or unsure of what to write next. Instead of stopping, keep writing through the block, even if it's just to describe your character's surroundings or internal thoughts. Sometimes, pushing through these moments leads to a breakthrough.

Avoid Multitasking: Multitasking is the enemy of flow. During your writing session, focus solely on your writing. Avoid checking emails, switching between tasks, or jumping to research. Stay present with the words on the page, and trust that you can deal with other tasks later.

Practice Letting Go of Judgment: If you find yourself judging your writing or overthinking each sentence, remind yourself to let go. Flow is about trusting the process and allowing ideas to come naturally. You can always revise and polish later—right now, your goal is to keep the momentum going.

Example: Set a timer for 30 minutes and commit to writing continuously during that time. Even if you hit a moment where you're unsure of what to write, keep your fingers moving. Describe a character's thoughts, explore an unexpected scene, or write dialogue—even if you're not sure it's perfect. The goal is to stay in motion, trusting that the flow will return.

Step 4: Cultivating Flow Through Routine

Flow is easier to achieve when writing becomes a consistent practice. Just as Zen practitioners develop mindfulness through regular meditation, writers can train their brains to enter flow more easily through routine and habit. Creating a regular writing schedule helps establish the conditions for flow to become a natural part of your creative process.

How to Practice:

Write at the Same Time Every Day: Consistency is key to cultivating flow. Try to write at the same time each day, even if it's only for 20 or 30 minutes. This routine signals to your brain that it's time to focus, making it easier to slip into a flow state.

Develop Pre-Writing Rituals: Create a ritual that helps you transition into writing mode. This could be making a cup of tea, lighting a candle, or doing a quick breathing exercise. Over time, this ritual becomes associated with writing, helping you enter a focused state more quickly.

Track Your Writing Sessions: Keep a journal or log of your writing sessions, noting when you experience flow and what conditions helped you get there. Tracking your progress can help you identify patterns that support or hinder your ability to enter flow.

Be Patient with the Process: Flow is not something that happens every time you sit down to write. Be patient with yourself, and trust that with regular practice, you'll experience flow more frequently. Even on days when the words don't come easily, the act of showing up to write is part of the journey.

Example: Create a simple writing routine that works for your schedule. For example, you might decide to write every morning for 30 minutes, starting with a cup of coffee and a few deep breaths. Over time, this consistent practice makes it easier to enter a flow state, as your brain begins to associate this time with creative focus.

Step 5: Embracing Imperfection in the Flow

One of the hallmarks of flow is the ability to create without self-consciousness or judgment. In flow, you're not worried about whether your writing is perfect—you're simply immersed in the process of creation. Embracing this mindset is key to sustaining flow and producing work that feels authentic and inspired.

How to Practice:

1. **Embrace the First Draft as Discovery:** The first draft is about discovery, not perfection. Allow yourself to explore ideas, characters, and plot twists without worrying about whether they're right. Flow is often about letting the story take unexpected turns.
2. **Resist the Urge to Edit as You Write:** Editing while writing can pull you out of the flow state. Instead, focus on getting the words down, and save revisions for later. Trust that you'll have time to polish and refine once the draft is complete.
3. **Accept That Some Writing Sessions Will Be Messy:** Not every writing session will be perfect or productive. Sometimes, flow will come easily, and other times it will be harder to find. Accept this as part of the creative process, and don't let one difficult session discourage you.
4. **Find Joy in the Process:** Flow is about enjoying the act of creation. Let yourself get lost in the process of

writing, and focus on the joy of bringing a story to life. The more you can connect with that joy, the more likely you are to find flow.

Example: As you write, remind yourself that this is just a first draft—a chance to explore, experiment, and discover. Let go of the need to edit or refine, and allow your ideas to flow naturally. If you hit a rough patch, keep going, knowing that you can revise and polish later.

Writing in flow is a deeply rewarding experience that allows you to tap into your most creative and inspired self. By adopting the principles of Zen focus—mindfulness, simplicity, and presence—you can cultivate the conditions that make flow more likely to occur. Through preparation, routine, and letting go of judgment, you'll find that writing becomes less of a struggle and more of a natural, joyful process.

The practice of Zen focus teaches us that flow is not about forcing creativity—it's about creating the mental and physical space for creativity to arise naturally. By entering each writing session with mindfulness and intention, you open the door to flow, allowing your story to unfold with clarity, ease, and purpose.

Ultimately, writing in flow is about being fully present with your story, trusting your instincts, and allowing the process of creation to take you where it will. By embracing this state of focus, you can produce work that feels authentic, inspired, and true to your artistic vision.

Merging Mind and Story: Creating with Intent

In Zen philosophy, there is an understanding that true mastery comes from the union of the mind and action. Whether practicing martial arts, calligraphy, or tea ceremony, the practitioner enters a state of mindfulness where the mind and the task become one. In the context of writing, this same principle applies: true mastery in storytelling comes from merging your mind with your story, creating with a clear sense of purpose and intent.

When you write with intent, every element of your story serves a greater purpose. The characters, plot, themes, and setting align harmoniously with your vision, and every word you write contributes to the story's core message or emotional truth. This intentional approach to storytelling goes beyond simply stringing together plot points—it involves deeply considering what you want to convey and how you want the audience to feel or think. By merging mind and story, you bring clarity, coherence, and depth to your work, allowing your narrative to resonate with meaning and purpose.

In this chapter, we will explore how to write with intent, focusing on the mental clarity and purpose required to merge your mind with your story. By being intentional about what you write and how you write it, you can create stories that are not only engaging but also impactful, with a message that resonates long after the final page is turned.

The Power of Intent in Storytelling

Writing with intent means having a clear understanding of what your story is about and what you want to achieve with it. This goes beyond plot mechanics or character development—it's about crafting a narrative that aligns with a central purpose or theme. When you write with intent, you approach each scene, character, and decision with mindfulness, ensuring that every element serves the story's larger goals.

Here's why intent is essential in storytelling:

1. **Clarifying Your Vision:** Writing with intent helps you clarify your vision for the story. It forces you to consider the larger message or emotional journey you want to convey and ensures that every choice you make serves that vision.

2. **Creating Meaningful Stories:** When you write with intent, you imbue your stories with deeper meaning. Readers or viewers can sense when a story is crafted with purpose, and this resonance creates a lasting emotional or intellectual impact.

3. **Maintaining Consistency:** Intent helps maintain consistency throughout the narrative. When you know what your story is trying to achieve, it becomes easier to ensure that all elements—plot, characters, themes, and tone—work together harmoniously.

4. **Guiding Your Creative Choices:** Intent provides a guiding light for decision-making during the writing process. Whether it's determining a character's arc, choosing a setting, or deciding how to end the story, your intent helps steer your creative choices in the right direction.

Step 1: Defining Your Intent

The first step to creating with intent is to define the purpose or message of your story. This involves looking beyond plot details and identifying the deeper themes or emotional truths that you want to explore. Understanding the intent behind your story gives you a clear direction, allowing you to craft every element in alignment with that purpose.

How to Practice:

1. **Ask What the Story Is Really About:** To define your intent, ask yourself: What is this story really about,

on a deeper level? Consider the emotional, philosophical, or thematic core of the narrative. Is it about love and loss? The search for identity? The struggle for justice? Defining this core will guide all your creative decisions.

2. **Identify the Emotional Journey:** Every story involves an emotional journey—whether it's a character's personal growth, a relationship's evolution, or a broader societal shift. What is the emotional arc you want your audience to experience? Identifying this journey helps clarify your story's intent and ensures that each scene contributes to that arc.

3. **Focus on the Message or Theme:** Think about the larger message or theme you want to convey through your story. This doesn't mean you need to preach or moralize, but having a thematic throughline helps you stay focused on what matters most in the narrative. Whether it's a commentary on human nature, a reflection on society, or an exploration of personal growth, this theme will shape the story's intent.

4. **Write a Statement of Intent:** To solidify your intent, try writing a brief statement that encapsulates what you want to achieve with the story. This could be something like, *"This story explores the tension between personal ambition and moral responsibility, following a protagonist who must decide between pursuing their dreams and doing what's right."* This statement serves as a touchstone throughout the writing process, reminding you of your story's core purpose.

Example: If your story is about a detective uncovering a conspiracy, the deeper intent might be about the nature of truth and deception. Your statement of intent could be: *"This story examines the cost of uncovering the truth and the moral ambiguities of justice."* This intent will guide how you develop the plot, the characters, and the resolution.

Step 2: Aligning Every Element with Intent

Once you've defined your story's intent, the next step is to align every element of the narrative with that intent. This means ensuring that your characters, plot, themes, and even the setting work together to serve the larger purpose of the story.

How to Practice:

1. **Align Character Arcs with Intent:** Consider how your characters' journeys reflect the story's central theme or message. If your story is about redemption, for example, your protagonist's arc should mirror that theme, with their personal growth tied to the larger intent. Similarly, secondary characters should complement or challenge the protagonist's journey, reinforcing the story's core message.

2. **Ensure the Plot Serves the Theme:** The events of the story should be more than just action or conflict—they should contribute to the exploration of the story's deeper themes. Ask yourself: How does each plot point reflect the intent of the story? If a scene doesn't align with the story's purpose, consider revising or cutting it.

3. **Use Setting to Reinforce Intent:** The setting can play a powerful role in reinforcing your story's intent. If your story explores themes of isolation, for example, a remote, desolate environment can enhance that feeling. Think about how the world you create—whether real or fictional—supports the emotional or thematic core of the narrative.

4. **Let Dialogue Reflect the Story's Purpose:** Dialogue is another way to subtly reinforce the story's intent. Characters' conversations should not only advance the plot but also reflect the themes and emotional undercurrents of the story. Whether through direct discussion or subtext, dialogue should be aligned with the narrative's purpose.

Example: In a story about the pursuit of truth, every element can reinforce that theme. The protagonist's arc might involve their growing realization of the moral complexities of their search. The plot might feature moments where the protagonist uncovers half-truths, false leads, or moral dilemmas that challenge their beliefs. The setting—a city shrouded in fog and darkness—could symbolize the ambiguity of truth, while dialogue could explore characters' differing views on what it means to be honest or just.

Step 3: Writing with Clarity and Purpose

Writing with intent also means writing with clarity and purpose. When you know what you want to convey, your writing becomes more focused, direct, and impactful. Every scene, character interaction, and piece of description should serve the story's overall goals.

How to Practice:

Eliminate Unnecessary Scenes or Details: When revising your work, ask yourself whether each scene, detail, or subplot contributes to the story's intent. If something feels extraneous or distracting, consider cutting or simplifying it. The goal is to keep the narrative focused and clear, with every element serving the larger purpose.

Avoid Over-Explaining: Writing with intent doesn't mean hitting the audience over the head with your theme or message. Trust your readers to engage with the story's deeper meanings without needing to over-explain. Subtlety often makes a theme more powerful, allowing readers to discover it for themselves.

Focus on Emotional Resonance: Writing with intent often involves tapping into the emotional heart of the story. Make sure your writing reflects the emotional journey of the characters and the larger themes. Whether through character actions, descriptions, or dialogue, aim to evoke emotions that align with your story's purpose.

Trust in the Process of Discovery: Even when writing with intent, allow yourself the flexibility to discover new ideas or directions as you write. Sometimes, the deeper purpose of your story becomes clearer as you explore it. Trust in this process of discovery, knowing that your intent will evolve as the story unfolds.

Example: Imagine you're writing a scene where the protagonist confronts an antagonist. Instead of focusing on a simple exchange of dialogue, consider how the scene serves the larger theme. If your story is about the cost of ambition, you might use this confrontation to explore the moral compromises the characters have made. The dialogue, setting, and character actions should all contribute to this deeper exploration, keeping the story's intent at the forefront.

Step 4: Merging Intuition and Intent

While intent provides a clear direction for your story, it's important not to lose sight of the intuitive, creative side of writing. Merging mind and story means balancing intention with intuition—allowing the story to flow naturally while keeping your purpose in mind.

How to Practice:

Trust your Instincts: Writing with intent doesn't mean rigidly adhering to a pre-determined plan. Allow your instincts to guide you as you write. If a character surprises you or the plot takes an unexpected turn, trust that these discoveries can deepen your understanding of the story's intent.

Stay Open to Change: Your initial intent may evolve as you write. Stay open to new ideas or directions that emerge during the writing process. Sometimes, the deeper purpose of a story reveals itself through the act of creation, leading to unexpected but meaningful shifts in direction.

Balance Structure and Flow: Writing with intent requires balancing the structure of your story with the natural flow of creativity. Use your intent as a guide, but allow room for spontaneity and discovery. This balance between structure and flow often leads to the most authentic, powerful storytelling.

Reflect on Your Intent as You Revise: During revision, revisit your initial intent and consider whether the story has evolved in a way that enhances or changes that purpose. If necessary, adjust scenes, characters, or themes to better align with the story's deeper message.

Example: While writing, you may initially intend for your protagonist to find redemption by the end of the story. However, as the narrative progresses, you realize that the character's arc is more complex than you originally thought. Rather than resisting this change, you embrace it, allowing the story's deeper theme of self-acceptance to emerge naturally. This balance between intuition and intent leads to a richer, more layered narrative.

Step 5: Revising with Intent

The process of revision is where your intent truly comes into focus. During revision, you can refine your story to ensure that every element aligns with its purpose. This is the stage where you merge your mind with the story, bringing clarity and coherence to the narrative.

How to Practice:

Revisit Your Statement of Intent: As you revise, keep your statement of intent in mind. Does each scene, character, and plot point serve the story's purpose? If something feels out of alignment, revise or cut it to strengthen the narrative.

Look for Opportunities to Deepen Themes: During revision, you may discover new opportunities to reinforce the story's themes. Look for moments where you can subtly weave in the message or emotional journey without being overt. Sometimes, a simple line of dialogue or a descriptive detail can bring the theme into sharper focus.

Clarify the Emotional Arc: Revisit the emotional journey of your characters and ensure that their arcs align with the story's intent. If a character's growth or transformation feels unclear, refine their arc to better reflect the emotional heart of the story.

Ensure a Satisfying Resolution: The resolution of your story should reflect its deeper themes and emotional journey. Whether the ending is hopeful, bittersweet, or tragic, it should feel like a natural conclusion to the story's intent. Revisit the final scenes to ensure they deliver a satisfying resolution that resonates with the audience.

Example: During revision, you may realize that a subplot involving a secondary character feels disconnected from the story's main theme. By revising the subplot to align with the protagonist's journey—perhaps by making the secondary character's struggles mirror the protagonist's—you strengthen the overall coherence of the narrative.

Merging mind and story through intentional writing is about more than just crafting a coherent plot—it's about infusing your narrative with meaning, purpose, and emotional depth. By defining your story's intent and aligning every element with that purpose, you create a narrative that resonates on a deeper level, leaving a lasting impact on the audience. Zen philosophy teaches us that true mastery comes from mindfulness and clarity of purpose.

In storytelling, this means approaching each word, scene, and character with intention, ensuring that everything serves the larger goal of the narrative. When you write with intent, you create stories that are not only engaging but also meaningful—stories that reflect the human experience in all its complexity and beauty.

Ultimately, writing with intent allows you to craft stories that speak to the core of what it means to be human. By merging mind and story, you create narratives that are authentic, purposeful, and unforgettable.

The Power of Contrast: Using Light and Shadow in Storytelling

In the world of visual art, light and shadow are essential tools used to create depth, highlight focal points, and convey mood. Similarly, in storytelling, contrast—whether between characters, emotions, themes, or narrative elements—adds complexity and richness to the narrative. Much like the interplay of light and shadow in a painting, contrast in a story helps define the emotional landscape, underscore themes, and guide the audience's experience.

In Zen philosophy, balance is achieved through the recognition of opposites—yin and yang, light and dark, stillness and movement. These opposites coexist in harmony, each defining the other. In storytelling, this idea is equally powerful. Light and shadow, in the metaphorical sense, represent the contrasts in characters, themes, and emotional arcs that give a story its depth and resonance.

In this chapter, we'll explore how to use contrast in your storytelling to create richer, more compelling narratives. Whether it's through character dynamics, thematic oppositions, or the pacing of scenes, contrast allows you to draw attention to important elements, evoke emotional complexity, and engage the audience in a more profound way.

The Role of Contrast in Storytelling

Contrast serves as a tool for highlighting differences, creating tension, and deepening the emotional or thematic impact of a story. By placing opposing forces or ideas in juxtaposition, contrast draws the audience's attention to key moments, characters, or themes, amplifying their significance.

Here are some key ways contrast functions in storytelling:

1. **Creating Emotional Depth:** Contrast between opposing emotions, such as joy and sorrow or hope and despair, creates emotional richness. When moments of light are followed by darkness—or vice versa—the emotional impact is heightened, allowing the audience to experience a wider range of feelings.
2. **Highlighting Themes:** Thematic contrasts, such as good versus evil, freedom versus control, or tradition versus progress, help clarify the story's central message. By placing these opposites in tension with one another, you invite the audience to reflect on the deeper meaning of the narrative.
3. **Building Tension and Conflict:** Contrast between characters—whether through their personalities, motivations, or goals—creates conflict, which drives the plot forward. This opposition between characters not only generates tension but also reveals key aspects of their personalities and arcs.
4. **Guiding the Audience's Focus:** Just as light in a painting draws attention to the focal point, contrast in storytelling guides the audience's focus. By juxtaposing moments of intensity with quieter, more reflective scenes, you create a rhythm that keeps the audience engaged and highlights the most important parts of the narrative.

Step 1: Using Contrast in Characterization

One of the most effective ways to use contrast in storytelling is through character dynamics. Characters who contrast with one another, either through their personalities, values, or goals, create compelling tension and conflict. These contrasts can also reveal deeper truths about the characters, highlighting their strengths, weaknesses, and internal struggles.

How to Practice:

1. **Create Foil Characters:** A foil is a character who contrasts with the protagonist in order to highlight certain qualities of the main character. This contrast can bring out key aspects of the protagonist's personality, values, or flaws. For example, a protagonist who is reserved and introspective might be

contrasted with a foil who is outspoken and impulsive, creating tension while highlighting the protagonist's inner conflict.

2. **Contrast Hero and Villain Motivations:** The conflict between a hero and villain is often most compelling when their motivations contrast sharply. For example, a hero who fights for freedom might face a villain who seeks control or domination. This contrast not only drives the central conflict but also underscores the story's themes.

3. **Juxtapose Character Strengths and Weaknesses:** Characters who have contrasting strengths and weaknesses can create a dynamic ensemble. For example, one character might be physically strong but emotionally vulnerable, while another is emotionally resilient but physically fragile. These contrasts add complexity to their interactions and development.

4. **Highlight Emotional Oppositions:** Characters who experience contrasting emotions can deepen the emotional complexity of a scene. For example, one character might feel hope while another feels despair, or one might be filled with anger while another remains calm. These emotional contrasts create tension and reveal deeper layers of each character's emotional state.

Example: In a story about two brothers, one might be calm, strategic, and thoughtful, while the other is hot-headed, impulsive, and quick to act. Their contrasting personalities lead to conflict, but also allow for moments where they balance each other out. The contrast between their approaches to life can highlight the central themes of the story—perhaps the tension between control and chaos or thought versus action.

Step 2: Thematic Contrast for Deeper Meaning

Thematic contrast is a powerful way to explore opposing ideas or values within your story. By setting two or more themes in opposition to each other, you create tension that prompts the audience to reflect on the deeper meaning of the narrative. These thematic contrasts often resonate long after the story is over, leaving the audience with something to contemplate.

How to Practice:

1. **Explore Opposing Worldviews:** Contrast can be used to explore conflicting worldviews or ideologies within a story. For example, a narrative might contrast a character who values individual freedom with one who believes in collective responsibility. These opposing worldviews create thematic tension that forces both characters (and the audience) to question their beliefs.

2. **Juxtapose Light and Dark Themes:** Stories that deal with both light and dark themes—such as hope and despair, love and hate, or innocence and corruption—often leave a lasting emotional impact. By weaving these contrasting themes throughout the narrative, you allow the audience to experience the full spectrum of human emotion and thought.

3. **Use Symbolism to Represent Opposites:** Symbolism is an effective way to reinforce thematic contrasts. For example, a story about life and death might use recurring symbols such as blooming flowers to represent life and wilting flowers to represent death. These visual contrasts serve as a constant reminder of the story's deeper themes.

4. **Let Themes Collide in the Climax:** The climax of the story is often where thematic contrasts reach their peak. The opposing ideas or values that have been building throughout the narrative collide, forcing the protagonist to make a choice or take a stand. This moment of resolution can be deeply satisfying when it reflects the core themes of the story.

Example: In a dystopian story, you might contrast themes of individualism versus conformity. One character might rebel against a highly controlled society, fighting for personal freedom, while another character believes that conformity is necessary for the greater good. The tension between these opposing themes drives the narrative, leading to a climax where the protagonist must decide whether to sacrifice personal freedom for societal stability or continue the fight for individual rights.

Step 3: Using Contrast in Plot Structure and Pacing

Contrast in plot structure and pacing is key to creating a dynamic, engaging narrative. By alternating between moments of action and moments of stillness, or by juxtaposing fast-paced sequences with slower, more introspective scenes, you create a rhythm that keeps the audience invested. This contrast also allows you to highlight key moments in the story, making them feel more impactful.

How to Practice:

1. **Alternate between Action and Stillness:** In stories with a lot of action, moments of stillness can provide necessary emotional depth and reflection. Conversely, in more introspective narratives, moments of action can inject energy and momentum. Alternating between these contrasting rhythms creates a balance that keeps the audience engaged.

2. **Build Tension with Quiet Moments:** Sometimes, the quietest moments in a story can be the most tension-filled. Contrast high-intensity action scenes with moments of eerie calm, where the characters (and the audience) are left waiting for something to happen. This use of contrast builds suspense and amplifies the impact of the next dramatic event.

3. **Contrast Clarity with Confusion:** In mysteries or thrillers, alternating between moments of clarity and moments of confusion can enhance the story's intrigue. A scene where the protagonist seems to gain important information can be followed by a scene that throws everything into question, keeping the audience on edge and maintaining a sense of mystery.

4. **End on a Contrasting Note:** The conclusion of your story can be particularly impactful if it contrasts sharply with what came before. For example, a story that has been largely dark and tragic might end on a note of hope, offering the audience a sense of resolution or redemption. Alternatively, a hopeful story might end with a surprising twist of tragedy or loss, leaving a bittersweet aftertaste.

Example: In a heist movie, the plot might alternate between high-stakes action sequences, such as the robbery itself, and quieter, more introspective moments where the characters reflect on their motivations and the potential consequences of their actions. The contrast between these fast-paced and slow-paced scenes creates tension, allowing the audience to catch their breath between intense moments while deepening their understanding of the characters.

Step 4: Contrast in Setting and Imagery

The setting and imagery of a story can be used to create powerful contrasts that reinforce the emotional or thematic content of the narrative. Just as light and shadow in visual art create depth and highlight important elements, contrasting settings and imagery can shape the tone and atmosphere of your story.

How to Practice:

1. **Juxtapose Opposing Environments:** Contrast between settings can enhance the emotional journey of the characters. For example, a story might begin in a bright, idyllic setting that contrasts with the dark, chaotic world the characters later encounter. This shift in setting mirrors the characters' internal struggles and highlights the changes they undergo.

2. **Use Light and Dark Imagery:** Imagery that contrasts light and dark can evoke strong emotional responses. A scene where a character is surrounded by darkness might symbolize fear, isolation, or uncertainty, while a scene bathed in light could represent hope, clarity, or revelation. Alternating between these contrasting images adds visual and emotional texture to the story.

3. **Create Oppositions in Weather or Time of Day:** Weather and time of day can also serve as symbolic contrasts in storytelling. A stormy night might represent chaos or danger, while a clear morning might symbolize new beginnings. Using these natural contrasts can subtly reinforce the mood or themes of a scene.

4. **Highlight the Protagonist's Internal World with External Contrasts:** The external world of the story can be used to reflect the protagonist's internal state. For example, a character who feels trapped or overwhelmed might be placed in a setting that is confining or chaotic, while a character who experiences a moment of peace or clarity might be shown in a serene, open environment. These contrasts help externalize the protagonist's emotional journey.

Example: In a post-apocalyptic story, you might contrast the bleak, desolate landscape of the ruined city with brief flashes of natural beauty—perhaps a lone flower growing amid the rubble or a distant view of untouched wilderness. This contrast emphasizes the theme of survival and resilience, showing that even in the darkest circumstances, life and hope can persist.

Step 5: Emotional Contrast for Greater Impact

One of the most powerful ways to use contrast in storytelling is through emotional shifts. By juxtaposing moments of intense emotion—such as joy, sorrow, fear, or relief—you can heighten the audience's emotional engagement with the story. These shifts create emotional peaks and valleys, allowing for greater impact and resonance.

How to Practice:

1. **Shift between Opposing Emotions:** Alternating between contrasting emotions can create emotional complexity. For example, a character might experience a moment of triumph followed by a sudden realization of loss, or a scene of joy might be interrupted by an unexpected tragedy. These emotional contrasts keep the audience engaged and invested in the characters' journeys.
2. **Create Emotional Reversals:** Emotional reversals—where a character's emotions change rapidly in response to a sudden event—can be particularly effective in generating contrast. A character who feels safe and secure might suddenly be thrown into danger, or a moment of despair might be interrupted by a surprising act of kindness or hope.
3. **Contrast Internal and External Emotions:** Sometimes, the contrast between what a character feels internally and what they express externally can create emotional tension. A character who appears calm and collected on the surface might be experiencing deep turmoil or fear internally. This emotional contrast adds layers of complexity to the character and invites the audience to look beneath the surface.
4. **End with an Emotional Shift:** The final moments of a story can be particularly impactful if they involve an emotional shift. A story that has been filled with tension and conflict might end on a note of resolution and peace, providing emotional closure for the audience. Conversely, a story that has been relatively calm might end with a sudden emotional twist, leaving the audience with a lingering sense of unease or surprise.

Example: In a story about a family reunion, you might contrast moments of joy and nostalgia with underlying tensions and unresolved conflicts. A scene where the family laughs together around the dinner table might be followed by a quiet conversation where two characters confront the pain and distance that has grown between them over the years. This emotional contrast deepens the audience's connection to the characters and highlights the complexity of family relationships.

Just as light and shadow create depth and dimension in visual art, contrast in storytelling brings complexity, emotional resonance, and meaning to your narrative. By juxtaposing characters, themes, emotions, and settings, you create a dynamic interplay that guides the audience's focus and deepens their engagement with the story. In Zen philosophy, opposites exist in harmony, each defining the other. In storytelling, contrast serves a similar function, highlighting the most important aspects of the narrative and bringing balance to the emotional and thematic elements. Whether you are exploring the tension between characters, the opposition of themes, or the shifts in emotional tone, contrast allows you to craft a story that is both nuanced and impactful.

Zen in Rewriting: Embracing Change in the Story

Rewriting is an integral part of the creative process, yet it often feels like a daunting challenge. For many writers, the idea of tearing apart their initial drafts, reworking characters, revising dialogue, or even discarding entire sections can evoke resistance. However, in Zen philosophy, change and impermanence are seen as natural and necessary aspects of life. The act of letting go and embracing transformation is essential to growth, understanding, and mastery.

In writing, too, there is wisdom in embracing change. Rewriting is not a sign of failure but a process of refinement, a chance to bring your story closer to its true form. By adopting a Zen-like approach to rewriting—one of mindfulness, acceptance, and openness—you allow your story to evolve, improving its clarity, depth, and resonance. Rewriting becomes less about fixing mistakes and more about discovering the story's full potential.

In this chapter, we'll explore how to approach rewriting with a sense of calm, openness, and purpose, applying Zen principles to transform what might seem like a daunting task into an opportunity for creative growth. By embracing change and letting go of attachment to the first draft, you can unlock the true essence of your story and refine it into something even more powerful.

The Importance of Rewriting in the Creative Process

Rewriting is where much of the true magic of storytelling happens. While the first draft allows you to explore ideas, characters, and themes, it is often rough and incomplete. Rewriting is your opportunity to clarify, deepen, and polish the narrative. Just as a Zen artist refines a piece of calligraphy or a sculptor shapes a block of stone, the process of rewriting hones your story into its most authentic form.

Here's why rewriting is essential:

Clarifying the Story's Intent: The first draft is often an exploration of ideas, but it may not fully reflect the story's deeper intent. Rewriting allows you to clarify your vision, ensuring that every element of the story aligns with its core message or theme.

Improving Structure and Flow: The structure of a story may need significant revision after the first draft. Rewriting gives you the chance to rearrange scenes, adjust pacing, and ensure that the plot unfolds in a coherent and engaging way.

Deepening Characters and Themes: The first draft often scratches the surface of characters and themes. Rewriting allows you to delve deeper into character motivations, relationships, and arcs, while also refining the themes that give the story its emotional resonance.

Polishing Language and Dialogue: While the first draft focuses on getting ideas down, rewriting is where you polish your language, tighten dialogue, and enhance the overall quality of the prose.

Rewriting is an opportunity to take your story from raw to refined, from concept to execution. By embracing this process, you can elevate your narrative to its fullest potential.

Step 1: Cultivating a Mindful Approach to Rewriting

In Zen, mindfulness is the practice of being fully present and aware of the moment, without judgment or attachment. When applied to rewriting, mindfulness allows you to approach the process with calm and clarity, rather than frustration or resistance. By being mindful, you can objectively assess your story and make the changes necessary to improve it.

How to Practice:

1. **Detach from the First Draft:** One of the biggest challenges in rewriting is letting go of attachment to the first draft. Mindfulness helps you detach from the belief that your initial draft is precious or untouchable. Accept that the first draft was just a starting point, and embrace the idea that the story can evolve.

2. **Focus on the Present Task:** When rewriting, avoid becoming overwhelmed by the scope of the changes needed. Instead, focus on one task at a time—whether it's revising a single scene, clarifying a character's arc, or tightening dialogue. By being fully present with each task, you can approach it with greater clarity and purpose.

3. **Observe Without Judgment:** Mindfulness involves observing without judgment. As you rewrite, take a step back and evaluate your story objectively. Instead of criticizing yourself for mistakes or weaknesses in the first draft, simply observe what needs to be improved and approach it with curiosity and openness.

4. **Create a Rewriting Ritual:** Establish a rewriting routine that promotes mindfulness. This could involve setting aside a quiet time and place for rewriting, starting with a few deep breaths, or engaging in a short meditation before you begin. Creating this space allows you to approach rewriting with a calm, focused mind.

Example: Before diving into your rewrite, sit quietly for a moment and take a few deep breaths. Let go of any frustration or attachment to the first draft, and approach the task with openness and curiosity. Focus on one chapter or scene at a time, observing what works and what needs to change without judgment. Trust that the rewriting process will lead you to a stronger, clearer version of the story.

Step 2: Letting Go of What No Longer Serves the Story

In Zen, the concept of *mujō* (impermanence) teaches that everything is in a constant state of change, and clinging to what no longer serves us only causes suffering. In writing, this means recognizing when certain scenes, characters, or plot elements no longer serve the story and having the courage to let them go.

How to Practice:

1. **Identify What's Essential:** As you rewrite, ask yourself what is truly essential to the story. Which scenes, characters, or plot points are central to the narrative's core message or emotional journey? By identifying what's essential, you can focus your efforts on refining those elements while cutting or revising anything that detracts from the story's purpose.

2. **Be Willing to Cut or Revise:** One of the hardest parts of rewriting is cutting or significantly revising sections of the story that you've become attached to. However, letting go of these elements can often lead to a more focused and impactful narrative. Trust that by removing what no longer serves the story, you are making room for something better.

3. **Recognize When You're Holding On Out of Attachment:** Sometimes, writers hold on to certain scenes or characters simply because they were part of the original vision. Ask yourself if you're holding on to a particular element out of attachment rather than because it serves the story. If it no longer fits, let it go.

4. **Revise with Purpose:** When revising, make changes with a clear purpose in mind. Rather than simply tweaking for the sake of tweaking, ask yourself how each revision strengthens the story's intent, emotional impact, or clarity.

Example: You might have a beautifully written scene that you love, but upon reflection, you realize it doesn't advance the plot or contribute to the character's journey. As difficult as it may be, cutting this scene frees the story from unnecessary weight, allowing the more essential elements to shine.

Step 3: Embracing Change as Part of Growth

In Zen, change is viewed as a necessary part of growth and transformation. In storytelling, too, change—whether in the narrative, characters, or themes—is essential for deepening the story's impact. By embracing change as part of the rewriting process, you allow your story to evolve into its best form.

How to Practice:

View Rewriting as Evolution, Not Correction: Rather than seeing rewriting as simply "fixing" mistakes from the first draft, view it as part of the story's natural evolution. Each revision brings you closer to the heart of the narrative, allowing the story to grow and develop in unexpected ways.

Be Open to New Directions: During the rewriting process, you may discover new ideas, characters, or plot developments that you hadn't considered in the first draft. Be open to these new directions, even if they require significant changes. Sometimes, the act of rewriting leads to creative breakthroughs that deepen the story.

Allow Characters to Evolve: Just as your story evolves through rewriting, your characters may also grow in ways you hadn't anticipated. Be willing to let your characters change, developing more complex motivations, relationships, or arcs as the story takes shape.

Embrace Uncertainty: Rewriting often involves moments of uncertainty, where you're not sure if a change will work or if a new direction is the right one. Embrace this uncertainty as part of the creative process. Trust that the story will reveal its true form as you continue to revise and refine.

Example: During your rewrite, you might realize that a secondary character has the potential to play a much larger role in the story than originally planned. While this change may require significant revisions to the plot, embracing this new direction can lead to a more layered and engaging narrative.

Step 4: Revising with Clarity and Intent

Rewriting is an opportunity to refine the clarity and intent of your story. Just as Zen practitioners seek to remove distractions and unnecessary elements from their practice, rewriting allows you to strip away anything that clouds the story's core message, creating a narrative that is focused, clear, and purposeful.

How to Practice:

1. **Revisit the Story's Core Intent:** As you rewrite, keep the story's core intent or theme in mind. What is the heart of the story? What emotional or thematic journey are you trying to convey? By revisiting this intent regularly, you can ensure that every scene, character, and plot point aligns with the story's purpose.

2. **Clarify Character Motivations and Arcs:** One of the key elements of rewriting is refining your characters' motivations and arcs. Ensure that each character's journey is clear and purposeful, and that their actions and decisions align with their core motivations.

3. **Tighten Pacing and Structure:** Rewriting gives you the chance to improve the pacing and structure of your story. Look for areas where the narrative drags or feels rushed, and adjust the pacing to create a more balanced flow. Ensure that the structure supports the emotional and thematic progression of the story.

4. **Polish Language and Dialogue:** Finally, use rewriting as an opportunity to polish the language and dialogue. Focus on making the prose clear, concise, and impactful. Dialogue should feel natural and purposeful, reflecting the characters' personalities and emotional states.

Example: During your rewrite, you may realize that a character's motivations in the first draft were unclear or inconsistent. By revisiting the character's arc and refining their motivations, you can ensure that their actions are driven by a clear internal logic, making the story more cohesive and emotionally resonant.

Step 5: Trusting the Process of Rewriting

Zen teaches the importance of trust—trusting the process, trusting the moment, and trusting yourself. In rewriting, trust is equally important. Trust that the changes you make are leading the story in the right direction, and trust that the process of revision will ultimately bring your story to its most authentic form.

How to Practice:

1. **Trust Your Instincts:** Throughout the rewriting process, trust your instincts as a storyteller. If something feels off or doesn't resonate with the story's intent, listen to that feeling. Similarly, trust when a change feels right, even if it requires significant revisions.

2. **Be Patient with the Process:** Rewriting takes time, and it's important to be patient with yourself and the story. Trust that each draft brings you closer to the final version, even if the process feels slow or uncertain at times.

3. **Embrace the Imperfect Nature of Drafts:** No draft, even after multiple revisions, will be perfect. Trust that the story's imperfections are part of its evolution, and focus on making each draft better rather than striving for perfection.

4. **Celebrate Progress:** Rewriting can be a long and sometimes difficult process, so it's important to celebrate the progress you make along the way. Each change, no matter how small, brings you closer to your vision. Recognize and appreciate the growth that happens with each draft.

Example: As you rewrite, you may find yourself questioning certain changes or directions. Instead of second-guessing every decision, trust that your instincts are guiding the story in the right direction. Be patient with the process, and trust that each draft brings you closer to the story's true form.

Rewriting is not simply about fixing what's wrong—it's about embracing change as an essential part of the creative process. By adopting a Zen approach to rewriting, you can let go of attachment to the first draft, embrace new directions, and refine your story with clarity and purpose. In Zen, change is not something to be feared but something to be embraced as a natural part of growth and transformation. Similarly, in storytelling, rewriting allows your story to evolve into its truest form. By cultivating mindfulness, letting go of what no longer serves the story, and trusting the process, you can approach rewriting with a sense of calm, openness, and purpose. Ultimately, rewriting is an act of discovery—an opportunity to uncover the deeper layers of your story and bring them to the surface. By embracing the changes that rewriting requires, you allow your story to grow and reach its full potential, transforming it into something more powerful, resonant, and authentic than you may have ever imagined.

Writing with Visual Precision: Crafting Each Scene in Detail

Great storytelling often begins with great visualization. A well-crafted scene allows readers to not only understand what's happening but to *see* it unfold in their minds. Visual precision—the ability to paint vivid, clear pictures with words—elevates your writing, helping to create immersive worlds, rich atmospheres, and compelling emotional experiences. Just as a filmmaker carefully composes each shot, a writer must shape each scene with intention and detail, using words to direct the audience's attention and evoke a strong sense of place, action, and emotion.

In Zen, there is an emphasis on being fully present and seeing things as they truly are—observing the details of the moment with mindfulness and clarity. This practice of precise observation can be applied to writing, allowing you to craft each scene with an eye for detail, atmosphere, and emotional resonance. Writing with visual precision doesn't mean overloading the reader with description but rather using well-chosen, specific details that bring the scene to life without overwhelming the flow of the story.

In this chapter, we'll explore how to craft each scene with visual precision, focusing on how to balance detail with pacing, how to direct the reader's attention, and how to create atmosphere and mood through vivid imagery.

The Power of Visual Precision in Storytelling

Visual precision involves creating clear, vivid, and immersive imagery that allows the reader to fully experience the world of the story. It's about more than just describing what the characters see—it's about choosing details that evoke emotion, set the tone, and deepen the reader's connection to the narrative. When used effectively, visual precision transforms a flat narrative into a rich, multi-dimensional experience.

Here are the key roles visual precision plays in storytelling:

Creating Immersion: Detailed, precise descriptions draw the reader into the world of the story, making them feel as though they are physically present in the scene. Whether you're describing a bustling city street, a quiet forest, or an intimate conversation, precise visuals help the reader fully engage with the setting and action.

Guiding Focus: Just as a camera lens focuses on specific elements in a film, visual precision allows the writer to guide the reader's attention to what's most important in the scene. By highlighting key details, you can shape how the reader experiences the moment.

Establishing Mood and Atmosphere: The choice of visual details can set the emotional tone for a scene. For example, dark, shadowy imagery might evoke fear or tension, while bright, warm descriptions can create a sense of comfort or hope. The atmosphere of a scene often hinges on the writer's ability to use precise, evocative imagery.

Revealing Character and Theme: Visual details can also reveal deeper insights into characters or themes. The way a character observes their surroundings or interacts with objects can reflect their internal state, while the recurring use of specific imagery can reinforce thematic elements.

Step 1: Focusing on Key Visual Details

When writing with visual precision, it's important to focus on the key details that will bring the scene to life. Rather than overwhelming the reader with a laundry list of descriptive elements, focus on the most important and evocative details—those that will enhance the mood, reveal character, or advance the plot.

How to Practice:

1. **Choose Specific, Concrete Details:** Vague descriptions can leave the reader grasping for a clear picture of the scene. Instead of saying, "The room was messy," describe the specific objects that create that sense of messiness: "Dirty clothes were piled high in the corner, and half-empty coffee cups lined the windowsill." These concrete details create a vivid image that sticks in the reader's mind.

2. **Use Details to Reflect Emotion:** Think about how the visual details of a scene can reflect the emotional state of the characters. For example, if a character is feeling anxious, you might focus on small, disjointed details that suggest unease—perhaps the flickering of a lightbulb or the sound of a distant, erratic drip.

3. **Limit Description to What's Essential:** While it's important to include enough detail to make the scene vivid, avoid overloading the reader with unnecessary information. Choose a few key elements that will create the desired effect and leave out the rest. This balance allows the reader's imagination to fill in the gaps while keeping the narrative moving.

4. **Direct the Reader's Gaze:** Just as a filmmaker controls what the audience sees in each frame, a writer can direct the reader's attention through the choice of details. Consider what the reader needs to notice in the scene. Is it the expression on a character's face, the way the light falls through a window, or an important object on the table? Use precise description to highlight these elements and guide the reader's focus.

Example: Instead of writing, *"The garden was beautiful,"* you might focus on specific elements that create that sense of beauty: *"The roses bloomed in wild, tangled clusters, their petals velvety and deep crimson, while ivy crept along the stone wall, casting long, delicate shadows in the late afternoon sun. A faint scent of jasmine hung in the air, blending with the earthy smell of damp soil."*

These details not only paint a vivid picture but also evoke the mood of the scene, allowing the reader to feel immersed in the environment.

Step 2: Balancing Description with Pacing

One of the challenges of writing with visual precision is finding the right balance between detail and pacing. While detailed descriptions can enhance a scene, too much description can slow down the action and make the narrative feel stagnant. The key is to use visual details in a way that enriches the scene without interrupting its flow.

How to Practice:

1. **Match the Pacing to the Scene's Purpose:** Consider the purpose of the scene when deciding how much detail to include. In slower, introspective scenes, you can take more time to describe the environment and create atmosphere. In fast-paced action scenes, keep the descriptions concise and focused, so the pacing remains dynamic.

2. **Weave Description into the Action:** Instead of stopping the action to describe the setting, try weaving visual details into the flow of the narrative. For example, as a character moves through a room, you can describe the objects they pass or interact with, allowing the description to feel natural and integrated with the action.

3. **Use Short, Punchy Descriptions in Action Scenes:** During moments of high tension or action, long descriptions can disrupt the pacing. In these scenes, opt for short, impactful descriptions that convey the essentials without slowing down the momentum. Think of these as quick, vivid snapshots that capture the intensity of the moment.

4. **Create Contrast with Pacing Shifts:** Sometimes, slowing the pacing to focus on visual detail can create a powerful contrast in the narrative. For example, after an intense action sequence, you might slow down the pacing with a quiet, descriptive scene that allows the characters (and the reader) to catch their breath and reflect on what has happened.

Example: In an action scene where a character is fleeing from danger, you might describe the environment in short, sharp bursts: *"The alley was narrow and dark, its brick walls slick with rain. Her breath came in ragged gasps as her footsteps echoed off the pavement, the shadows behind her shifting as if they had a life of their own."*

This description is concise but effective, conveying the setting without slowing the pace of the chase.

Step 3: Creating Atmosphere and Mood through Imagery

Atmosphere and mood are essential components of any scene, and visual precision is one of the most powerful tools for creating these elements. By carefully selecting the imagery you use, you can evoke a specific emotional response from the reader, whether it's tension, serenity, fear, or joy.

How to Practice:

1. **Use Light and Shadow to Set the Mood:** Light and shadow can dramatically influence the mood of a scene. Soft, warm lighting might create a sense of intimacy or comfort, while harsh, stark lighting can evoke tension or unease. Similarly, the use of shadows can create mystery or fear. Think about how light and shadow play a role in your scene and use them to enhance the emotional tone.

2. **Choose Colors with Emotional Resonance:** Colors carry emotional weight, and using color in your descriptions can subtly influence the reader's mood. For example, bright, vivid colors can evoke energy and excitement, while muted or dark tones can create a sense of melancholy or foreboding. Consider how the color palette of your scene aligns with its emotional content.

3. **Pay Attention to Sensory Details Beyond Sight:** While visual precision focuses on what the reader can see, other sensory details—such as sound, smell, touch, and taste—can also contribute to the atmosphere. The distant sound of thunder, the smell of rain on asphalt, or the texture of rough stone beneath a character's fingers can all add depth and emotional texture to the scene.

4. **Use Nature to Reflect Emotion:** The natural world often serves as a mirror for the emotional states of characters. A stormy sky might reflect internal turmoil, while a clear, star-filled night could represent peace or clarity. By aligning the external environment with the internal emotions of the characters, you can create a deeper connection between the reader and the story.

Example: To create an eerie, unsettling atmosphere, you might describe a scene like this: *"The moon hung low in the sky, casting a pale, sickly light over the empty street. The wind whispered through the trees, their branches twisting like gnarled fingers against the inky blackness. Every creak and rustle seemed amplified in the silence, as if the night itself were holding its breath, waiting for something to happen."*

This description uses light, shadow, and sound to evoke a sense of foreboding, drawing the reader into the mood of the scene.

· · · ·

STEP 4: REVEALING CHARACTER through Visual Detail

Visual precision can also be used to reveal character traits, emotions, and development. The way a character observes their surroundings, interacts with objects, or even describes a scene can provide insight into their personality, mood, or state of mind. By paying attention to how characters engage with their environment, you can add depth to their portrayal.

How to Practice:

1. **Show Character Emotions Through Observation:** A character's emotional state can be reflected in how they perceive their surroundings. For example, a character who is feeling anxious might notice small, disjointed details in a room, while a character who is calm might take in the scene with broader, more relaxed observations.

2. **Reveal Character Traits Through Interaction:** How a character interacts with their environment can reveal key aspects of their personality. A meticulous character might arrange objects in perfect order, while

a carefree character might leave items scattered haphazardly. These small details give the reader clues about who the character is without needing to explicitly state it.

3. **Use Symbolic Objects to Reflect Inner Conflict:** Sometimes, objects in a scene can serve as symbols of a character's internal struggle or desires. A mirror might reflect a character's fractured sense of identity, or a locked door could represent a barrier they are trying to overcome. These symbolic details add layers of meaning to the scene.

4. **Let Characters See the World Differently:** Different characters may observe the same environment in entirely different ways, based on their personalities, backgrounds, or emotional states. Consider how each character's perspective shapes what they notice and how they describe it. This variation adds richness to both the characters and the world they inhabit.

Example: If a character is feeling overwhelmed, you might describe the scene from their point of view in a fragmented, anxious way: *"The room felt too small, the walls closing in around her. Papers cluttered the desk, their edges crumpled and torn. The ticking of the clock was too loud, each second dragging on like an eternity. She couldn't focus—couldn't breathe."*

This description uses the character's perception of the environment to reflect their internal state of anxiety and overwhelm.

Step 5: Refining Visual Precision through Revision

Writing with visual precision often requires careful revision. The first draft may include either too little or too much detail, or the descriptions may not fully capture the mood or atmosphere you intended. By revisiting your scenes during revision, you can refine your descriptions, ensuring they are vivid, purposeful, and aligned with the emotional tone of the story.

How to Practice:

1. **Assess Each Scene for Visual Clarity:** During revision, read through each scene and assess whether the visual details are clear and evocative. Are there any vague or generic descriptions that could be replaced with more specific, concrete imagery? Look for opportunities to sharpen your descriptions.
2. **Cut Unnecessary Description:** Sometimes, the first draft includes too much description, which can bog down the pacing. During revision, identify any details that don't contribute to the scene's mood, action, or emotional impact, and cut or condense them to streamline the narrative.
3. **Enhance Atmosphere and Emotion:** Revisit scenes where the atmosphere or emotional tone feels flat or underdeveloped. Use visual precision to heighten the mood—whether through changes in lighting, color, sensory details, or the natural environment.
4. **Fine-Tune Symbolism and Visual Themes:** If your story includes recurring symbols or visual themes, ensure that they are consistent and intentional throughout the narrative. Look for opportunities to subtly reinforce these elements through visual detail without overemphasizing them.

Example: During revision, you might realize that a description of a character's bedroom feels generic and doesn't reflect their personality. In the revised version, you could add specific details that reveal more about who they are: *"Posters of vintage jazz musicians covered the walls, their edges curled from years of sunlight. A stack of vinyl records sat next to an old turntable, and a well-worn armchair, patched with faded fabric, stood in the corner. The faint scent of tobacco and cedar lingered in the air."*

These details create a vivid sense of place while also revealing the character's tastes and lifestyle.

Writing with visual precision is about more than just describing what happens—it's about crafting scenes that engage the reader's senses, evoke emotion, and immerse them fully in the world of the story. By focusing on key details, balancing description with pacing, and using imagery to create atmosphere and reveal character, you can transform your writing into a rich, multi-layered experience. Zen teaches us to be fully present and aware of the moment, observing the details of life with clarity and intention. By applying this mindfulness to your writing, you can approach each scene with the same level of focus and precision, ensuring that every word serves a purpose and every image contributes to the story's emotional and thematic depth. Ultimately, writing with visual precision allows you to take your readers on a journey—not just through the plot, but through the vivid, textured world you've created.

Characters as Reflections of Self: The Zen of Understanding Others

In storytelling, characters are more than just fictional constructs. They are mirrors reflecting facets of the human condition—our desires, fears, ambitions, and flaws. Every character we create embodies a part of ourselves or the world we observe, and through them, we explore the complexities of identity, relationships, and the human spirit. Zen philosophy, with its emphasis on interconnectedness and self-awareness, offers valuable insights into understanding others through the lens of ourselves.

Just as Zen encourages us to look inward to gain insight into the external world, writing characters invites us to tap into our own emotions, experiences, and perceptions. By understanding ourselves, we gain a deeper understanding of our characters, allowing them to become authentic, complex beings who resonate with readers on a profound level. This chapter will explore the Zen-like process of using characters as reflections of the self, emphasizing the interconnectedness between the writer's inner world and the characters they create.

The Interconnectedness of Self and Character

In Zen, the concept of non-duality teaches that the self is not separate from the world around us. We are connected to everything, and our perceptions shape our reality. Similarly, characters in a story are extensions of the writer's inner world, shaped by the writer's thoughts, emotions, and experiences. Understanding characters begins with understanding the self.

Here's why the interconnectedness between self and character matters:

1. **Creating Authentic Characters:** When you draw from your own emotions, experiences, and worldview, your characters become more authentic and multidimensional. They are not just vehicles for plot advancement but fully realized individuals with their own internal lives, shaped by the same forces that shape you.
2. **Exploring Different Aspects of the Self:** Each character represents a different aspect of the writer's psyche. Whether it's a reflection of your strengths, insecurities, dreams, or fears, characters allow you to explore parts of yourself in a way that's both personal and universal.
3. **Empathy and Understanding:** By seeing characters as reflections of the self, you develop empathy for them—even the antagonists. This empathy allows you to write with nuance, understanding the motivations, fears, and desires that drive each character's actions, making them more relatable and human.
4. **Universal Connection:** The more deeply you connect with your characters, the more likely they are to resonate with readers. Human emotions and experiences are universal, and when you write characters with emotional truth, readers will recognize pieces of themselves in those characters, creating a powerful connection.

Step 1: Looking Inward to Create Outward

To create authentic, multidimensional characters, you must first look inward. Zen practice encourages self-reflection and awareness, and the same approach can be applied to writing. By exploring your own emotions, fears, motivations, and beliefs, you gain the material needed to breathe life into your characters.

How to Practice:

1. **Explore Your Own Emotional Landscape:** Before creating a character, take time to explore your own emotions. How do you react to fear, joy, anger, or grief? What are your insecurities, your deepest desires, or the challenges you face? By understanding your own emotional responses, you can infuse your characters

with similar depth.

2. **Use Personal Experiences as a Foundation:** Think about key moments in your life—challenges you've overcome, relationships that have shaped you, or experiences that have left a lasting impact. These moments can serve as inspiration for your characters' journeys. Whether it's the fear of failure, the joy of success, or the pain of loss, these emotions are universal, and using them as a foundation makes your characters more relatable.

3. **Embrace Vulnerability:** Writing characters as reflections of the self requires vulnerability. You must be willing to expose parts of yourself, including your fears and flaws. By allowing your characters to embody these aspects, you create emotionally honest and compelling stories.

4. **Understand Your Own Motivations:** What drives you? What are your goals, dreams, and fears? By understanding your own motivations, you can create characters with clear, compelling motivations of their own. Whether it's the desire for success, love, or revenge, characters who are driven by deep, personal motivations feel more authentic and layered.

Example: If you've experienced the fear of failure in your own life, you might create a character who is driven by a fear of not being good enough. Perhaps they constantly strive for perfection, avoiding risks to protect themselves from potential failure. This emotional foundation creates a character who is relatable and complex, because their fears and desires reflect real human experiences.

Step 2: Seeing Characters as Mirrors

In Zen, the concept of self-awareness extends beyond the individual. We learn about ourselves through our relationships with others. Similarly, characters often act as mirrors, reflecting different aspects of ourselves and each other. By seeing characters as reflections—of yourself and of one another—you can create dynamic relationships and internal conflicts that drive the story.

How to Practice:

Explore the Shadow Self: In Jungian psychology, the "shadow" refers to the parts of ourselves that we repress or deny. When writing characters, consider how each one reflects a different part of your shadow self—your insecurities, fears, or negative traits. These characters provide an opportunity to explore parts of yourself that you might not be comfortable confronting directly.

Create Characters Who Contrast with One Another: Just as characters reflect different aspects of the self, they can also reflect contrasting qualities in each other. Consider how one character's traits—such as optimism, generosity, or confidence—might reflect or oppose another character's traits, such as pessimism, selfishness, or insecurity. These contrasts create dynamic relationships and tension.

Examine Relationships as Reflections: In Zen, relationships are often seen as a reflection of our internal world. Consider how your characters' relationships mirror their internal struggles. For example, a character who struggles with trust issues might have a strained relationship with someone they love, reflecting their internal battle between vulnerability and self-protection.

Let Characters Teach You About Yourself: As you write, allow your characters to reveal new insights about your own inner world. Sometimes, characters surprise us, behaving in ways we didn't anticipate. These moments often reflect something within us that we hadn't fully acknowledged. Embrace these revelations as opportunities for self-discovery.

Example: You might create two characters—one who is fiercely independent and another who is deeply insecure about their reliance on others. Their relationship could reflect an internal conflict within yourself: the desire for self-sufficiency versus the fear of being alone. As these characters interact, their contrasting traits reveal more about each other and, by extension, more about the writer's own internal struggles.

Step 3: Developing Empathy for All Characters

Zen emphasizes compassion and empathy, not only for others but for oneself. In storytelling, this means developing empathy for all your characters, including antagonists. Every character, no matter how flawed or villainous, has a story, a set of motivations, and a perspective that is shaped by their experiences. By approaching your characters with empathy, you create well-rounded, believable individuals who feel human, even in their darkest moments.

How to Practice:

Understand Your Antagonist's Motivations: Rather than viewing antagonists as purely evil or malicious, explore their motivations with empathy. What drives them to act the way they do? What fears, desires, or past traumas shape their behavior? By understanding their motivations, you create more nuanced, complex antagonists who feel human rather than one-dimensional.

Give Every Character a Justification for Their Actions: Even if a character's actions seem misguided or harmful, they likely have a reason for behaving the way they do. Try to put yourself in their shoes—how do they justify their choices? What do they believe they are gaining or protecting? This empathy makes all characters, even minor ones, feel real and relatable.

Embrace Flaws and Weaknesses: Just as you must be willing to explore your own flaws, you must also embrace the flaws of your characters. No one is perfect, and characters who are overly idealized or flawless often feel flat. Allow your characters to make mistakes, grapple with their weaknesses, and grow from their struggles.

Consider Each Character's Perspective: Every character in your story has their own perspective, shaped by their unique experiences and worldview. Even if you don't agree with their actions, approach their perspective with empathy. What led them to see the world this way? How do they justify their choices? By understanding their perspective, you can write characters with depth and complexity.

Example: Your antagonist might be a ruthless businessperson who manipulates others for personal gain. Rather than portraying them as purely evil, you could explore their backstory, revealing that they grew up in poverty and developed a fear of scarcity. Their ruthless behavior is driven by a deep-seated fear of losing everything they've worked for. This motivation adds layers to the character, making them more than just a villain—they become a complex individual whose actions, while harmful, are rooted in fear and survival.

Step 4: Writing Characters as Reflections of the World

Just as characters reflect the self, they can also reflect the world around them—its values, conflicts, and social structures. In Zen, the self and the world are interconnected, and by understanding one, we gain insight into the other. Similarly, by creating characters who reflect societal issues, cultural norms, or larger themes, you can use storytelling to explore the complexities of the world.

How to Practice:

1. **Use Characters to Explore Societal Issues:** Characters can serve as vehicles for exploring larger societal or cultural issues. Whether it's inequality, prejudice, power dynamics, or environmental concerns, characters can embody the struggles and conflicts that exist in the world around them. Through their experiences, you can comment on these broader themes.

2. **Reflect Cultural Norms and Values:** Consider how your characters reflect or challenge the cultural norms and values of their society. A character who rebels against societal expectations might represent the desire for freedom or individualism, while a character who adheres to tradition might reflect the comfort found in stability and order.

3. **Create Characters Who Embody Larger Themes:** Just as characters can reflect personal struggles, they can also embody larger, universal themes such as love, loss, sacrifice, or redemption. By aligning your characters with these themes, you create a narrative that speaks to broader human experiences, allowing readers to connect with the story on multiple levels.

4. **Use Dialogue and Interaction to Reflect Social Dynamics:** How your characters interact with one another can reveal deeper social dynamics. For example, dialogue between characters of different social classes, genders, or backgrounds can highlight issues of privilege, power, or inequality. By carefully crafting these interactions, you can explore complex social dynamics within your story.

Example: In a story set in a dystopian society, your protagonist might struggle against a rigid system of control, representing themes of freedom and oppression. Their journey could reflect larger societal issues, such as the loss of individual rights or the impact of authoritarianism on personal identity. Through their experiences, you explore not only their internal conflict but also the societal forces shaping their world.

Step 5: Revising Characters with Self-Awareness

Creating characters as reflections of the self is an ongoing process that often requires revision and self-awareness. Just as Zen encourages continuous self-reflection and growth, writing characters is a dynamic process in which you must be willing to revise, refine, and deepen your understanding of both yourself and your characters.

How to Practice:

Reflect on How Characters Have Evolved: During revision, take time to reflect on how your characters have evolved throughout the writing process. Are they still true to their original conception, or have they grown in ways that surprise you? Consider how their journey mirrors your own growth as a writer and person.

Deepen Characters Through Internal Conflict: Characters often become more complex through internal conflict. Revisit your characters' internal struggles and ask yourself if these conflicts are fully realized. Are they grappling with their fears, desires, or contradictions in a meaningful way? Deepening their internal conflict can add layers to their development.

Align Characters with the Story's Themes: Ensure that your characters' journeys are aligned with the story's overarching themes. If a character feels disconnected from the main narrative, consider revising their arc to better reflect the story's emotional or thematic core.

Be Open to Change: Just as in Zen, where change is embraced as part of growth, be open to changing your characters as you revise. You may find that a character needs to take a different path or that their role in the story shifts. Embrace these changes as part of the creative process.

Example: During revision, you might realize that your protagonist's internal conflict isn't fully explored. By revisiting their backstory and motivations, you discover new layers to their struggle—perhaps their fear of failure is rooted in a deeper fear of disappointing their family. This added layer of internal conflict makes the character more relatable and their journey more compelling.

Writing characters as reflections of the self is a deeply personal and profound process. Just as Zen teaches us to look inward to understand the world, writing encourages us to explore our own inner landscape to create characters who resonate with universal truths. Through self-awareness, empathy, and reflection, you can create characters who are not just fictional constructs but fully realized individuals, each with their own motivations, struggles, and desires. By embracing the interconnectedness between the self and others, you gain a deeper understanding of your characters, allowing them to reflect the complexities of the human experience. Whether exploring personal fears and desires, societal issues, or larger themes, your characters become mirrors through which both you and your readers can see the world more clearly. Ultimately, the Zen of understanding others through characters is about embracing the complexity of human nature.

The Art of Visual Metaphor: Symbolism in Storytelling

In storytelling, symbols act as a bridge between the tangible world of the narrative and the intangible realm of deeper meaning. Visual metaphors and symbols allow writers to infuse their stories with layers of significance, subtly communicating themes, emotions, and character arcs without overtly stating them. Like the brushstrokes of a Zen painter, where each stroke conveys both form and meaning, symbols in storytelling serve as simple yet profound tools for enriching the narrative.

In Zen philosophy, much is communicated through silence, suggestion, and simplicity. The same principles apply to the use of symbolism in writing. By embedding visual metaphors in the narrative, a writer can evoke complex ideas and emotions while allowing the reader to discover meaning on their own terms. This chapter explores the art of using visual metaphor and symbolism in storytelling, focusing on how to incorporate meaningful symbols that elevate your story and resonate with your audience on a deeper level.

The Power of Symbolism in Storytelling

Symbolism allows a story to transcend its literal meaning and engage with broader, universal themes. When used effectively, symbols provide insight into characters, foreshadow events, and reinforce the emotional core of a narrative. Visual metaphors, in particular, help to create a rich sensory experience that makes the story more vivid and resonant for the audience.

Here's why symbolism is such a powerful tool in storytelling:

1. **Evoking Deeper Meaning:** Symbols allow writers to communicate complex ideas and emotions without needing to state them explicitly. By using metaphors and visual imagery, you can evoke themes such as love, loss, freedom, or fear in a way that feels organic and subtle.

2. **Creating Emotional Resonance:** Well-chosen symbols can evoke powerful emotional responses from readers, drawing them into the emotional world of the story. When a symbol recurs throughout the narrative, it reinforces the emotional stakes and helps readers connect with the characters on a deeper level.

3. **Foreshadowing and Thematic Unity:** Symbols can be used to foreshadow key events, hinting at what is to come without giving away too much. They also provide thematic unity, linking seemingly disparate elements of the story together in a way that feels cohesive and intentional.

4. **Engaging the Reader's Imagination:** Symbolism encourages readers to engage with the story on a more active level, inviting them to interpret the underlying meanings and make connections between the visual imagery and the narrative's themes.

. . . .

STEP 1: IDENTIFYING Core Themes for Symbolism

To use symbolism effectively, you must first identify the core themes or messages of your story. Symbols should serve as visual metaphors for these deeper themes, enhancing the narrative by reinforcing the emotional or philosophical ideas you want to convey.

How to Practice:

1. **Define the Central Themes:** What are the main themes of your story? Is it about love and sacrifice, the passage of time, or the search for identity? By identifying the central themes, you can choose symbols that reflect and reinforce these ideas throughout the narrative.

2. **Align Symbols with Emotional Arcs:** Consider how symbols can be tied to the emotional journeys of

your characters. For example, a character going through a personal transformation might be associated with symbols of rebirth or renewal, such as the changing seasons or a phoenix rising from the ashes.

3. **Use Simple, Universal Symbols:** While symbols can be personal, they are most effective when they tap into universal human experiences. Symbols such as light and darkness, water, fire, or the moon carry deep emotional and cultural significance across time and place. These universal symbols can be adapted to fit the unique context of your story.

4. **Choose Symbols that Evolve:** Symbols can evolve over the course of the story, reflecting changes in the characters or themes. A symbol that begins with one meaning might take on new significance as the narrative progresses, deepening the audience's understanding of the story.

Example: If your story explores themes of freedom and confinement, you might use birds as a recurring symbol. Early in the story, a bird trapped in a cage could represent the protagonist's feeling of being trapped in their circumstances. As the character grows and gains agency, you might show a bird flying freely, symbolizing their newfound freedom.

Step 2: Embedding Visual Metaphors in the Setting

The setting of your story provides a natural canvas for visual metaphors and symbols. By embedding symbolic elements in the environment, you can create a rich visual landscape that reinforces the themes and emotions of the narrative without drawing attention away from the action.

How to Practice:

Use Natural Elements as Symbols: Nature is full of potent symbols that can be incorporated into the setting. Water, for example, often symbolizes change, emotion, or purification, while fire represents destruction or transformation. Think about how natural elements in the setting can reflect the internal or external conflicts of the characters.

Align Setting with Character's Emotional State: The environment can serve as a metaphor for a character's internal state. A stormy night might reflect a character's inner turmoil, while a calm, sunny day could symbolize a moment of peace or clarity. By aligning the setting with the emotional arc of the scene, you add an additional layer of meaning.

Use Objects as Symbols: Everyday objects in the setting can take on symbolic meaning if used thoughtfully. A cracked mirror might symbolize a fractured sense of identity, while a locked door could represent a character's emotional barriers or secrets. These objects don't need to be over-explained—let their significance emerge naturally as the story unfolds.

Create Contrast with Symbolic Settings: Sometimes, contrast can enhance the symbolism of a setting. For example, a scene of violence or conflict set in a peaceful, idyllic garden might emphasize the starkness of the action, highlighting the themes of innocence lost or the fragility of peace.

Example: If your protagonist is experiencing a deep sense of isolation, you might set a scene in a vast, empty landscape—perhaps a barren desert or an open sea—where the sheer scale of the environment mirrors their emotional detachment from the world around them.

Step 3: Incorporating Symbolism into Character Development

Symbols can also be woven into character development, serving as metaphors for the characters' internal struggles, growth, or transformation. By associating characters with specific symbols, you create a visual shorthand for their emotional and psychological journey.

How to Practice:

Assign a Symbol to Each Character: Consider giving each of your main characters a symbolic element that reflects their personality or journey. For example, a character who is constantly searching for answers might be associated with light or fire, while a character who is mysterious or secretive might be linked to shadows or water.

Use Clothing and Accessories as Symbols: What a character wears can serve as a subtle symbol of their identity or emotional state. A character who wears a necklace with sentimental value might be holding on to the past, while a character who removes a piece of jewelry may be letting go of an old identity.

Evolve the Symbol as the Character Grows: As characters evolve, the symbols associated with them can also change. For example, a character who begins the story wearing dark, heavy clothing might shift to lighter, more colorful attire as they undergo personal growth. These symbolic changes visually reinforce the character's transformation.

Use Symbolic Actions to Reveal Character: Sometimes, a character's actions can carry symbolic meaning. A character who plants a tree might be seeking stability or a new beginning, while a character who shatters a mirror might be rejecting an old self or confronting the truth. These actions don't need to be explicitly explained—their symbolic meaning will resonate with readers on a subconscious level.

Example: If your protagonist is someone who has always followed the rules and lived a rigid, predictable life, you might introduce a symbol of control—such as a tightly wound pocket watch. As the story progresses and they begin to embrace uncertainty and spontaneity, you could have a scene where they abandon the watch, symbolizing their willingness to let go of control.

Step 4: Using Recurring Symbols for Thematic Cohesion

One of the most effective ways to use symbolism in storytelling is through repetition. When a symbol recurs throughout the narrative, it creates a sense of thematic cohesion, linking different parts of the story together and reinforcing the central message or emotional arc.

How to Practice:

1. **Introduce the Symbol Early:** To create a recurring symbol, introduce it early in the story, even if its significance isn't immediately clear. As the narrative progresses, the symbol can take on new layers of meaning, deepening its impact on the reader.
2. **Repeat the Symbol in Key Moments:** Use the symbol during important moments of character development or plot progression. Its recurrence will signal to the reader that this symbol is tied to the story's larger themes, and it will help reinforce the emotional resonance of these moments.
3. **Evolve the Symbol Over Time:** As the characters and story evolve, the meaning of the symbol can shift. A symbol that once represented loss might come to symbolize acceptance or growth by the end of the story. This evolution keeps the symbol dynamic and meaningful throughout the narrative.
4. **Use the Symbol in the Climax or Resolution:** The climax or resolution of the story is an ideal place to bring the symbol full circle. Its presence in the final moments of the narrative can provide emotional closure and reinforce the story's themes in a powerful way.

Example: If a recurring symbol in your story is a key, it might first appear as a literal object—a key to a locked room. Over time, the key could take on metaphorical significance, representing access to hidden truths or unlocking one's potential. In the climax, the protagonist might finally use the key to open a door, symbolizing their acceptance of a new reality or their readiness to face a long-buried secret.

Step 5: Allowing Room for Interpretation

One of the most beautiful aspects of symbolism is its ability to invite multiple interpretations. Just as a Zen koan invites reflection and contemplation, symbols in storytelling should not be overly explained or rigid in their meaning. By leaving room for the reader to interpret symbols in their own way, you create a more engaging and personal experience.

How to Practice:

Resist the Urge to Over-Explain: Allow symbols to speak for themselves. Avoid explaining their meaning too explicitly in the narrative, as this can diminish their impact. Trust that your readers will understand and interpret the symbolism based on their own experiences and perspectives.

Encourage Ambiguity: Some symbols are most effective when their meaning is ambiguous or open to interpretation. This ambiguity invites readers to engage more deeply with the story, reflecting on what the symbol means to them personally. For example, a symbol like a mirror might represent self-reflection, vanity, or illusion, depending on how the reader interprets it.

Let the Symbol Carry Emotional Weight: Symbols should evoke emotion without needing explanation. A recurring symbol—a faded photograph, a dying plant, a flickering candle—can resonate with readers on an emotional level, even if they don't fully understand its meaning right away.

Encourage Discussion and Reflection: The best symbols linger in the reader's mind long after the story is over, prompting reflection and discussion. By allowing your symbols to remain somewhat open-ended, you encourage readers to think more deeply about the story's themes and emotional resonance.

Example: In a story where the symbol of a river is used to represent change and the passage of time, you might leave it up to the reader to decide whether the river symbolizes positive growth or the inevitability of loss. By allowing the river's meaning to remain open to interpretation, you create space for the reader to reflect on their own relationship with change and time.

Incorporating visual metaphor and symbolism into your storytelling allows you to communicate deeper meanings and emotions in a subtle, evocative way. Just as Zen encourages contemplation and the appreciation of simplicity, the use of symbols in writing invites readers to engage with the story on multiple levels, finding personal meaning in the imagery and metaphors.

Symbols enhance the narrative by reinforcing themes, guiding emotional responses, and providing a sense of unity and cohesion throughout the story. Whether through natural elements, recurring objects, or character-driven actions, symbols serve as a visual language that speaks to both the conscious and subconscious mind.

Ultimately, the art of symbolism in storytelling is about trusting the reader's ability to interpret and find meaning in the symbols you create. By embedding rich, layered metaphors in your story, you elevate the narrative, creating a more immersive, thought-provoking, and emotionally resonant experience for your audience.

Zen and the Act of Listening: Hearing Your Characters Speak

In Zen practice, the act of listening is more than simply hearing words; it is about being fully present and attuned to the nuances of silence, sound, and the space between them. True listening requires openness, mindfulness, and a quieting of the self in order to understand what is being communicated on deeper levels. When applied to writing, this concept of deep listening becomes essential for hearing your characters speak in a way that feels authentic, true to their nature, and reflective of the world they inhabit.

Writing believable dialogue is a skill that goes beyond crafting clever lines or witty banter. It involves creating space for your characters to reveal their personalities, emotions, and desires through their words. By listening carefully to your characters, you allow them to express themselves naturally, giving life to their voices in a way that resonates with readers.

This chapter will explore the Zen-like process of listening to your characters, highlighting how to tune into their voices, capture their unique rhythms of speech, and create dialogue that is both true to the character and integral to the story. Through mindful listening, you can unlock the authentic voice of each character, allowing their individuality to shine through and their conversations to feel grounded in reality.

The Importance of Listening to Your Characters

Listening to your characters is essential for creating dialogue that feels natural, engaging, and true to who they are. It's not about forcing your own words or ideas onto them, but rather about stepping back and allowing their voices to emerge. Just as Zen teaches us to listen without judgment or expectation, writing dialogue requires openness to the nuances of character speech, tone, and intention.

Here's why listening is so important when writing characters:

Authentic Dialogue: When you listen carefully to your characters, their dialogue feels authentic and true to their personalities. Each character speaks in a way that reflects their background, beliefs, and emotional state, rather than sounding like a mouthpiece for the author.

Character Development: Dialogue is one of the most powerful tools for character development. By listening to your characters speak, you gain insight into their inner worlds—their desires, fears, motivations, and conflicts. This, in turn, informs how they interact with other characters and navigate the story.

Emotional Resonance: Listening allows you to tune into the emotional undertones of your characters' words. The way a character speaks—whether with anger, vulnerability, hesitation, or joy—reveals their emotional state and adds depth to their relationships with others.

Subtext and Unspoken Communication: In Zen, much is communicated through what is left unsaid. Similarly, in writing, listening to the subtext of your characters' dialogue helps you capture the unspoken emotions and intentions that lie beneath the surface. This adds complexity to the dialogue, allowing readers to engage with the deeper layers of the conversation.

Step 1: Quieting the Writer's Mind to Hear the Character's Voice

In order to truly hear your characters speak, you must first quiet your own mind. Just as Zen meditation encourages practitioners to let go of distractions and mental noise, writing dialogue requires you to quiet your own inner voice so that you can be fully present with the character. This means setting aside your preconceived notions about what the character should say or how the conversation should unfold, and instead allowing the character's voice to guide you.

How to Practice:

1. **Start with Character Immersion:** Before writing dialogue, spend time immersing yourself in the

character's world. What are their core motivations, desires, and fears? How do they see the world, and how does this influence the way they communicate? By grounding yourself in the character's mindset, you can better understand how they would speak.

2. **Let Go of Preconceptions:** Approach the scene with an open mind, without forcing specific lines of dialogue or outcomes. Trust that the character's voice will emerge naturally if you give them the space to speak. Be willing to let the conversation take unexpected turns, even if it deviates from your original plan.

3. **Listen Without Judgment:** As your character begins to speak, listen to their words without immediately editing or critiquing them. Let the conversation flow freely, allowing the character's voice to develop organically. You can always revise later, but during the initial drafting, focus on capturing the essence of their voice.

4. **Engage in Dialogue, Not Monologue:** Remember that conversation is a two-way exchange. Pay attention to how your character responds to others, not just what they say. How do they react to being questioned, challenged, or supported? Listening to their responses in the moment will help you craft dialogue that feels dynamic and alive.

Example: If you're writing a scene where two characters are arguing, resist the urge to pre-plan each character's retorts. Instead, place yourself in the mindset of each character and let the argument unfold naturally. What emotions are driving their words—frustration, fear, guilt? By listening to the emotional undercurrent of the conversation, you'll capture a more authentic and spontaneous exchange.

• • • •

STEP 2: TUNING INTO Each Character's Unique Voice

Just as every person has their own way of speaking, each character in your story should have a unique voice that reflects their personality, background, and worldview. Listening to your characters means paying attention to their individual speech patterns, word choices, and rhythms, so that their dialogue feels distinct and true to who they are.

How to Practice:

Consider the Character's Background: A character's upbringing, education, culture, and life experiences all influence the way they speak. A character who grew up in a formal, traditional household might speak with more structured, measured language, while a character who spent their youth on the streets might have a more casual, colloquial tone.

Capture Their Speech Rhythm: Pay attention to the natural rhythm of each character's speech. Some characters might speak in short, clipped sentences, while others might be more verbose or meandering. Does the character speak quickly when they're excited, or do they take their time, carefully choosing their words? These details add texture and authenticity to the dialogue.

Listen for Word Choices and Tone: Word choice can reveal a great deal about a character's personality and mood. A character who uses precise, technical language might be analytical or intellectual, while a character who speaks in metaphors or colorful expressions might have a more creative or emotional nature. Tone, too, can reveal the character's emotional state—whether they're sarcastic, defensive, sincere, or playful.

Allow for Imperfections: Real people don't speak in perfect sentences, and neither should your characters. Allow for the natural imperfections of speech—pauses, interruptions, hesitations, or repetitions. These moments of imperfection make the dialogue feel more realistic and grounded in the character's experience.

Example: Imagine two characters from different social backgrounds—one a university professor, the other a mechanic. The professor might speak with formal, academic language, while the mechanic might use more practical, no-nonsense expressions. Their distinct voices not only reflect their individual backgrounds but also add depth to their relationship, as their differing communication styles create both tension and connection.

Step 3: Listening for Subtext and Unspoken Emotions

In Zen, silence and stillness often carry as much meaning as words. The same is true in dialogue, where what is left unsaid can be just as powerful as the spoken words. Listening to your characters means tuning into the subtext of their conversations—the emotions, intentions, and desires that simmer beneath the surface.

How to Practice:

Identify What's Not Being Said: Pay attention to what your characters are not saying, and why. Is a character avoiding a particular subject because it's too painful to discuss? Are they holding back their true feelings in order to protect themselves or others? This subtext adds depth to the conversation and gives the reader insight into the character's inner world.

Let Actions Speak for Themselves: Sometimes, a character's body language or actions convey more than their words. A character who says, "I'm fine," while avoiding eye contact or fidgeting with their hands might be masking their true feelings of anxiety or fear. Listening to these non-verbal cues helps you capture the full emotional scope of the scene.

Use Silence Purposefully: Moments of silence in dialogue can be powerful tools for conveying tension, uncertainty, or reflection. A pause between lines can signal that a character is grappling with a difficult decision or processing their emotions. These silences create space for the reader to interpret the unspoken meaning behind the words.

Layer Meaning into the Conversation: Dialogue with subtext often has multiple layers of meaning. On the surface, the characters might be talking about something mundane, but beneath the surface, they are grappling with deeper issues. This layering creates complexity and invites readers to engage with the emotional and psychological dimensions of the conversation.

Example: In a scene where two characters are discussing plans for a vacation, the subtext might reveal that one character is deeply uncertain about the future of their relationship. While the words exchanged are light-hearted and focused on the logistics of the trip, their hesitant pauses and avoidance of eye contact suggest that there are unspoken doubts and fears beneath the surface. This creates tension and emotional depth without needing to explicitly state the character's concerns.

Step 4: Allowing Characters to Change and Evolve

Characters, like real people, evolve over time. As they grow and change throughout the story, their dialogue should reflect this evolution. Listening to your characters means staying attuned to how their voices shift in response to their experiences, relationships, and emotional journeys.

How to Practice:

Track Character Growth: As your characters develop and undergo challenges, their speech patterns, word choices, and tone may change. A character who starts off shy and reserved might become more confident and assertive as they gain strength, while a character who begins with a playful, carefree attitude might adopt a more serious tone after experiencing loss or hardship.

Reflect Emotional Shifts in Dialogue: Characters' emotions often fluctuate over the course of a conversation or scene. A character who begins a conversation feeling hopeful might become defensive or withdrawn if they feel misunderstood or rejected. Listening for these emotional shifts helps you capture the ebb and flow of dialogue in a realistic and engaging way.

Allow Relationships to Shape Dialogue: Relationships between characters naturally evolve over time, and this evolution should be reflected in their dialogue. Characters who once spoke to each other with formal politeness might adopt a more relaxed, intimate tone as their bond deepens, while characters whose relationship is deteriorating might speak more curtly or with tension.

Embrace Moments of Transformation: Sometimes, a single conversation can serve as a turning point for a character, marking a moment of transformation or self-realization. In these moments, listen for how the character's voice might shift, signaling their internal change. This could be a shift in the way they express themselves, the words they choose, or the tone they adopt.

Example: At the beginning of a story, a character who is grappling with low self-esteem might speak hesitantly, using uncertain language like "I think" or "Maybe." As they grow more confident over the course of the story, their dialogue might become more direct and assertive, with shorter, more definitive statements. This change in dialogue mirrors their internal transformation, allowing the reader to track their growth.

Step 5: Revising Dialogue with a Mindful Ear

Just as Zen practice emphasizes continual mindfulness and reflection, the process of revising dialogue requires you to return to your characters' voices with fresh ears. During revision, listen carefully to the dialogue you've written, ensuring that it feels true to the character and the moment. This is where you refine and polish the voices of your characters, making sure they resonate with clarity and purpose.

How to Practice:

1. **Read Dialogue Aloud:** One of the best ways to test the authenticity of dialogue is to read it aloud. This allows you to hear the rhythm, pacing, and natural flow of the conversation. If the dialogue feels stilted or unnatural, revise it until it sounds like something the character would realistically say.

2. **Check for Consistency in Voice:** During revision, ensure that each character's voice remains consistent throughout the story. A character who speaks in a casual, laid-back tone in one scene shouldn't suddenly adopt formal, elaborate language in the next unless there's a clear reason for the shift. Listen for any inconsistencies and revise accordingly.

3. **Refine Subtext and Emotion:** Revisit scenes where the emotional stakes are high, and listen for the subtext beneath the words. Are the characters' emotions coming through in their dialogue, even if they're not explicitly stated? If a scene feels flat, consider revising to add more emotional depth through tone, word choice, or pauses in the conversation.

4. **Eliminate Excess or Redundancy:** In revision, be mindful of dialogue that feels excessive or redundant. Characters don't need to say everything—they can leave things unsaid, trusting the reader to pick up on the subtext. Trim any unnecessary dialogue that doesn't serve the scene or character development.

Example: During revision, you might notice that a character's dialogue feels overly formal in a moment of emotional vulnerability. By reading the scene aloud, you recognize that the character would likely speak more simply and directly in such a moment, given their emotional state. You revise the dialogue to reflect this, making it feel more natural and aligned with the character's inner experience.

The Zen practice of listening requires presence, mindfulness, and a deep attentiveness to the subtle nuances of communication. When applied to writing, this approach allows you to hear your characters' voices with clarity, capturing their emotions, personalities, and desires in a way that feels authentic and true. Listening to your characters is not about imposing your voice on them, but about creating space for their voices to emerge naturally. By tuning into their unique speech patterns, capturing the subtext of their conversations, and allowing them to evolve over time, you create dialogue that resonates with emotional depth and realism. Ultimately, the art of listening in writing is about trusting the characters to speak for themselves.

Achieving Balance in Story Structure: A Holistic Approach

In Zen, balance is a fundamental principle that governs all aspects of life. It teaches us that harmony comes from finding equilibrium between opposing forces—between action and stillness, light and shadow, or expansion and contraction. In storytelling, this same sense of balance is crucial to creating a narrative that flows naturally, maintains tension, and resonates emotionally with readers. Achieving balance in story structure involves crafting a story that feels complete and harmonious, where every element—plot, character, pacing, and theme—works in tandem to create a unified whole.

A balanced story doesn't mean every moment needs to be equal in intensity or importance. Instead, it means finding the right proportions, allowing moments of action to be offset by reflection, and ensuring that tension and release occur in a way that sustains the reader's engagement. Just as a Zen garden incorporates contrasting elements—rock and water, order and spontaneity—so too should a story blend its various components in a way that feels both dynamic and grounded.

In this chapter, we will explore how to achieve balance in story structure through pacing, character development, theme, and emotional arcs. By approaching storytelling from a holistic perspective, you can create narratives that are not only compelling but also harmonious and resonant.

The Importance of Balance in Story Structure

Story structure is the framework that holds a narrative together, guiding the reader through the unfolding events and emotional journeys of the characters. Achieving balance within this structure ensures that the story progresses in a way that feels natural, keeping the reader engaged while allowing space for reflection and emotional depth.

Here's why balance is essential in story structure:

Sustaining Reader Engagement: A well-balanced story keeps the reader engaged by alternating between moments of tension and release. Too much action without pause can overwhelm the reader, while too much reflection without forward movement can cause the narrative to stagnate. A balanced structure allows for both momentum and contemplation.

Maintaining Pacing: Pacing is crucial to how a story feels to the reader—whether it's fast-paced and thrilling, or slow and meditative. Achieving balance in pacing ensures that the story never feels rushed or dragging, but instead flows naturally between high-energy scenes and quieter moments of introspection.

Enhancing Emotional Impact: Balanced story structure allows for emotional build-up and release, ensuring that key moments of tension or catharsis land with the greatest impact. By giving characters and readers time to process events, you create emotional depth and resonance.

Harmonizing Plot and Character Development: A well-balanced story structure ensures that both plot and character development are given equal weight. The external events of the story should drive the internal growth of the characters, while the characters' emotional journeys should shape the unfolding plot.

Step 1: Creating Balance between Action and Reflection

One of the key aspects of a balanced story structure is finding the right rhythm between action and reflection. Action drives the plot forward, creating momentum and tension, while reflection allows the characters—and the reader—to process those events, deepening the emotional and thematic impact of the story.

How to Practice:

1. **Alternate between High-Intensity and Low-Intensity Scenes:** Too much action in succession can overwhelm the reader, while too much reflection can slow the story's pace. Strive to create a rhythm by alternating between high-intensity scenes, such as action sequences or moments of dramatic conflict, and

lower-intensity scenes, where characters have time to reflect, recover, or plan.

2. **Use Reflection to Deepen Character Development:** Reflection scenes give characters the space to process their emotions, question their motivations, or reconsider their goals. These quieter moments add depth to the characters and ensure that their actions are rooted in personal growth or conflict.

3. **Allow for Emotional Release After Climax:** After moments of high tension, such as the story's climax or a major turning point, it's important to provide a period of emotional release. This allows the reader to process the intensity of the scene and prepares them for the resolution of the story.

4. **Consider the Overall Story Arc:** When mapping out your story, ensure that there is a balance between scenes that push the plot forward and those that explore the emotional or thematic aspects of the narrative. Every story arc should have moments of action balanced with moments of introspection, ensuring that the story remains engaging without feeling rushed or shallow.

Example: In a story about a detective solving a murder, you might balance action-packed scenes of chasing suspects or confronting criminals with quieter scenes where the detective reflects on the case, revisits clues, or grapples with their own emotional stakes. This balance keeps the tension high while also allowing for deeper character exploration.

• • • •

STEP 2: HARMONIZING Plot and Character Development

A well-balanced story ensures that plot and character development work in harmony, with each influencing the other. The external events of the plot should be driven by the characters' desires, choices, and internal conflicts, while the characters' emotional growth should be shaped by the unfolding events of the story.

How to Practice:

1. **Align Plot Points with Character Arcs:** Each major plot point should align with a significant moment in the characters' emotional or psychological journeys. For example, the inciting incident might force the protagonist to confront a personal fear, while the climax could reflect a moment of self-realization or transformation.

2. **Use External Conflict to Highlight Internal Struggles:** External events—whether it's a battle, a mystery, or a quest—should reflect the characters' internal struggles. The external conflict becomes a metaphor for the internal journey, allowing the plot to reveal deeper layers of the characters' personalities and motivations.

3. **Give Characters Agency in the Plot:** Balanced story structure ensures that characters are active participants in the plot, rather than passive bystanders. Allow your characters to make choices that drive the plot forward, and show how those choices reflect their internal growth or conflicts.

4. **Let Plot and Character Arcs Evolve Together:** As the plot unfolds, the characters should evolve in response to the events they experience. Similarly, the characters' emotional growth should influence how the plot progresses. This interplay between plot and character creates a dynamic, cohesive narrative.

Example: In a coming-of-age story, the protagonist's internal struggle to find their identity might be mirrored by external challenges, such as navigating new relationships or overcoming societal expectations. The key plot points—first love, a personal failure, a moment of rebellion—align with the protagonist's internal journey of self-discovery, creating a balanced structure where plot and character development are intertwined.

Step 3: Balancing Pacing Throughout the Narrative

Pacing is the rhythm of the story—the speed at which events unfold and the way in which tension builds and releases. A balanced narrative ensures that pacing feels natural, with moments of intensity balanced by moments of calm. This prevents the story from feeling rushed or sluggish and keeps the reader engaged throughout.

How to Practice:

Start with Momentum, Then Vary the Pace: The opening of your story should grab the reader's attention with a strong inciting incident or compelling situation. After that, vary the pace by alternating between fast-moving scenes and slower, more reflective moments. This keeps the reader invested while allowing for breathing room.

Build Tension Gradually: In a well-paced story, tension builds gradually over time, leading to moments of high stakes and intensity. Avoid resolving conflicts too quickly—let the tension simmer and evolve, giving the characters (and readers) time to feel the weight of the situation before reaching a resolution.

Slow Down for Emotional Moments: Slower pacing is often necessary for emotionally charged scenes, where characters are processing grief, love, fear, or doubt. Give these moments the space they need to resonate fully with the reader, without rushing to the next plot point.

Use Pacing to Control the Reader's Experience: The pace of the story should align with the emotional arc you want the reader to experience. Fast pacing can create excitement, urgency, or chaos, while slow pacing can evoke reflection, sadness, or anticipation. Adjust pacing to match the mood and tone of each scene.

Example: In a thriller, the pacing might be fast during action scenes, such as a high-stakes chase or confrontation. However, after these moments of intensity, the pace might slow as the protagonist reflects on their next move, or as they deal with the emotional aftermath of a dangerous situation. This balance creates a dynamic, engaging narrative that doesn't feel rushed or overwhelming.

Step 4: Weaving Themes throughout the Story

Themes are the underlying ideas or messages that give a story its deeper meaning. A well-balanced story structure ensures that themes are woven organically throughout the narrative, rather than being forced or overly emphasized. This thematic balance allows the story to resonate on both an intellectual and emotional level.

How to Practice:

1. **Introduce Themes Early:** The central themes of your story should be introduced early, even if they are only hinted at in the beginning. As the story progresses, these themes can be explored more fully through the characters' actions, decisions, and internal conflicts.

2. **Let Themes Emerge Naturally:** Avoid being too heavy-handed with thematic elements. Instead, allow themes to emerge naturally through the story's events, dialogue, and symbolism. Readers should feel the weight of the themes without being explicitly told what they are.

3. **Use Characters to Explore Themes:** Each character can represent a different perspective on the story's themes, allowing for multiple angles of exploration. For example, in a story about justice, one character might believe in personal vengeance, while another upholds the law, and a third questions the morality of both approaches. This diversity of viewpoints creates thematic depth.

4. **Reflect Themes in the Story's Climax and Resolution:** The climax and resolution of the story should bring the central themes to the forefront. The choices the characters make and the outcomes they experience should reflect the thematic questions posed throughout the narrative, offering a sense of closure or revelation.

Example: In a story about redemption, the theme might be subtly introduced through small moments of forgiveness or second chances early in the narrative. As the story progresses, the theme becomes more pronounced, with the protagonist facing decisions that challenge their belief in redemption. By the climax, the protagonist's ultimate choice reflects the story's exploration of whether true redemption is possible, creating thematic cohesion.

Step 5: Balancing Emotional Arcs for Maximum Impact

A balanced story structure ensures that the emotional arcs of the characters—and the readers—are carefully calibrated. Just as in life, emotions in a story ebb and flow, with moments of joy, sorrow, anger, and hope all woven together. Achieving balance in the emotional arc allows for powerful moments of catharsis and connection.

How to Practice:

1. **Map Out Emotional Peaks and Valleys:** When planning your story, map out the key emotional beats, identifying moments of high intensity (such as conflict or revelation) and moments of emotional release (such as reconciliation or quiet reflection). Ensure that these emotional peaks and valleys are spaced out to create a satisfying rhythm.

2. **Avoid Emotional Monotony:** Too much of one emotion—whether it's constant tension or unrelenting sadness—can lead to emotional fatigue for the reader. Balance intense emotional moments with quieter, more subtle scenes that offer a contrast and allow the reader to process the characters' emotional journey.

3. **Create Emotional Arcs for Secondary Characters:** While the protagonist's emotional arc is central, secondary characters should also have their own emotional journeys. These arcs add depth to the story and provide a broader emotional landscape for the reader to engage with.

4. **Use Emotional Restraint for Greater Impact:** Sometimes, the most powerful emotions are conveyed not through grand gestures, but through moments of restraint. A character holding back tears, a strained silence between two people, or a subtle gesture of reconciliation can carry immense emotional weight. Balance emotional outbursts with moments of quiet intensity for maximum impact.

Example: In a family drama, the emotional arc might build towards a climactic confrontation where long-buried resentments are brought to the surface. However, after this intense moment, the emotional pace might slow as the characters begin to process what was said and work towards healing. This balance of tension and release creates an emotionally satisfying narrative.

Achieving balance in story structure is about creating a narrative that feels harmonious, dynamic, and emotionally resonant. Just as Zen emphasizes the importance of balance in all aspects of life, storytelling requires a careful equilibrium between plot and character, action and reflection, tension and release.

By approaching storytelling from a holistic perspective, you can craft narratives that flow naturally and maintain the reader's engagement while allowing space for emotional depth and thematic exploration. Balance ensures that no element of the story overwhelms the others, creating a unified whole where plot, character, pacing, and theme work together seamlessly. Ultimately, a balanced story structure invites readers on a journey that feels both satisfying and meaningful—where every scene, every character, and every emotional beat contributes to a larger, cohesive narrative.

Crafting a Cinematic Mind: Writing for Screen and Scene

In today's storytelling landscape, writers often juggle the mediums of prose and screenwriting, blending literary techniques with the visual demands of cinema. Writing for the screen requires a shift in thinking—a move from internal reflection to external action. Instead of describing a character's internal thoughts or painting expansive landscapes with words, the screenwriter must convey meaning through visual cues, dialogue, and action. This shift involves developing a "cinematic mind"—the ability to think in terms of scenes, images, and visual moments that speak to the audience through what is seen and heard, not just what is described.

In Zen practice, simplicity, clarity, and presence are paramount. Similarly, writing for the screen requires a focus on the essentials: every scene, line of dialogue, and image must serve a purpose, contributing to the story's emotional and visual impact. Crafting a cinematic mind allows you to write in a way that embraces the visual, telling stories through the lens of a camera rather than the confines of the page. This chapter will explore how to cultivate a cinematic mindset, emphasizing the use of visual storytelling, scene composition, and the principles of writing with clarity and purpose for the screen.

The Power of Visual Storytelling in Screenwriting

Unlike novels or short stories, screenwriting demands that the writer think visually. The screen is a medium of sight and sound, where every detail—the lighting, set design, camera angles, and actors' expressions—conveys meaning. As a writer, you are responsible for crafting scenes that unfold in the audience's mind as clearly as they will on the screen.

Here's why visual storytelling is so crucial in screenwriting:

1. **Show, Don't Tell:** The old adage applies especially to screenwriting. Instead of relying on inner monologue or descriptive prose to convey emotions, a screenwriter uses images, actions, and dialogue to show what characters are feeling, thinking, or experiencing.
2. **Creating Memorable Visual Moments:** In film and television, certain images or sequences can linger in the audience's mind long after the story ends. These visual moments—whether it's a striking landscape, a symbolic gesture, or a character's reaction—create a lasting emotional impact that transcends words.
3. **Economy of Storytelling:** Screenwriting requires brevity. Every scene must serve the story, with no wasted dialogue or unnecessary exposition. A cinematic mind is one that is focused, efficient, and able to communicate complex ideas through simple, powerful imagery.
4. **Using the Camera as a Storytelling Tool:** In screenwriting, the camera becomes an extension of the narrative. How a scene is framed, the angle of the shot, and what is shown (or not shown) all influence how the audience experiences the story. Writing for the screen means thinking not only about what happens but also how it is visually presented.

Step 1: Thinking in Terms of Scenes and Shots

To cultivate a cinematic mind, begin by thinking of your story in terms of scenes and shots, rather than paragraphs or pages of description. Scenes are the building blocks of screenplays, and each scene is composed of visual moments—specific shots that convey the action, mood, and meaning.

How to Practice:

1. **Break the Story Into Visual Beats:** Instead of thinking about a story as a sequence of events, break it down into key visual moments, or "beats." These are the moments when something changes for the

character or when an important piece of information is revealed. Focus on how these moments look and feel on screen.

2. **Imagine the Camera's Perspective:** When writing a scene, think about where the camera is placed. Is it close to the character's face to capture an emotional reaction, or does it pull back to show the full scope of a setting or situation? The camera's perspective influences how the audience interprets the scene, so consider what the shot should reveal.

3. **Use Visual Symbols:** In cinematic storytelling, objects, settings, or gestures can serve as symbols that convey deeper meaning. A close-up of a key turning in a lock, for example, can symbolize secrecy, entrapment, or a turning point. Incorporate these visual symbols to add layers of meaning without relying on dialogue.

4. **Craft Action Through Movement:** Screenwriting is about movement. Whether it's the physical movement of characters or the progression of the story, every scene should have a sense of forward motion. Use action to propel the narrative, revealing character traits and advancing the plot through what the characters do, rather than what they say.

Example: In a suspense thriller, instead of writing a lengthy explanation of a character's growing paranoia, you might show it through a series of shots: a close-up of the character's trembling hands, their wide-eyed glance around the room, the sudden flicker of a shadow passing by the window. These visual cues tell the audience everything they need to know about the character's emotional state without a single line of dialogue.

Step 2: Writing Dialogue with a Cinematic Mindset

In screenwriting, dialogue must be purposeful, succinct, and revealing. Characters speak because they need to, not because the writer needs to explain something. Great dialogue advances the plot, reveals character, and reflects the subtext of a scene, all while sounding natural and believable.

How to Practice:

Keep It Brief and Punchy: Screenwriting is about economy, and that applies especially to dialogue. Characters should speak in short, meaningful sentences that get to the point. Avoid long monologues unless they serve a specific dramatic purpose.

Reveal Subtext through Dialogue: In film, what characters don't say is often more important than what they do say. Use subtext to reveal the true emotions and intentions behind a character's words. A character might say, "I'm fine," but their tone, body language, and the visual context of the scene tell the audience otherwise.

Let the Action Speak for Itself: Dialogue should never be used to explain what the audience can already see. If a character is running through a rain-soaked street, we don't need them to say, "I'm wet and cold." Trust the visuals to convey the situation and keep dialogue focused on what adds to the emotional or narrative tension.

Use Dialogue to Build Tension and Conflict: Dialogue is often a form of verbal sparring between characters, where power dynamics, hidden motives, or emotional wounds are revealed. Listen to how your characters interact and let their conversations build tension, even when they're discussing something mundane.

Example: In a romantic drama, instead of having a character confess their love with a long, flowery speech, you might use a simple, understated exchange. The tension builds not through what is said but through the pauses, glances, and nervous gestures. The audience feels the weight of the moment because the dialogue is restrained, leaving room for the visuals and the actors' performances to carry the emotion.

Step 3: Building Atmosphere and Mood Through Visuals

Atmosphere is an essential part of cinematic storytelling. Whether you're writing a gritty crime drama or a sweeping epic, the mood of the story is conveyed through the setting, lighting, sound, and overall visual tone. A cinematic mind understands that these elements are as important as dialogue and plot in shaping the audience's emotional experience.

How to Practice:

Choose Settings That Reflect the Theme: The setting of a scene can do more than provide a backdrop—it can reinforce the story's themes and emotional tone. A crumbling building might symbolize decay or lost hope, while a sunlit meadow might evoke peace or renewal. Consider how the setting contributes to the story's mood and meaning.

Use Lighting and Color as Storytelling Tools: In film, lighting and color are powerful tools for setting the mood. A dimly lit room with shadows creeping along the walls creates a sense of danger or uncertainty, while bright, warm lighting might evoke comfort or nostalgia. When writing a scene, think about how lighting and color can reflect the emotional tone of the moment.

Let Sound Enhance the Atmosphere: While screenwriters don't typically dictate specific sound choices, you can suggest the mood through auditory details. Is there a constant, oppressive hum in the background? The sound of distant thunder building tension? These auditory cues can enhance the atmosphere and deepen the audience's immersion in the scene.

Show Don't Tell—Even With Mood: Instead of describing how a character feels or how the setting looks, let the visuals do the work. A character sitting alone in a dark room, head in hands, tells the audience more about their despair than any amount of descriptive prose. Use actions and visuals to create the atmosphere without explicitly stating it.

Example: In a horror film, rather than relying on characters to verbalize their fear, you might build the atmosphere through setting and sound: the creaking of old floorboards, flickering lights casting strange shadows, the echo of footsteps in an empty hallway. The tension builds through these visual and auditory elements, drawing the audience deeper into the story's mood without needing to explain the characters' fear.

Step 4: Structuring a Story Cinematically

Cinematic storytelling involves structuring the narrative in a way that is visually dynamic and emotionally engaging. The structure of a screenplay is typically more rigid than that of a novel, adhering to a three-act format or similar framework. However, within this structure, there is room for creativity, and a cinematic mind knows how to use this framework to build tension, develop characters, and deliver a powerful emotional arc.

How to Practice:

1. **Use the Three-Act Structure as a Foundation:** The classic three-act structure—setup, confrontation, and resolution—provides a solid foundation for building a cinematic story. In Act 1, establish the world and introduce the central conflict. In Act 2, escalate the tension and challenges. In Act 3, bring the story to a climax and resolve the conflict. Each act should have its own emotional arc, with the tension building and releasing in waves.

2. **Focus on Visual Setups and Payoffs:** A cinematic story often relies on visual setups and payoffs—planting a visual or narrative clue early on and paying it off later in the story. For example, if a character is shown nervously fiddling with a key in the first act, that key might become crucial in the climax. These visual callbacks create a sense of continuity and satisfaction for the audience.

3. **Ensure Every Scene Serves the Story:** In screenwriting, every scene must have a purpose. If a scene doesn't move the plot forward, reveal something new about the characters, or build tension, it likely doesn't belong. A cinematic mind is ruthless in cutting unnecessary scenes, ensuring that each moment contributes to the overall narrative.

4. **Build to a Visual and Emotional Climax:** The climax of a cinematic story is both a visual and emotional peak. It's where the tension reaches its highest point, and the characters face their greatest challenge. When structuring your story, build toward this moment with increasing stakes and escalating tension, ensuring that the climax delivers both visually and emotionally.

Example: In a mystery film, the three-act structure might look like this: Act 1 introduces the protagonist, a detective, and sets up the central mystery. Act 2 sees the detective following leads, facing obstacles, and uncovering dark secrets. Act 3 builds to the climax, where the detective confronts the antagonist in a tense, visually striking showdown. The visual payoff might be a symbolic image—perhaps a broken watch that was a key clue, now revealed in a moment of emotional and narrative resolution.

Step 5: Revising with a Cinematic Lens

Once the initial draft is complete, revising with a cinematic lens allows you to refine the story, ensuring that each scene, line of dialogue, and visual moment contributes to the overall narrative. A cinematic mind looks for opportunities to tighten the pacing, enhance the visuals, and clarify the emotional beats of the story.

How to Practice:

1. **Trim Excess Dialogue and Description:** In revision, focus on cutting any dialogue or description that isn't essential. Screenwriting thrives on brevity, so eliminate any lines or scenes that don't serve the story. Trust the visuals to convey meaning, and let the actors bring the subtext to life.

2. **Clarify Visual and Emotional Arcs:** Ensure that the visual storytelling aligns with the emotional journey of the characters. Are the key visual moments supporting the themes and emotions of the story? If a character undergoes a transformation, is that reflected visually in the way they're presented on screen?

3. **Strengthen Setups and Payoffs:** Look for opportunities to tighten the story's setups and payoffs. If you've planted a visual or narrative clue early on, make sure it pays off in a satisfying way. These moments of continuity create a cohesive and engaging narrative.

4. **Polish Scene Transitions:** In film, how one scene transitions to the next is crucial to the flow of the story. Look for ways to create smooth, dynamic transitions between scenes—whether through visual match cuts, thematic connections, or changes in pacing. These transitions help maintain the narrative momentum and keep the audience engaged.

Example: During revision, you might realize that a scene where two characters discuss their plans could be cut entirely, as the same information is conveyed through their actions in a later scene. By trimming this unnecessary dialogue, you streamline the story and keep the focus on the visual and emotional beats that matter most.

Crafting a cinematic mind means thinking visually, economically, and purposefully. Writing for the screen involves more than just telling a story—it's about showing it in a way that engages the audience through sight, sound, and movement. By focusing on visual storytelling, writing tight and meaningful dialogue, building atmosphere, and structuring the narrative with clarity and purpose, you create stories that come alive on screen. A cinematic mindset invites you to embrace simplicity, clarity, and presence—qualities that align with Zen principles. Each scene, each shot, and each line of dialogue is an opportunity to communicate meaning and emotion without excess. Through mindful attention to the visual and emotional landscape of your story, you can craft narratives that not only entertain but also resonate deeply with the audience. Ultimately, writing for screen and scene requires you to think like a director, capturing moments of beauty, tension, and transformation with the precision of a camera lens. By honing your cinematic mind, you become not just a storyteller, but a visual artist, capable of bringing your story to life in a way that is dynamic, powerful, and unforgettable.

The Peace of Completion: Letting Go of the Story

In Zen philosophy, one of the core teachings is learning to let go—to release attachment to outcomes and embrace the natural flow of life. This idea of letting go extends to all aspects of existence, including the creative process. For writers, reaching the end of a story can feel like a moment of triumph, but it can also evoke feelings of loss, uncertainty, or anxiety. How do you know when the story is truly finished? How do you move on after dedicating so much of yourself to its creation?

Letting go of a story is an act of peace. It means accepting that the narrative has reached its conclusion, that the characters have walked their paths, and that the creative process has come full circle. While the urge to hold on, revise endlessly, or seek perfection is common, true fulfillment comes from understanding that the story, like all things, has its natural endpoint. The peace of completion is found in embracing the impermanence of the creative process and knowing that you have done your best with the story.

In this chapter, we will explore the Zen-like peace that comes with completing a story. We'll look at how to let go of your work with a sense of closure, how to trust the journey you've taken, and how to move forward into new creative endeavors without lingering attachments or doubts.

The Significance of Completion in the Creative Process

Completion is not just about typing "The End" at the bottom of the page. It's about reaching a point where the story feels whole—where it has achieved its intended emotional and thematic impact. Letting go of the story means releasing it into the world, whether through publication, sharing with readers, or simply moving on to the next creative project.

Here's why embracing completion is important:

Honoring the Creative Cycle: Just as every story has a beginning, middle, and end, so too does the creative process itself. Honoring the cycle of creation means knowing when it's time to finish, allowing the work to stand on its own, and moving forward without dwelling on what could have been.

Avoiding Perfectionism: Perfectionism can be the enemy of completion. The desire to keep revising or "fixing" a story indefinitely can prevent you from ever finishing. Accepting that no story will ever be perfect allows you to find peace in completion and let go of the need for endless revisions.

Creating Space for New Ideas: Holding on to a completed story can prevent you from exploring new creative possibilities. Letting go frees up mental and emotional space, allowing you to dive into fresh ideas and new projects with renewed energy and inspiration.

Trusting the Process: Trust is a key component of Zen practice. Trust that the story is complete, that you have done your best, and that its imperfections are part of its unique character. By trusting the process, you can release attachment to the outcome and find peace in the act of creation itself.

Step 1: Recognizing When the Story is Complete

Knowing when a story is complete can be challenging. There may always be more you could add, another layer you could explore, or a line of dialogue you could refine. But part of achieving peace in completion is recognizing when the story has fulfilled its purpose and when further changes would no longer serve its heart.

How to Practice:

1. **Listen to the Story's Natural Rhythm:** Every story has a rhythm—a natural flow that guides its progression. As you approach the end, pay attention to whether the story feels like it's reaching a point of closure. Are the major themes resolved? Have the characters reached the end of their emotional arcs? If the story feels like it's winding down, trust that instinct.

2. **Evaluate the Emotional and Thematic Impact:** A story is complete when it has achieved the emotional and thematic impact you intended. Reflect on the core themes and emotional beats of the narrative. Have they been fully explored and resolved? If so, the story is likely ready for completion.

3. **Trust Your Intuition:** Often, you'll feel an intuitive sense that the story is complete, even if it's not perfect. Trust your creative instincts. If you feel a sense of closure or contentment when reading the final pages, it's a sign that the story has reached its natural conclusion.

4. **Resist the Urge for Endless Tweaks:** It's tempting to keep tweaking sentences or adding new scenes, but at some point, these changes no longer enhance the story's core. When you reach this point, it's time to stop. Minor imperfections are part of the story's character, and continuing to revise may only dilute its authenticity.

Example: In a story about a character's journey of self-discovery, the narrative might feel complete once the protagonist has faced their greatest challenge, learned an essential truth about themselves, and made a pivotal choice that reflects their growth. Even if there are minor details you could tweak, if the character's emotional journey feels complete, it's time to let go of the story.

Step 2: Embracing Imperfection as Part of the Story's Essence

Zen teaches us to embrace imperfection as part of the natural order of life. In storytelling, this concept applies to the work itself. No story will ever be flawless, but its imperfections are part of what make it unique. Learning to accept these imperfections and seeing them as intrinsic to the story's character can bring a sense of peace in letting go.

How to Practice:

Acknowledge the Beauty of Imperfection: Imperfections in a story—whether it's a slightly awkward phrase, a scene that could be more polished, or a subplot that feels underdeveloped—are part of the creative process. Embrace these imperfections as evidence of the story's humanity and authenticity, rather than seeing them as flaws that need to be fixed.

Stop Chasing Perfectionism: Perfectionism is an unattainable goal. If you try to make every detail of the story flawless, you may never finish. Accept that the story, in its current form, is enough. By releasing the need for perfection, you free yourself to let go and move on.

Celebrate the Journey, Not Just the Destination: The creative process is about more than just the finished product. Reflect on the journey you took in writing the story—the moments of inspiration, the challenges you overcame, the growth you experienced as a writer. The story's imperfections are a testament to that journey, and embracing them allows you to find peace in completion.

Find Meaning in the Story's Authenticity: Sometimes, it's the imperfections in a story that make it feel real and relatable. A character's flaws, a moment of awkwardness, or an unresolved question can add depth and texture to the narrative. Letting go of the need to "fix" these imperfections allows the story to remain true to itself.

Example: Imagine a story where the pacing is slightly uneven in the middle, but the emotional climax lands powerfully. Rather than obsessing over the pacing, you might choose to embrace the imperfection, knowing that the heart of the story remains intact. The imperfect pacing becomes part of the story's unique rhythm, adding to its authenticity.

Step 3: Releasing the Story into the World

Once a story is complete, the next step is to release it—whether through publication, sharing with others, or simply acknowledging it as a finished work. Releasing the story means letting go of your control over it, allowing it to live on its own and make its way into the world, where it will be interpreted and experienced by others.

How to Practice:

1. **Trust the Story's Ability to Stand on Its Own:** Just as a Zen practitioner trusts the natural flow of life, trust that your story can stand on its own. It doesn't need to be perfect to resonate with readers. By releasing it, you give it the opportunity to connect with others and find its place in the world.

2. **Accept that Readers Will Bring Their Own Interpretations:** Once you release a story, it no longer belongs solely to you. Readers will interpret it through their own experiences and emotions, and their interpretations may differ from your intentions. Embrace this as part of the story's journey and trust that it will resonate in ways you may not have anticipated.

3. **Let Go of Attachment to Outcomes:** Whether the story is published, praised, criticized, or met with silence, its worth is not defined by external validation. By letting go of attachment to outcomes, you find peace in knowing that the act of creating the story was meaningful in itself.

4. **Celebrate the Completion:** Completion is an achievement in and of itself. Take time to celebrate the fact that you have brought the story full circle—from idea to execution to release. This moment of celebration allows you to honor the story and your creative effort before moving on to new projects.

Example: If you've finished writing a short story and decide to share it with a group of readers, trust that their responses will be varied. Some may love it, some may offer critique, and others may interpret it in unexpected ways. Let go of the need to control how the story is received, and instead celebrate the fact that it has now taken on a life of its own.

Step 4: Moving On to New Creative Projects

Letting go of a story creates space for new ideas and creative projects to emerge. The peace of completion allows you to move forward without being weighed down by the past. By fully embracing the end of one creative endeavor, you open yourself to the possibilities of the next.

How to Practice:

1. **Clear Your Mind and Workspace:** After completing a story, take time to clear both your mental and physical workspace. This might involve tidying up your writing environment, organizing notes, or simply reflecting on the story's completion. This act of clearing creates space for new ideas to flow in.

2. **Cultivate Curiosity for New Ideas:** Letting go of one story allows you to approach new ideas with curiosity and openness. What creative possibilities excite you? What new stories are waiting to be told? By shifting your focus to new projects, you reinvigorate your creative energy.

3. **Avoid Lingering Attachments:** It's easy to get stuck in the past, revisiting old stories or wondering if you could have done things differently. Let go of these attachments and trust that the story is complete as it is. Focus your attention on the creative future rather than dwelling on what has already been finished.

4. **Embrace the Next Creative Cycle:** Just as the completion of one story marks the end of a creative cycle, it also signals the beginning of the next. Embrace this new cycle with excitement and openness, knowing that the lessons learned from your previous project will inform and inspire your next one.

Example: After finishing a novel, you might spend a few days reflecting on the story's completion and clearing your workspace. Once you feel ready, you turn your attention to new ideas—perhaps brainstorming a completely different genre or form. By letting go of the previous project, you create mental and emotional space for fresh inspiration to emerge.

The peace of completion comes from embracing the natural end of the creative process and letting go of your attachment to the story. In Zen, letting go is an act of acceptance—accepting imperfection, trusting the journey, and releasing control over the outcome. In writing, this means finding peace in the story's completion, allowing it to exist as it is, and moving forward with a sense of fulfillment and clarity. Letting go of a story is not about abandoning it, but about recognizing that it has reached its full expression. By releasing the story into the world and allowing yourself to move on, you honor both the creative process and your growth as a writer. The peace of completion is found in knowing that every story, like every aspect of life, has its time—and that by letting go, you make room for new stories to unfold. In the end, letting go of the story is a powerful act of trust and surrender.

Staying Present in the Creative Process: Avoiding Distractions

In the modern world, distractions are everywhere. Whether it's the constant ping of notifications, the pull of social media, or the demands of daily life, it's easy to become overwhelmed and pulled away from the creative process. For writers and creators, staying present—fully immersed in the task at hand—is essential for bringing ideas to life and achieving a state of flow. Zen philosophy emphasizes mindfulness, being fully engaged in the moment without judgment or attachment to external noise. This same principle applies to creativity. When distractions are minimized, and the mind is focused, the creative process becomes smoother, deeper, and more fulfilling.

In this chapter, we will explore how to stay present in the creative process by cultivating mindfulness, reducing distractions, and developing habits that allow for sustained focus. By learning to avoid distractions, both internal and external, you can tap into a state of flow, where ideas flourish, and your writing feels effortless and inspired.

The Importance of Presence in Creativity

Being present in the creative process means giving your full attention to the task at hand, whether it's writing, brainstorming, or revising. Creativity thrives when the mind is focused and free from distractions, allowing ideas to flow naturally. However, distractions—both digital and mental—can easily disrupt this focus, leading to frustration, writer's block, or a sense of disconnection from the work.

Here's why staying present is so important in the creative process:

1. **Deep Focus Leads to Flow:** When you are fully present, you can enter a state of flow—a mental state where creativity comes effortlessly, and time seems to disappear. In this state, ideas are generated with ease, and the act of creation feels almost meditative.

2. **Minimizing Mental Clutter:** Distractions create mental clutter, which makes it harder to connect with your ideas or characters. By staying present, you clear away the noise and focus on what truly matters in the moment—your story, your characters, and the world you are building.

3. **Enhancing Creativity and Problem-Solving:** The more focused and present you are, the more creative solutions you can find to challenges in your work. Staying present allows you to think more clearly and deeply, opening up new possibilities for your narrative or characters.

4. **Reducing Stress and Overwhelm:** Distractions can lead to feelings of stress, overwhelm, and frustration. When you stay present, you can approach your creative work with a sense of calm and clarity, reducing the pressure to multitask or juggle competing demands.

. . . .

STEP 1: CULTIVATING Mindfulness in the Creative Process

Mindfulness, the practice of being fully present and aware in the moment, is a powerful tool for staying focused during the creative process. By cultivating mindfulness, you can train your mind to stay anchored in the present, even when distractions arise.

How to Practice:

1. **Start with a Mindful Breathing Exercise:** Before diving into your writing session, take a few moments to practice mindful breathing. Close your eyes, take a deep breath in, and slowly exhale. Focus on your breath and let go of any thoughts or worries. This simple practice helps calm the mind and center your focus, preparing you for a more productive creative session.

2. **Set an Intention for Your Session:** At the beginning of each writing session, set a clear intention. What do

you hope to accomplish? Whether it's writing a specific scene, revising a chapter, or brainstorming new ideas, having a clear intention helps you stay focused and present in your work.

3. **Engage Fully with the Present Moment:** As you write, notice how your mind engages with the task at hand. Are you fully focused on the scene, or are you mentally drifting? If you find yourself getting distracted, gently bring your attention back to the present moment, reminding yourself of your intention. The more you practice this, the easier it becomes to stay focused.

4. **Practice Non-Judgment:** When distractions arise—whether they are external (such as noise) or internal (such as self-doubt)—practice observing them without judgment. Acknowledge the distraction, and then let it go without getting caught up in it. This practice of non-judgment allows you to maintain focus without becoming frustrated or discouraged.

Example: Before starting a writing session, you might spend a few minutes practicing mindful breathing and setting the intention to complete a specific scene. During the session, if you notice your mind wandering or feeling the urge to check your phone, acknowledge the distraction without judgment, take a deep breath, and return your focus to the scene. Over time, this practice of mindfulness strengthens your ability to stay present.

Step 2: Reducing External Distractions

External distractions—such as notifications, background noise, or interruptions—can quickly pull you out of the creative zone. Reducing or eliminating these distractions is key to staying focused and present in the writing process.

How to Practice:

1. **Create a Distraction-Free Workspace:** Set up a writing space that minimizes external distractions. This could mean turning off your phone, blocking distracting websites, or finding a quiet environment where you won't be interrupted. A clutter-free, calm workspace allows you to focus more easily.

2. **Set Boundaries for Your Creative Time:** Let others know when you are in a creative session and ask for minimal interruptions. This could be as simple as setting specific hours for your writing and communicating these boundaries to family, friends, or colleagues. The clearer you are about your creative time, the easier it will be to protect it from distractions.

3. **Use Focus Tools:** If digital distractions are a problem, consider using tools that help you stay focused. Apps like "Focus@Will," "Freedom," or "Forest" can block distracting websites, create timed focus sessions, or provide background music that enhances concentration.

4. **Embrace the Power of Silence:** Sometimes the best way to stay present is to embrace silence. Turn off any unnecessary background noise, such as TV or music, and allow yourself to write in a quiet space. Silence can help you focus more deeply on the rhythm of your writing and the emotions of your characters.

Example: You might create a designated writing space in a quiet room, free from clutter and distractions. Before starting, turn off your phone, use an app to block distracting websites, and let others in your household know that you'll be unavailable for the next hour. By creating this intentional environment, you reduce external distractions and make it easier to stay present with your writing.

Step 3: Managing Internal Distractions

Internal distractions—such as self-doubt, perfectionism, or racing thoughts—can be just as disruptive as external ones. Learning to manage these internal distractions is essential for staying present and focused in the creative process.

How to Practice:

Acknowledge and Release Negative Thoughts: When negative thoughts arise (e.g., "This isn't good enough," "I'll never finish this"), acknowledge them without judgment, and then release them. You might say to yourself, "I see this thought, but it's not helpful right now," and then refocus on your writing.

Practice Self-Compassion: Be kind to yourself when internal distractions arise. Writing can be challenging, and it's natural to experience moments of doubt or frustration. Instead of criticizing yourself, practice self-compassion by reminding yourself that it's okay to have off days. What matters is showing up and continuing the creative process.

Use Mindful Refocusing Techniques: When your mind starts to wander, use a mindful technique to bring yourself back to the present. This could involve taking a few deep breaths, rereading the last sentence you wrote, or visualizing the scene in your mind's eye. These small actions help anchor you back in the moment.

Break Large Tasks into Smaller Steps: Overwhelm can lead to procrastination or distraction. If a writing project feels too big, break it down into smaller, manageable steps. Focus on completing one task at a time, such as writing a single paragraph or brainstorming character traits. This approach makes the creative process feel more manageable and less daunting.

Example: If you find yourself overwhelmed by self-doubt during a writing session, pause and take a few deep breaths. Acknowledge the thought (e.g., "I'm not sure this scene is working"), and then release it without judgment. Refocus by breaking the task into a smaller step, such as revising one paragraph or visualizing the next scene in your mind. By managing internal distractions mindfully, you can stay present and keep moving forward.

Step 4: Developing Habits for Sustained Focus

Staying present in the creative process requires developing habits that support sustained focus. By creating routines and practices that encourage mindfulness, you can train your mind to remain focused, even when distractions are present.

How to Practice:

Establish a Daily Writing Routine: Having a consistent writing routine helps signal to your brain that it's time to focus. Whether it's early in the morning or late at night, choose a time when you are least likely to be distracted and commit to writing during that time every day. This routine helps you develop a habit of presence and focus.

Set Time Limits for Creative Sessions: Sometimes, knowing that you only have a limited amount of time can enhance focus. Use a timer to set specific writing intervals (e.g., 25 minutes of focused writing, followed by a short break). This technique, known as the Pomodoro Technique, helps maintain focus by creating structured work periods with intentional breaks.

Prioritize Movement and Breaks: Sitting for long periods can lead to physical and mental fatigue. Incorporate short breaks into your writing routine, using them to stretch, take a walk, or simply rest your eyes. These moments of movement and relaxation refresh your focus and prevent burnout.

Reflect on What Worked and What Didn't: After each writing session, take a few moments to reflect on what worked and what didn't. Were there certain distractions that pulled you away? Did you feel more focused at certain times of the day? By reflecting on your habits and distractions, you can adjust your approach to enhance future creative sessions.

Example: You might establish a daily writing routine in the morning, committing to a 90-minute session. During this time, you use the Pomodoro Technique, working for 25-minute intervals and taking 5-minute breaks to stretch or walk around. After the session, you reflect on how focused you felt and whether any distractions affected your work. By developing these habits, you train your mind to stay present and focused over time.

Step 5: Embracing Flow and Letting Go of Perfectionism

One of the greatest challenges to staying present is the desire for perfection. Perfectionism can lead to overthinking, second-guessing, or procrastination, all of which disrupt the creative process. To stay present, it's important to let go of perfectionism and embrace the flow of ideas as they come.

How to Practice:

1. **Let Go of the Need to Be Perfect:** Accept that the first draft doesn't need to be perfect. The goal of the creative process is not to produce flawless work immediately, but to explore ideas, take risks, and let the story evolve naturally. By letting go of perfectionism, you free yourself to stay present in the act of creation.
2. **Trust the Flow of Ideas:** When you're fully present, ideas will come naturally. Trust this flow, even if it feels messy or imperfect. The creative process is iterative, and the more you stay engaged, the more refined your ideas will become over time.
3. **Focus on Progress, Not Outcome:** Instead of fixating on the final product, focus on the progress you're making in each session. Celebrate small victories—whether it's completing a scene, discovering a new character trait, or finding the perfect line of dialogue. Staying present in these small moments of progress keeps you motivated and connected to the creative process.
4. **Allow for Imperfection in the Creative Journey:** Creativity is rarely a straight line. There will be moments of frustration, confusion, and doubt. Embrace these imperfections as part of the journey, knowing that they contribute to the richness and authenticity of the final work. By staying present through the ups and downs, you maintain your connection to the creative flow.

Example: During a writing session, you might feel frustrated that a scene isn't coming together as smoothly as you'd like. Instead of giving in to perfectionism, remind yourself that it's okay for the first draft to be rough. Focus on making progress, even if it's imperfect, trusting that you can revise and refine the scene later. By staying present with the creative flow, you allow the ideas to unfold naturally.

Staying present in the creative process requires mindfulness, focus, and a commitment to avoiding distractions—both external and internal. By cultivating mindfulness, creating a distraction-free environment, managing internal thoughts, and developing habits that support sustained focus, you can tap into a state of flow where creativity flourishes. Zen teaches us the importance of being fully engaged in the present moment, without attachment to outcomes or distractions. In writing, this same principle applies: the more present you are with your work, the more connected you become.

Time is an essential element in storytelling. It governs the pace of a narrative, defines character development, and shapes the structure of a plot. In Zen, time is often seen as fluid, with the past, present, and future all interconnected in a natural flow. To write with an awareness of time is to create a narrative that feels seamless, where events unfold naturally, and the reader is carried along by the story's progression.

Understanding the flow of time in writing involves more than just managing pacing. It means recognizing how time influences every aspect of your story—how characters grow and change, how tension builds and resolves, and how each scene connects to the next in a way that feels organic. Whether your narrative spans hours, days, or generations, the way you handle time will determine the reader's experience of the story's rhythm and emotional depth.

In this chapter, we will explore how to write with a sense of natural progression, allowing time to flow organically within your narrative. We'll cover pacing, character growth over time, the structure of plot arcs, and the subtle art of transitions between scenes and events. By mastering the flow of time, you can create stories that feel alive, evolving in a way that captivates and resonates with readers.

The Importance of Time in Storytelling

Time is the invisible framework upon which a story is built. Whether a narrative is told in linear fashion or jumps between moments in the past and future, the progression of time shapes how the story unfolds and how readers experience it. When time flows naturally, the story feels cohesive, and the reader can follow the narrative without feeling rushed or disoriented.

Here's why time is so crucial in storytelling:

1. **Creating Pacing and Momentum:** Time dictates the pacing of a story. It determines when to slow down for reflection and when to speed up for action. Properly managing the flow of time keeps the reader engaged, maintaining a balance between tension and release.

2. **Developing Characters Over Time:** Characters grow and change as time progresses. Whether it's over the course of a single day or many years, time allows for emotional and psychological development. Characters' experiences and the passage of time shape their motivations, relationships, and transformations.

3. **Building Tension and Resolution:** Time is essential for building tension and delivering resolution. A well-timed reveal, a moment of suspense that lingers just long enough, or a slow build toward an emotional climax all depend on the careful management of time within the narrative.

4. **Creating a Seamless Reading Experience:** A story that flows naturally through time feels immersive. Readers are not distracted by disjointed scenes or awkward transitions; instead, they are carried effortlessly through the events, fully engaged in the unfolding of the narrative.

Step 1: Pacing the Story with the Flow of Time

Pacing refers to the speed at which a story moves, and it is directly influenced by how time is handled within the narrative. A well-paced story doesn't rush through important moments or linger too long on unnecessary details. Instead, it allows the reader to experience the unfolding events in a way that feels natural and satisfying.

How to Practice:

1. **Vary the Pace According to the Scene's Purpose:** Not every scene needs to move at the same speed. Action scenes often require a faster pace, with shorter sentences and quick transitions, while reflective

moments benefit from a slower pace, allowing the reader to absorb the emotional weight of the scene. Adjust the flow of time based on the needs of each scene.

2. **Use Time Compression and Expansion:** Sometimes, it's necessary to compress time, summarizing hours, days, or even years in a single sentence or paragraph to keep the story moving. At other times, you may want to expand time, slowing down to focus on a key moment, such as a character's internal struggle or an intense confrontation. Mastering this ebb and flow of time adds texture to the narrative.

3. **Avoid Rushing Key Moments:** Important moments—such as turning points, emotional revelations, or climactic scenes—should not be rushed. Allow the reader to linger in these moments, experiencing the full weight of what is happening. This may involve slowing down the narrative with descriptive detail, internal dialogue, or a careful exploration of the character's emotions.

4. **Balance Fast-Paced and Slow-Paced Scenes:** A well-paced story alternates between fast-paced and slow-paced scenes to maintain variety and engagement. After an action-packed sequence, a slower scene allows the reader to catch their breath and reflect on the significance of what has just occurred. This balance keeps the narrative dynamic.

Example: In an adventure novel, the pace might speed up during a chase scene, with short, rapid sentences that mimic the urgency of the moment: *"He ran. Footsteps thundered behind him. He ducked into an alley, heart pounding."* Once the chase ends, the pace might slow down as the character reflects on what has happened, with longer sentences that invite introspection: *"His chest heaved as he caught his breath. The world around him seemed to pause, and in that moment of stillness, he realized just how close he'd come to losing everything."*

Step 2: Allowing Characters to Evolve Over Time

Character development is deeply tied to the passage of time. As characters experience the events of the story, they change, learn, and grow. A character who remains static feels unrealistic; it's through the passage of time that characters reveal new facets of themselves, confront challenges, and undergo transformation.

How to Practice:

1. **Track Emotional and Psychological Growth:** Characters should evolve in response to the events of the story. Whether it's gradual growth or a sudden revelation, time allows characters to process experiences and emerge changed. Track how your characters' emotions, thoughts, and behaviors shift over time, ensuring that their growth feels natural and earned.

2. **Reflect Passage of Time Through Physical and Environmental Changes:** Time affects not only characters' internal worlds but also their physical appearance, relationships, and environment. As time passes, show the subtle signs of change—whether it's graying hair, deepening friendships, or a home that evolves as the characters do. These changes reflect the passage of time in a tangible way.

3. **Use Time Skips to Show Development:** Sometimes, it's necessary to skip ahead in time—whether it's weeks, months, or even years—to show significant changes in the characters or their circumstances. When using time skips, make sure to provide enough context for the reader to understand what has happened during the gap. This can be done through dialogue, reflection, or brief narrative exposition.

4. **Anchor Key Moments to Specific Points in Time:** Ground important character moments in specific points of time—whether it's a life event (such as a birthday or anniversary), a season (such as winter or spring), or a turning point in the character's journey. These temporal markers help readers feel the significance of time passing and add weight to the character's development.

Example: In a coming-of-age novel, a character might start as a naive, hopeful teenager but gradually evolve into a more cynical, self-assured adult. Over the course of several years, their relationships, ambitions, and outlook on life change in response to the events they experience. The passage of time is marked by significant life events, such as graduation, moving to a new city, or a breakup, each of which leaves a lasting impact on the character's growth.

Step 3: Structuring the Plot for Natural Progression

A well-structured plot has a sense of natural progression, where events unfold logically and build toward a satisfying conclusion. Time plays a critical role in this structure, guiding the reader through the highs and lows of the narrative and ensuring that each event feels like a natural consequence of what has come before.

How to Practice:

1. **Establish a Clear Timeline:** Even if your story doesn't follow a strict chronological order, having a clear timeline helps maintain consistency and coherence. Map out key events and decide when and how they unfold, ensuring that the timeline makes sense within the world of your story.

2. **Build to Climactic Moments Gradually:** The climactic moments of your story should feel like the natural culmination of everything that has come before. Allow time for tension and stakes to build, gradually escalating the conflict until it reaches its peak. Rushing into the climax too quickly can undermine its emotional impact.

3. **Use Time as a Source of Tension:** Time itself can be a source of tension in your story. Whether it's a ticking clock, a looming deadline, or the slow passage of time that wears down a character's resolve, time can create urgency, suspense, and pressure, driving the narrative forward.

4. **Provide a Sense of Closure Over Time:** As the story approaches its conclusion, time should bring a sense of closure, both for the plot and for the characters. Loose ends should be tied up, conflicts resolved, and characters given the opportunity to reflect on the journey they've taken. A well-timed resolution feels satisfying and earned.

Example: In a mystery novel, the structure of the plot might revolve around the passing of days as the detective works to solve a case. Each day brings new clues, suspects, and challenges, with time ticking down toward a final revelation. As the deadline for solving the case approaches, the tension builds, with each scene leading naturally to the next, until the climactic moment when the mystery is finally unraveled.

Step 4: Mastering Transitions between Scenes and Events

Transitions between scenes and events are crucial for maintaining the flow of time in a narrative. Poorly handled transitions can make the story feel disjointed, while smooth transitions help the reader move seamlessly from one moment to the next, maintaining immersion in the story.

How to Practice:

Use Temporal Markers to Guide Transitions: Temporal markers—such as "the next morning," "later that evening," or "three months later"—help orient the reader and provide clarity about the passage of time. These markers ensure that transitions between scenes feel natural and prevent confusion.

Weave Transitions Into the Narrative Flow: Instead of abruptly cutting from one scene to the next, look for ways to weave transitions into the narrative itself. This could involve using a character's reflection, a change in setting, or a shift in mood to guide the reader from one moment to the next.

Align Transitions With Emotional Beats: The timing of transitions should align with the emotional arc of the scene. If a character has just experienced a major revelation or emotional breakthrough, allow for a natural pause before moving on to the next event. Conversely, if a scene ends on a cliffhanger or moment of high tension, a quick transition to the next scene can maintain momentum.

Vary the Length and Style of Transitions: Not every transition needs to be the same. Some scenes may require a brief, one-line transition to keep the story moving quickly, while others may benefit from a more gradual, reflective transition. Varying the style and length of transitions keeps the narrative dynamic and engaging.

Example: In a historical fiction novel, transitions between scenes might be marked by changes in the seasons or significant historical events. After a pivotal battle, the narrative might transition to "three months later, as winter settled over the land," signaling the passage of time and the emotional shift in the characters. This transition not only moves the story forward but also reflects the changing mood and tone of the narrative.

Step 5: Embracing the Rhythm of Time in the Narrative

Writing with a sense of natural progression means embracing the rhythm of time in your story. Time is not just a tool for organizing events; it's a living element of the narrative, shaping the mood, tone, and emotional depth of the story.

How to Practice:

1. **Find the Natural Rhythm of Your Story:** Every story has its own rhythm—whether it's fast-paced and action-driven or slow and contemplative. Pay attention to the flow of time within your narrative and adjust the pacing to match the emotional beats of the story.

2. **Let Time Create Emotional Resonance:** The passage of time often deepens the emotional resonance of a story. Moments of reflection, nostalgia, or longing are made more powerful by the awareness of time passing. Use time to evoke emotions such as loss, hope, or regret, allowing characters and readers to feel the weight of the moments they experience.

3. **Trust in the Unfolding of Events:** Writing for natural progression means trusting in the unfolding of events. Don't rush through the narrative to get to the next plot point. Allow scenes to breathe, characters to evolve, and tension to build naturally over time. The more you trust the flow of time in your story, the more engaging and meaningful the narrative will become.

4. **Embrace Silence and Stillness:** Sometimes, the most powerful moments in a narrative come in the quiet spaces between events. Moments of silence or stillness, where time seems to pause, can be just as important as moments of action. Use these pauses to reflect on the significance of what has occurred and to prepare for what comes next.

Example: In a literary novel, time might flow slowly, allowing for deep emotional reflection and exploration of the characters' inner worlds. The narrative might linger on small, quiet moments—a character watching the sunset, contemplating a decision, or remembering a past love. These moments of stillness give the story a meditative quality, allowing the reader to fully absorb the emotional depth of the characters' experiences. The flow of time is at the heart of every story, shaping its structure, pacing, and emotional depth. Writing for natural progression means embracing the rhythm of time, allowing events to unfold organically and characters to evolve in a way that feels real and resonant. By mastering the flow of time, you can create narratives that captivate readers, carrying them along on a journey that feels both seamless and emotionally satisfying. In Zen, time is seen as fluid and interconnected, and the same is true in storytelling. Each moment in a story is connected to the next, building toward a larger whole. By paying attention to the passage of time, the pacing of events, and the emotional development of characters, you can write stories that flow naturally and leave a lasting impact on your readers. Ultimately, writing for natural progression means trusting the process—trusting that the story will unfold in its own time, that characters will grow as they experience the passage of time, and that the narrative will reach its conclusion when the moment is right. By embracing the flow of time, you create stories that feel alive, evolving, and deeply human.

Conflict is at the heart of every compelling story. It drives the plot, challenges characters, and engages readers by creating tension and suspense. In Zen philosophy, conflict is not something to be feared or avoided, but rather an inevitable part of the journey toward understanding and growth. In writing, conflict serves a similar purpose—it is the engine that propels characters forward, forcing them to confront their limitations, desires, and fears. Ultimately, conflict becomes a path to resolution, guiding the narrative toward a satisfying conclusion.

Visualizing the conflict in a story means understanding its deeper purpose and how it affects every aspect of the narrative. Conflict is not just about external struggles—battles, confrontations, or disagreements—but also about the internal turmoil that characters experience as they face challenges and make difficult decisions. Whether it's a conflict between characters, within a character, or against external forces, visualizing this tension allows you to shape the narrative in a way that feels dynamic and meaningful.

In this chapter, we will explore how to visualize conflict in storytelling, using it as a powerful tool to drive the narrative and lead characters toward resolution. We will look at the different types of conflict, how to create visual metaphors for conflict, and how conflict can be woven into the story as a path toward personal and narrative growth.

The Role of Conflict in Storytelling

Conflict is essential for creating drama, tension, and movement in a story. It forces characters to act, make decisions, and evolve. Without conflict, there is no reason for the plot to progress or for characters to change. Conflict creates stakes and emotional engagement, making the reader invested in the outcome of the story.

Here's why conflict is so crucial in storytelling:

1. **Driving the Plot Forward:** Conflict creates obstacles that characters must overcome. Whether it's a physical challenge, an emotional dilemma, or a philosophical debate, these obstacles propel the plot forward by creating situations that demand action.
2. **Developing Character Arcs:** Conflict forces characters to confront their flaws, fears, and desires. It is through these struggles that characters grow and change, developing emotional depth and complexity. A well-written conflict reveals the true nature of a character.
3. **Creating Tension and Engagement:** Readers become emotionally invested in a story when they care about the outcome of the conflict. Tension builds as the stakes increase, keeping readers engaged and eager to see how the conflict will be resolved.
4. **Leading to Resolution:** Conflict sets the stage for resolution. Without it, there can be no meaningful resolution or character growth. The resolution of the conflict provides closure, answering the central questions of the story and leaving the reader with a sense of satisfaction.

Step 1: Identifying the Core Conflict

Every story has a core conflict—a central struggle that drives the narrative. This conflict can take many forms, including external conflicts (character vs. character, character vs. society, character vs. nature) and internal conflicts (character vs. self). Understanding the core conflict is the first step in visualizing how it will unfold throughout the story.

How to Practice:

1. **Determine the Main Source of Tension:** Ask yourself what the primary source of tension is in the story. Is it a conflict between two characters with opposing goals? Is it an internal struggle within the protagonist as

they wrestle with their own fears or insecurities? Identifying the core conflict helps you focus the narrative.

2. **Consider Both External and Internal Conflicts:** Most stories feature both external and internal conflicts. For example, a character might be fighting against an oppressive regime (external conflict) while also dealing with their own doubts about their ability to lead a rebellion (internal conflict). Think about how these layers of conflict interact and shape the story.

3. **Define the Stakes:** What does the character stand to gain or lose if they succeed or fail in resolving the conflict? High stakes make the conflict more engaging and give the reader a reason to care about the outcome. The greater the risk, the more invested the reader will be in seeing how the conflict is resolved.

4. **Visualize the Conflict's Arc:** Imagine the progression of the conflict over the course of the story. How does it escalate? What obstacles does the character face? How does the conflict evolve, becoming more complex as the story unfolds? Visualizing the arc of the conflict allows you to structure the narrative in a way that builds tension toward a climax.

Example: In a science fiction story, the core conflict might be a battle between humanity and an alien race for control of a dwindling resource (external conflict). At the same time, the protagonist, a reluctant leader, may struggle with their own self-doubt and guilt over past decisions (internal conflict). The stakes are high—if the protagonist fails, humanity faces extinction. The progression of the conflict sees the protagonist facing increasingly difficult choices, leading to a final showdown that tests both their leadership skills and their moral integrity.

Step 2: Creating Visual Metaphors for Conflict

Conflict can be visualized not only through action and dialogue but also through metaphors and symbols. These visual representations of conflict add layers of meaning to the narrative, allowing readers to engage with the story on a deeper level. A visual metaphor can be an object, a setting, or even a recurring motif that symbolizes the tension and struggle at the heart of the story.

How to Practice:

1. **Use Symbols to Represent Conflict:** Look for objects or images that can serve as metaphors for the central conflict. For example, a broken mirror might symbolize a character's fractured sense of self, while a stormy sea might represent the tumultuous nature of a relationship. These symbols can appear throughout the story, reinforcing the theme of conflict.

2. **Create Contrasting Visuals:** Conflict often arises from contrast or opposition. You can visualize conflict by creating contrasting images—light and dark, calm and chaos, growth and decay. These visual contrasts reflect the opposing forces in the narrative and heighten the tension.

3. **Reflect Internal Conflict Through the Setting:** The environment or setting can mirror a character's internal conflict. For example, a character who feels trapped in their life might be shown living in a cramped, cluttered space. As the character works through their internal struggles, the setting might change to reflect their growth—perhaps moving to an open, airy environment that symbolizes freedom.

4. **Use Recurring Visual Motifs:** A recurring visual motif can serve as a reminder of the central conflict throughout the story. For example, if the protagonist is haunted by a past mistake, you might show a recurring image, such as a locked door or an old photograph, that symbolizes their unresolved guilt. Each time the motif appears, it reminds the reader of the ongoing internal struggle.

Example: In a fantasy story, the central conflict between the forces of good and evil might be represented visually through light and shadow. The antagonist might be surrounded by darkness, while the protagonist is bathed in light. However, as the protagonist faces moral dilemmas, the visual imagery could shift—perhaps shadows begin to creep into the protagonist's world, symbolizing the internal conflict between their desire to do good and the temptation to take a darker path.

Step 3: Escalating Conflict to Build Tension

Conflict should escalate over the course of the story, increasing in intensity as the stakes rise and the characters face greater challenges. An effective escalation of conflict keeps readers engaged, building tension until the story reaches its climactic moment. To escalate conflict, introduce new obstacles, raise the stakes, and deepen the complexity of the characters' struggles.

How to Practice:

1. **Introduce New Obstacles:** As the story progresses, introduce new challenges or complications that prevent the character from easily resolving the conflict. These obstacles force the character to adapt, make difficult decisions, and push beyond their limits.
2. **Raise the Stakes at Key Moments:** As the conflict escalates, the consequences of failure should become more severe. Early in the story, the stakes might be relatively low—perhaps the character risks losing a job or a relationship. By the midpoint or climax, the stakes should be much higher—life, death, or the fate of an entire community might be at risk.
3. **Deepen the Internal Conflict:** External conflict often mirrors a character's internal struggles. As the external conflict escalates, the character's internal conflict should become more pronounced. The character might face moments of self-doubt, ethical dilemmas, or conflicting desires, adding layers of complexity to their journey.
4. **Build Toward a Climax:** The conflict should escalate toward a climactic moment, where the tension reaches its peak. This is the moment when the character must make a pivotal choice, confront their greatest fear, or face the ultimate antagonist. The climax serves as the turning point for both the external conflict and the character's internal arc.

Example: In a thriller, the protagonist might initially be dealing with a minor criminal investigation. As the story progresses, they uncover a conspiracy that puts their life—and the lives of others—at risk. Each new discovery raises the stakes, and the protagonist's internal conflict deepens as they question their own morality and motivations. By the climax, the protagonist is forced to confront not only the villain but also their own inner demons, leading to a high-stakes resolution.

Step 4: Using Conflict as a Path to Resolution

Conflict is not an end in itself—it is a means to resolution. In Zen philosophy, challenges and struggles are seen as opportunities for growth and enlightenment. Similarly, in storytelling, conflict serves as the path that leads characters to greater understanding, transformation, or redemption. The resolution of the conflict brings closure to the narrative and provides a sense of emotional fulfillment for the reader.

How to Practice:

Allow Characters to Grow Through Conflict: The resolution of the conflict should reflect the character's growth. Whether the character overcomes external obstacles, makes peace with their internal struggles, or finds a new sense of purpose, the conflict should lead to meaningful change. Characters who emerge from conflict unchanged feel static and unconvincing.

Create a Satisfying Resolution: The resolution of the conflict should provide closure to the central questions of the story. While not all conflicts need to be resolved perfectly, the reader should feel that the character has reached a place of understanding or acceptance. The resolution should feel earned, not contrived.

Resolve Internal and External Conflicts Simultaneously: In many stories, the resolution of the external conflict is tied to the resolution of the internal conflict. For example, a character might defeat the antagonist (external conflict) by overcoming their own fear or doubt (internal conflict). Resolving both layers of conflict simultaneously creates a sense of completeness.

End on a Note of Growth or Transformation: The conclusion of the story should reflect the character's transformation as a result of the conflict. Whether the character has gained wisdom, strength, forgiveness, or self-acceptance, the resolution should leave the reader with a sense of closure and emotional satisfaction.

Example: In a historical drama, the protagonist might be a soldier fighting in a brutal war (external conflict). Throughout the story, they struggle with guilt over actions they took in the heat of battle (internal conflict). In the climactic moment, the protagonist is faced with a moral decision that forces them to confront their guilt. By choosing a path of redemption, they not only resolve the external conflict but also find peace within themselves. The resolution leaves the reader with a sense of closure, as the protagonist has grown through the conflict.

Step 5: Reflecting on the Purpose of Conflict in the Story

In Zen, conflict is seen as part of the journey toward understanding and enlightenment. In storytelling, conflict is a means of creating emotional depth, tension, and resolution. As you write, reflect on the deeper purpose of the conflict in your narrative. How does it serve the characters' growth? What does it reveal about their values, motivations, and desires?

How to Practice:

1. **Consider the Thematic Implications of Conflict:** Conflict is often tied to the central themes of the story. Reflect on how the conflict explores broader themes, such as justice, love, identity, or power. The resolution of the conflict should offer insight into these themes.
2. **Think About the Emotional Impact of Conflict:** Conflict engages readers on an emotional level. As you write, consider how the conflict will make readers feel—whether it evokes fear, excitement, empathy, or sorrow. The emotional stakes of the conflict should be clear and compelling.
3. **Use Conflict to Challenge Characters' Beliefs:** Conflict often forces characters to question their beliefs, values, or assumptions. Use the central conflict to challenge the characters' worldviews, pushing them to evolve and grow in unexpected ways.
4. **Ensure the Conflict Leads to Resolution:** The ultimate purpose of conflict is resolution. Whether the resolution is happy, tragic, or ambiguous, it should feel like the natural culmination of the conflict. Reflect on how the resolution brings the story full circle, providing closure for the characters and the reader.

Example: In a dystopian novel, the conflict between a repressive government and a group of rebels might explore themes of freedom, control, and sacrifice. The protagonist, initially reluctant to join the rebellion, is forced to confront their own fears and moral convictions as the conflict escalates. By the end of the story, the protagonist's internal struggle is resolved as they fully embrace the cause, leading to a resolution that ties together both the external and internal conflicts.

Conflict is more than just an obstacle in storytelling—it is the driving force that propels characters toward growth and resolution. Visualizing conflict allows you to create a dynamic narrative where tension builds, stakes are raised, and characters are transformed. Whether the conflict is external or internal, it serves as the path that leads to resolution, offering readers a satisfying emotional journey. In Zen philosophy, conflict is not something to be feared but embraced as part of the natural cycle of life. In writing, conflict provides the opportunity for characters to evolve, for themes to be explored, and for the story to reach a meaningful conclusion. By understanding the purpose of conflict and using it as a tool for character development and narrative progression, you can create stories that are not only engaging but also deeply resonant. Ultimately, conflict is the means through which characters—and readers—reach a deeper understanding of themselves and the world around them.

Writing the Hero's Transformation: A Zen Approach to Growth

In storytelling, the hero's transformation is often the most powerful and resonant part of the narrative. The journey from who they were at the beginning to who they become at the end is a testament to their growth, perseverance, and self-discovery. This transformation is deeply tied to the hero's internal and external conflicts, and how they navigate these challenges shapes their eventual evolution. In Zen philosophy, transformation is seen as a natural and ongoing process, rooted in self-awareness, mindfulness, and an acceptance of life's constant changes. Applying a Zen approach to writing the hero's transformation involves focusing on the gradual, mindful progression of the character's growth, allowing for moments of stillness, reflection, and awakening.

In this chapter, we will explore how to craft the hero's transformation by using a Zen perspective on growth. We will look at how internal and external conflicts shape transformation, the importance of self-awareness and reflection, and the need for balance between action and introspection. This approach to transformation emphasizes organic growth rather than forced or sudden change, allowing the hero to evolve in a way that feels natural, authentic, and emotionally impactful.

The Essence of Transformation in Storytelling

The hero's transformation is the heart of many narratives, from epic adventures to intimate character studies. This transformation usually involves a journey—physical, emotional, or spiritual—during which the hero faces challenges that force them to confront their fears, beliefs, and limitations. By the end of the story, the hero emerges transformed, often wiser, stronger, or more self-aware.

Here's why the hero's transformation is so important:

1. **Emotional Resonance:** Readers connect with stories where characters undergo meaningful growth. The hero's transformation allows readers to witness and feel the weight of change, making the story emotionally compelling and relatable.
2. **Character Arcs:** The transformation is the culmination of the hero's character arc—the emotional journey they take from beginning to end. A well-crafted transformation completes this arc, providing closure and fulfillment.
3. **Themes of Growth and Enlightenment:** Transformation is often tied to larger themes of growth, enlightenment, and self-discovery. It allows the story to explore deeper questions about identity, purpose, and the nature of change.
4. **Resolution of Conflict:** The hero's transformation is often tied to the resolution of the central conflict. As the hero changes, they are able to overcome the obstacles they face, whether these are external challenges or internal struggles.

· · · ·

STEP 1: DEFINING THE Hero's Starting Point

Before a hero can undergo transformation, it's important to define their starting point. Who are they at the beginning of the story? What are their flaws, limitations, or insecurities? What internal or external challenges do they face? The more clearly you understand the hero's starting point, the more meaningful their transformation will be by the end.

How to Practice:

1. **Identify the Hero's Core Flaws or Fears:** At the beginning of the story, the hero is often defined by certain

flaws, fears, or insecurities that prevent them from reaching their full potential. These could be fears of failure, feelings of inadequacy, or a stubborn attachment to outdated beliefs. Defining these core flaws helps set the stage for transformation.

2. **Understand Their Beliefs and Motivations:** The hero's beliefs and motivations at the start of the story are key to understanding their journey. What do they believe about themselves, the world, or their role in it? Are these beliefs limiting them in some way? As the story progresses, these beliefs will likely be challenged, leading to growth.

3. **Establish the Hero's Goals and Desires:** What does the hero want at the beginning of the story? Their initial goals and desires will likely evolve over time as they gain new insights and face challenges. By defining their starting goals, you create a framework for how these goals will change as they undergo transformation.

4. **Consider External Circumstances:** The hero's transformation is not only shaped by their internal struggles but also by the external circumstances they face. What challenges or conflicts do they encounter early on? How do these external factors influence their state of mind and their journey toward growth?

Example: In a fantasy story, the hero might start as a young, naive villager who dreams of adventure but fears responsibility. They may believe they are too small or insignificant to make a difference in the world. Their journey begins with a clear goal—perhaps seeking a magical artifact to prove their worth—but as the story unfolds, they are forced to confront deeper fears and insecurities, leading to a transformation from a hesitant dreamer to a confident leader.

Step 2: Allowing the Hero to Face Challenges Mindfully

In Zen, challenges and obstacles are seen as opportunities for growth, rather than something to be avoided. Similarly, in storytelling, the hero's transformation is often catalyzed by the challenges they face along their journey. These challenges force the hero to question their beliefs, confront their flaws, and make difficult choices that shape their evolution.

How to Practice:

Present External Challenges That Reflect Internal Struggles: External challenges, such as conflicts with other characters, dangerous environments, or impossible tasks, should reflect the hero's internal struggles. For example, if the hero fears vulnerability, they might face a situation that forces them to open up emotionally or risk failure.

Let the Hero Struggle: Transformation does not come easily. Allow the hero to struggle with their challenges—both internal and external. These struggles are essential for growth, as they force the hero to confront their limitations and push beyond them.

Encourage Moments of Reflection: In a Zen approach to growth, reflection is key. As the hero faces challenges, provide moments of stillness or introspection where they can reflect on their journey, their choices, and the lessons they are learning. These reflective moments deepen the emotional impact of the transformation.

Show Gradual Change: Transformation is rarely immediate or sudden. Instead, it unfolds gradually over time, as the hero faces new challenges and gains insights. Allow the hero's growth to happen naturally, rather than forcing a sudden change. Each challenge should bring them one step closer to their eventual transformation.

Example: In a sci-fi adventure, the hero might face a series of increasingly dangerous missions, each reflecting their internal fear of failure. Initially, they struggle, making mistakes and doubting their abilities. However, with each mission, they gain new skills, insights, and confidence. After each challenge, the hero has a moment of reflection—perhaps looking out at the stars or engaging in a quiet conversation with a mentor—that allows them to process their growth.

Step 3: Balancing Action with Introspection

A key part of a Zen approach to transformation is balancing action with introspection. While the hero's growth is often triggered by external events, their internal evolution happens during moments of reflection, stillness, or self-awareness. This balance between doing and being is essential for creating a transformation that feels both organic and profound.

How to Practice:

Give the Hero Space to Reflect: After moments of action or conflict, give the hero time to reflect on what has happened and how it affects them. These moments of introspection are where the hero processes their experiences and begins to internalize the lessons they are learning.

Explore the Hero's Internal Dialogue: Internal dialogue is a powerful tool for showing the hero's transformation. As the hero faces challenges, explore their thoughts, doubts, and realizations. How does their internal dialogue change over time? What new insights do they gain as they reflect on their journey?

Balance External and Internal Growth: The hero's external actions should be balanced with internal growth. As they take action in the external world—whether it's fighting an enemy, solving a mystery, or making a difficult decision—they should also be evolving internally. This internal growth might involve overcoming fear, letting go of ego, or embracing a new perspective.

Use Symbolic or Metaphorical Moments of Reflection: Sometimes, the hero's transformation can be visualized through symbolic or metaphorical moments. For example, a character might meditate, watch a sunset, or experience a dream that reflects their internal journey. These moments of stillness allow the hero's transformation to be felt on a deeper, more spiritual level.

Example: In a contemporary drama, the hero might be a workaholic who is forced to slow down after a health crisis. While they continue to face external challenges—such as dealing with work responsibilities and family dynamics—their real transformation happens during moments of introspection. These could be moments of stillness in nature, conversations with a therapist, or simply quiet reflection at home. Over time, they come to realize that their self-worth isn't tied to their productivity, leading to a transformation that balances action with inner peace.

Step 4: Guiding the Hero toward Enlightenment or Self-Acceptance

In Zen, the ultimate goal of transformation is enlightenment—an awakening to the true nature of oneself and the world. In storytelling, this might translate to a hero gaining self-awareness, wisdom, or a new understanding of their purpose. The hero's transformation is often about moving from ignorance to knowledge, from fear to courage, or from doubt to self-acceptance.

How to Practice:

1. **Create a Moment of Awakening:** The hero's transformation often culminates in a moment of awakening, where they gain a new understanding of themselves or their world. This moment can be subtle, such as a quiet realization, or dramatic, such as a life-altering decision. Either way, it should reflect the hero's growth and newfound wisdom.

2. **Focus on Self-Acceptance or Letting Go:** Transformation is often about letting go of old fears, beliefs, or attachments. In a Zen approach, the hero's transformation might involve letting go of the need for control, perfection, or approval. This letting go allows them to embrace who they truly are and find peace in the present moment.

3. **Tie the Transformation to the Resolution of Conflict:** The hero's transformation should be linked to the resolution of the story's central conflict. Whether it's an external battle or an internal struggle, the hero's growth allows them to resolve the conflict in a way that reflects their transformation. The resolution should feel earned and meaningful.

4. **End on a Note of Harmony or Balance:** The hero's transformation often leads to a sense of harmony or balance—whether that's within themselves, their relationships, or the world around them. This balance doesn't mean that everything is perfect, but it does suggest that the hero has found a sense of peace or clarity as a result of their journey.

Example: In a psychological thriller, the hero might be haunted by guilt over a past mistake. Throughout the story, they try to bury their guilt, avoiding responsibility and pushing others away. However, after confronting the consequences of their actions, they experience a moment of awakening, realizing that they must accept their past in order to move forward. This acceptance allows them to make amends and find a sense of peace, leading to a resolution that feels both redemptive and transformative.

Step 5: Reflecting on the Hero's Journey of Transformation

In Zen, the journey is just as important as the destination. The hero's transformation is not only about who they become at the end of the story but also about the process of growth they experience along the way. Reflecting on this journey allows you to appreciate the subtle moments of change, the struggles that shaped the hero, and the lessons they learned.

How to Practice:

1. **Reflect on the Hero's Growth Throughout the Story:** At the end of the story, take a moment to reflect on how the hero has changed. What internal and external challenges did they overcome? How did their beliefs, motivations, or fears evolve over time? This reflection helps highlight the significance of their transformation.

2. **Appreciate the Small Moments of Change:** Transformation is often gradual, with small moments of growth building toward the final awakening. Reflect on the smaller, quieter moments of change throughout the story—whether it's a shift in the hero's attitude, a decision to take a risk, or a moment of vulnerability.

3. **Explore the Impact of the Transformation on Others:** The hero's transformation often has a ripple effect, influencing the lives of other characters or the world around them. Reflect on how the hero's growth impacts their relationships, their community, or the broader world of the story. This adds depth and meaning to the transformation.

4. **End with a Sense of Continuity:** While the hero has undergone significant transformation, their journey doesn't necessarily end with the story. In a Zen approach, transformation is an ongoing process, with no fixed endpoint. Consider leaving the story with a sense of continuity—suggesting that the hero's growth will continue beyond the final page.

Example: In a romance novel, the hero might begin as someone afraid of intimacy due to past heartbreak. Over the course of the story, they face challenges that force them to confront their fear of vulnerability, eventually leading to a moment of awakening where they realize the importance of opening their heart to love again. This transformation not only allows them to find happiness in a new relationship but also deepens their understanding of themselves. As the story concludes, there is a sense that the hero's journey of self-discovery will continue, even as they embark on this new chapter of their life. Writing the hero's transformation through a Zen lens emphasizes growth as a natural, mindful process. It is not about forcing sudden change or creating dramatic moments of realization, but about allowing the character to evolve organically as they face challenges, reflect on their experiences, and gain self-awareness. By focusing on balance, introspection, and gradual growth, you create a transformation that feels authentic and emotionally resonant. In Zen, transformation is seen as an ongoing journey—there is no final destination, only continuous growth and learning. Similarly, the hero's transformation is not the end of their story, but a significant milestone in their lifelong journey of self-discovery and enlightenment.

Zen and the Journey Ahead: Continuously Evolving as a Storyteller

In Zen philosophy, the journey is as important—if not more important—than the destination. Life is seen as a continuous flow, a path without a fixed endpoint, where growth, learning, and transformation occur at every step. Similarly, in storytelling, the process of creation is ongoing, and the evolution of the storyteller is never complete. Every story written, every character crafted, and every lesson learned becomes part of a larger journey toward mastery and self-discovery. Just as characters evolve within a narrative, so too does the storyteller evolve with each story they tell.

This final chapter explores how the principles of Zen can guide you as a storyteller, not just in the act of writing, but in your ongoing journey as a creative individual. We will focus on embracing the creative process, cultivating mindfulness, allowing room for continuous growth, and finding peace in the evolution of your craft. By adopting a Zen approach, you can remain open to new ideas, embrace challenges as opportunities for growth, and maintain a sense of humility and curiosity throughout your journey as a storyteller.

The Journey of a Storyteller: Embracing the Path

Storytelling is both an art and a craft, one that evolves with practice, experience, and self-reflection. The journey of a storyteller is never truly finished. Each story you write is a step along the path of discovery, and each new project brings with it fresh challenges, insights, and opportunities for growth. The Zen approach to storytelling recognizes that this journey is continuous, without a defined endpoint, and that every experience—whether it be a triumph or a setback—contributes to the evolution of your creative self.

Here's why embracing the journey is so essential for storytellers:

Fostering Continuous Learning: As a storyteller, you are constantly learning—about your craft, your voice, and your own creative process. Each new project teaches you something new, whether it's a technique for developing characters, a method for structuring a plot, or a deeper understanding of your own creative instincts.

Embracing Impermanence and Change: Like life itself, the creative process is fluid and ever-changing. Some stories may come easily, while others may be more difficult to bring to life. Embracing the impermanence of success and struggle allows you to remain flexible and open to change, adapting as needed to continue growing.

Finding Joy in the Process, Not Just the Outcome: A Zen approach to storytelling emphasizes the importance of finding joy in the act of creation itself, rather than becoming overly focused on the final product. When you cultivate mindfulness and presence during the creative process, you experience each moment fully, allowing the act of storytelling to become a source of fulfillment in its own right.

Staying Open to New Possibilities: As you evolve as a storyteller, it's important to remain open to new ideas, genres, and techniques. Zen teaches us to approach life with a beginner's mind, free from preconceived notions or rigid expectations. By staying open to possibilities, you allow yourself to grow in unexpected and exciting ways.

Step 1: Cultivating Mindfulness in the Creative Process

Mindfulness—the practice of being fully present in the moment—is a cornerstone of Zen philosophy, and it can profoundly enhance your creative process. When you approach storytelling mindfully, you engage more deeply with your characters, themes, and ideas. You become more attuned to the flow of your story, less distracted by external pressures or internal doubts.

How to Practice:

1. **Set Intentions for Each Writing Session:** At the beginning of each writing session, take a moment to set an intention. This could be as simple as staying present, focusing on a particular scene, or exploring a character's emotional journey. By setting an intention, you ground yourself in the creative process and align

your energy with your goals.

2. **Write Without Judgment:** Mindful storytelling involves letting go of judgment during the drafting process. Rather than criticizing yourself for what you perceive as mistakes or imperfections, allow your ideas to flow freely. Trust that the revision process will provide the space for refinement later on.

3. **Stay Present with Your Characters:** As you write, focus on staying fully present with your characters. What are they experiencing in the moment? How are they feeling? By staying connected to your characters' emotions and experiences, you create a more authentic and engaging narrative.

4. **Take Breaks to Reflect and Recharge:** Mindfulness also involves recognizing when you need a break. If you find yourself feeling overwhelmed or stuck, step away from the page for a moment of reflection. Take a walk, practice mindful breathing, or meditate. These breaks help you return to your work with a fresh perspective and renewed energy.

Example: Imagine you're writing a complex scene where the protagonist is making a difficult decision. Rather than rushing through the scene, take a moment to ground yourself. Set an intention to fully explore the character's internal conflict. As you write, remain mindful of the character's emotions and thoughts, allowing them to unfold naturally. If you feel tension rising, take a brief break to center yourself before continuing. This mindful approach helps you stay connected to the emotional core of the scene.

· · · ·

STEP 2: EMBRACING GROWTH through Challenges

Challenges are inevitable in storytelling—whether it's writer's block, self-doubt, or navigating complex plot structures. However, Zen teaches that challenges are not obstacles, but opportunities for growth. By embracing the difficulties that arise during the creative process, you can evolve as a storyteller, learning from each experience and emerging stronger on the other side.

How to Practice:

1. **Reframe Challenges as Opportunities:** When faced with a creative challenge, such as a plot problem or a difficult character arc, reframe it as an opportunity for growth. Ask yourself, "What can I learn from this? How can this challenge help me grow as a storyteller?" This shift in perspective turns obstacles into stepping stones.

2. **Stay Patient and Persistent:** Transformation doesn't happen overnight. Stay patient with yourself as you work through challenges, knowing that persistence will lead to breakthroughs. The creative process is often slow and winding, but with patience, you can navigate the ups and downs with grace.

3. **Reflect on Past Challenges and Growth:** Take time to reflect on the challenges you've already overcome in your storytelling journey. What lessons did you learn from those experiences? How have they shaped the way you approach your current project? Reflecting on past growth helps reinforce your resilience and encourages you to keep moving forward.

4. **Seek Out New Challenges:** Growth happens when you push yourself beyond your comfort zone. Seek out new creative challenges, whether that's writing in a different genre, experimenting with a new narrative structure, or tackling a complex theme. These challenges not only expand your skills but also deepen your understanding of storytelling.

Example: Suppose you're working on a mystery novel, and you've reached a point where the plot feels tangled and difficult to resolve. Instead of feeling frustrated, approach this challenge with curiosity. Reframe it as an opportunity to improve your plotting skills. Take time to reflect on potential solutions, and don't be afraid to experiment with different approaches. Through this process, you may discover a new narrative technique or structure that enhances your storytelling.

Step 3: Embracing Impermanence and Letting Go

In Zen, impermanence is a fundamental truth of existence. Everything is constantly changing, and nothing remains the same. This idea of impermanence can be applied to storytelling as well, particularly in the way you approach each project. As a storyteller, it's important to recognize when it's time to let go—whether that's letting go of a draft, a story idea, or an attachment to a specific outcome.

How to Practice:

Let Go of Perfectionism: One of the most common struggles for storytellers is the pursuit of perfection. However, no story will ever be perfect. Let go of the need for flawless execution and embrace the imperfections in your work as part of the creative process. Perfectionism can stifle creativity, whereas imperfection allows for growth and discovery.

Recognize When a Story Is Complete: Knowing when to finish a story and move on is crucial for your growth as a storyteller. Sometimes, it's tempting to hold on to a project indefinitely, revising and tweaking in search of perfection. Instead, trust your instincts and let go when the story feels complete, even if it's not perfect.

Be Open to Change: Just as life is ever-changing, so too is your creative path. Be open to shifts in your storytelling style, genre, or themes. What you were passionate about a few years ago may no longer resonate with you today—and that's okay. Let go of old ideas that no longer serve you and embrace new creative directions.

Celebrate the Journey, Not Just the Destination: Instead of fixating on external validation—such as publishing success or critical acclaim—celebrate the journey of creation itself. Every story you write contributes to your growth as a storyteller, regardless of its outcome in the world. Letting go of attachment to outcomes allows you to find joy in the process.

Example: If you've been working on a novel for several years and find yourself endlessly revising without a sense of completion, take a moment to reflect. Are you holding on to the project out of fear or perfectionism? Consider whether it's time to let go and declare the story finished, even if it isn't perfect. By doing so, you free yourself to move forward and explore new creative possibilities.

Step 4: Remaining Open to Continuous Learning

In Zen, the concept of the "beginner's mind" encourages an attitude of openness, curiosity, and humility. Even as you gain experience as a storyteller, it's important to approach each new project with the mindset of a beginner, always open to learning and discovery. By staying curious and humble, you allow yourself to evolve continuously as a storyteller.

How to Practice:

1. **Approach Each Project with Curiosity:** Each story you write offers new opportunities for learning and growth. Approach every project with curiosity, asking yourself what new techniques, themes, or structures you can explore. By staying open to discovery, you keep your storytelling fresh and dynamic.
2. **Seek Feedback and Learn from Others:** One of the best ways to grow as a storyteller is to seek feedback from others. Whether it's from fellow writers, editors, or readers, constructive feedback helps you see your work from new perspectives. Be open to learning from others and integrating their insights into your craft.
3. **Embrace Lifelong Learning:** Storytelling is a craft that requires continuous learning. Stay engaged with new developments in the field, whether that's reading widely, studying new narrative techniques, or attending workshops and conferences. The more you learn, the more you evolve as a storyteller.
4. **Maintain a Sense of Humility:** No matter how experienced you become, it's important to remain humble and open to growth. Every story you write is a chance to improve and refine your skills. By maintaining a sense of humility, you stay open to the endless possibilities for growth in your storytelling journey.

Example: After completing a novel, you might seek feedback from a trusted writing group. Instead of becoming defensive or attached to your original draft, approach the feedback with an open mind. What can you learn from their perspectives? How might their insights help you improve as a storyteller? By embracing this feedback, you continue to evolve and refine your craft.

Step 5: Finding Peace in the Ongoing Journey

In Zen, peace is found not in reaching a final destination, but in embracing the present moment and the journey itself. As a storyteller, this means finding peace in the ongoing process of creation and growth. Rather than seeking validation or finality, embrace the continuous evolution of your storytelling path. Each story is a chapter in your larger journey as a creator, and every experience—whether positive or challenging—contributes to your growth.

How to Practice:

1. **Find Fulfillment in the Act of Creation:** Focus on the joy of storytelling itself, rather than fixating on external outcomes. Whether your story is published, praised, or goes unnoticed, the act of creation is its own reward. By finding fulfillment in the creative process, you cultivate a sense of peace and satisfaction.
2. **Celebrate Small Victories:** Throughout your storytelling journey, take time to celebrate the small victories—whether it's finishing a draft, overcoming a creative block, or discovering a new idea. These moments of celebration help you stay motivated and connected to the joy of storytelling.
3. **Accept the Uncertainty of the Journey:** The creative journey is full of uncertainty, with ups and downs, successes and failures. Accept this uncertainty as part of the process, and trust that every experience contributes to your growth as a storyteller. By embracing the unknown, you open yourself to new possibilities and directions.
4. **Stay Grounded in the Present Moment:** Instead of constantly looking ahead to the next project or goal, stay grounded in the present moment of creation. By being fully present with your current story, you create more authentically and connect more deeply with your characters and ideas.

Example: After completing a short story, you might feel uncertain about its future—whether it will be published or well-received. Instead of focusing on these external outcomes, take a moment to reflect on the joy you found in writing the story itself. Celebrate the fact that you completed it, and find peace in the knowledge that you are continuously evolving as a storyteller, no matter the outcome.

The journey of a storyteller is an ongoing, ever-evolving path. By embracing a Zen approach, you can navigate this journey with mindfulness, curiosity, and a sense of peace. Storytelling is not about reaching a final destination or achieving perfection; it is about growing, learning, and evolving with each new story you create. Through patience, self-reflection, and a willingness to face challenges, you can continuously refine your craft and deepen your connection to the stories you tell.

In Zen, life is seen as a flow—an endless process of change and transformation. As a storyteller, you are part of this flow, evolving with each new experience, idea, and project. By remaining open to the journey ahead, you allow yourself to grow in ways you never anticipated, discovering new depths of creativity and insight.

Ultimately, the Zen of storytelling teaches us that the process of creation is its own reward. Every story is an opportunity for growth, every challenge is a chance to learn, and every moment spent writing is a step along the path. As you continue on your journey as a storyteller, may you find peace in the act of creation, joy in the process, and fulfillment in the ever-unfolding story of your life.

Good luck in your storytelling.

Andrew

Don't miss out!

Visit the website below and you can sign up to receive emails whenever Andrew Parry publishes a new book. There's no charge and no obligation.

https://books2read.com/r/B-A-FROLC-SQNCF

BOOKS 2 READ

Connecting independent readers to independent writers.

About the Author

Andrew Parry is a writer and filmmaker with a profound love for film, particularly the genre of science fiction. His passion for the limitless possibilities of sci-fi drives both his storytelling and his creative vision. For Andrew, science fiction is more than just a genre—it's a way to explore the boundaries of human imagination, the future of technology, and the mysteries of the universe. Through his writing and filmmaking, Andrew seeks to create narratives that transport audiences to worlds filled with awe, wonder, and the thrill of discovery.

Read more at https://lonetrail.blog.